The Story of the Highgate Society

1966 – 2016

ACKNOWLEDGEMENTS

The editorial team who have put together this book owe a huge debt of gratitude to the members of the Highgate Society who have contributed to what we believe is an outstandingly successful community project. In particular we wish to place on record our gratitude for the generosity of the 130 of them whose names are listed on page 8 and of the organisations featured on pages 82 to 85. They have amazed us by being prepared to fund the full cost of this book's publication even before a page was printed.

The task of writing the bulk of the text has been shared between Michael Hammerson, Robin Fairlie, Tye Blackshaw and myself. In this we have been assisted by Martin Adeney, the Society's expert on the planning history of the Highgate Bowl, and by Nicky Gavron, Tony Baker and Ian Dungavell, each of whom has been critically involved in the Highgate voluntary organisations described in chapter 10. Thanks too to Catherine Budgett-Meakin who has given generous support to the editorial team and to Hilary Laurie who has provided invaluable editorial oversight.

Notwithstanding the number of names included in the index, the list of people mentioned in the book is far from complete. Limitations of space have prevented a deserved mention of hundreds of members, past and present, whose stalwart support for the Society over the years has contributed so much to its success. To the many whose involvement is not given the mention it deserves we can only apologise.

The writing of this book, no doubt like many others, has made us aware how wrong it is to assume that historical sources necessarily provide an accurate account even of comparatively recent historical events. The Highgate Society's quarterly magazine *Buzz* is only as accurate as the memories of its contributors and at times it has not proved as easy as we had expected to arrive at a balanced and accurate assessment, particularly of the events that occurred during the Society's earliest years.

We hope that the factual errors have been kept to a minimum but apologise for any which we have inadvertently made.

Richard Webber, Editor

Published 2016 by Northern Heights Publications on behalf of the Highgate Society

10A South Grove, London N6 6BS www.highgatesociety.com

ISBN 978-1-5262-0549-0

A CIP catalogue record for this book is available from the British Library.

Designed by Nicholas Moll Design www.nicholasmolldesign.co.uk Printed by Gomer Press

Life in a London village

The Story of the Highgate Society
1966 ~ 2016

EDITOR

Richard Webber

CONTENTS

Foreword   6

Introduction   9

SETTING THE SCENE

CHAPTER 1   Highgate and Highgate Village   13

CHAPTER 2   Early Protests (1930 - 1965)   19

THE STORY OF THE SOCIETY 1966-2016 AS RECORDED IN BUZZ

CHAPTER 3   The First Decade (1966 -1975)   31

CHAPTER 4   The Second Decade (1976 - 1985)   47

CHAPTER 5   The Third Decade (1986 - 1995)   59

CHAPTER 6   The Fourth Decade (1996 - 2005)   77

CHAPTER 7   The Fifth Decade (2006 - 2016)   97

ONGOING ISSUES

CHAPTER 8   Traffic and Transport   119

CHAPTER 9   Mansions for the Moneyed Classes   125

CHAPTER 10   The Widening of Voluntary Activities   135

CONCLUSIONS

CHAPTER 11   The Society in a Changing World   147

Index   158

List of illustrations   166

Illustration credits   168

Officers of the Highgate Society   169

End Notes   175

FOREWORD

Some while back now the Highgate Society invited me to address its members. This was in my capacity as President of "Civic Voice" - the association that represents Civic Societies across England.

I remember the evening well: a crowded room, an expectant, even earnest attention, a novice on the rostrum – me. I am always conscious, on occasions like that, that I am talking to people who have far more experience of civic struggles, their history, their planning laws and the social obstacles than I do.

Afterwards somebody was kind enough to thank me. He coughed, pulled up his trousers and politely began, "Well... nothing new there..."

But I heard new things. I met an informed, articulate and passionate audience. I learned about the extraordinary range of activities undertaken by the Highgate Society; from French evenings to life drawing classes, from historical walks to vetting 500 planning applications a year and fighting - and winning - appeals against developers with bottomless pockets.

There is a common view amongst planners, developers and journalists that amenity groups are little more than "nay-sayers", but this is an association with a long, dedicated history of understanding, loving and helping Highgate. No organisation better understands the special qualities that make this famous and beautiful part of London so successful.

Of course, from the outset, the story has included campaigns to preserve the best of Highgate: sometimes against those who see the leafy heights as an inconvenient obstacle on their way to the centre of London, or others who view its great and historic architecture as a nuisance stopping them making maximum profit.

Again and again, however, this account shows that the local community were ahead of their time – they recognized that the motor car was not the ultimate solution but the ultimate problem in our urban fabric, that the quality of a place would be reflected in its open spaces and fine buildings, that voluntary associations are the very things that are most fragile in any attempt to exploit an area and many other concerns that come from inhabiting a space rather than merely assessing it. They felt that some buildings that were seen as "out of date" would come to reflect the continuity and history of a place and increase its value – very much sooner than their would-be despoilers understood.

These issues continue to need vigilance. It's not a question of "not in my back yard" but "will you look at my back yard as carefully as possible please?" After all, if we, who live in a place, do not care for our immediate environment, who do we think will?

It is not a vice to be civic-minded, or caring, or a responsible community member, is it? It is surely one of the most significant old-fashioned and long established virtues, celebrated and respected by the Romans. Be a "citizen" not a mere inhabitant.

I am not a Highgate resident, just an outsider looking in. I stand amazed. This history shows that, far from being dull and worthy, the Highgate Society is an exciting and evolving association - a rewarding organisation to be involved with and, very often, an entertaining and worthwhile, uplifting organism.

I hope you read this "warts and all" account. I hope you conclude that you can play a part too.

The clear message is that the Highgate Society speaks for Highgate people. It does that best by involving as many residents as possible. So my own contribution here is "join!" Even if you do no more than read the magazine Buzz, or explore this excellent history, you will become aware that Highgate is a distinctive, vibrant, exciting place in which to live and it needs its citizens to celebrate that.

And there is nothing new there.

Griff Rhys-Jones
President, Civic Voice

Map One: Highgate Village

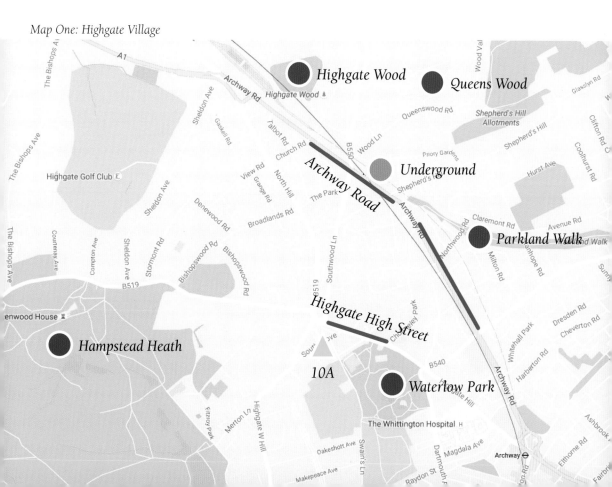

SUBSCRIBERS TO THE HISTORY OF THE HIGHGATE SOCIETY*

Martin Adeney

Timothy Ades

Robbie Hill and Harley Atkinson

David and Michele Badenoch

Richard and Dominique Bale

Ruth and Peter Benton

Judy Bernstein

Mrs J Bezzant

M Billington

Blackshaw Family

Mrs Inne Blake

Dinah Bond

William and Tricia Britain

Catherine Budgett-Meakin

Mary Burns

Ivor Burt

Mrs Margaret Butt

John Caird

Dr James Carne and Mrs Pearl Carne

Mr and Mrs Peter Charles

Elspeth Clements and David Porter

Dr Dennis Cowen and Mrs Judith Cowen J.P.

Sally Cox

Joanna Cox

Anthony R C Crawford

Kay Curtis

Kirsten de Keyser

Catherine Dobson

The family of Daphne and Alfred Doulton

Audrey and Richard Downer

Christopher Riley and Paul Dubois

Desiree and Daniel Eames

Judith and Robin Fairlie

Dr Simon Farmer and Dr Lucinda Carr

Elizabeth Fletcher

Patricia Fox

Elaine and Rod Garrod

Gibbs Familly

David Glasser

Harvey and Barbara Goldstein

M M and R D Good

Jane and Edmund Gordon

Andreas Hadjimamas

Michael Hammerson

Roxanne and Ivan Harbour

Peter and Vivienne Haynes

Ruth Hazeldine

Tessa and Ian Henghes

Della Ryness-Hirsch and Dan Hirsch

Stephen and Leila Hodge

John Rolfe Horton

Diane Jones

Anon

Tamar Karet and David Shelbourn

M J Kellet

Joanna and Steve Kennard

John Kennedy

Graham and Hilary Laurie

Nigel Legg

Matt and Jo Lewis

Sir Clive Lewis

Arvind Limaye

Peter Linden

Irene Mackay

Joy Elizabeth and Clare Manchester

Peter and Liz Mantle

June C Marson

Bettina Martin, Ella and Billy

Adrian Mayer

Sandra McAdam nee Merry

Kate McLay

Jim and Sheila Meikle

Selwyn Midgen

Anne and Tony Miles

Elizabeth Millar

Pat Moller

Maryilyn Monk

Jan Morgan

Anne and Philip Moser

P B Mostyn

Michael Mottram

Fergus Munro

James and Caroline Myddleton

Christine Nickles

Christina Nolan

Irene Norton

Stephen and Ceridwen Panke

Stanley Peart

Betty and Walter Pires

Antony and Arlene Polonsky

Carolyn and Simon Purves

Isabel Raphael

Marius and Mimi Reynolds

Penny Russell, Sarah Elizabeth and Helena Roberts

Bill Rodgers

Susan and Michael Rose

Rothenberg Family

The Ruggi Family

Jenny Russell

Gabriel Ryder

Charlotte and Geoffrey Salmon

Neil and Kate Shadwell

Trevor and Paula Shaw

Colin and Annie Sheaf

Tim and Shirley Shelton

Hazel and David Solomon

Marilyn Southey

Chii Steinhouse

Katherine M Stewart

Malcolm and Isobel Stokes

Ann Straker

Ursula Sullivan

Junko Nakata and Andrew Sulston

Sheila Sutherland

Gill Adams and Alan Taylor

Eleanor Thomas

Ray and Pauline Treen

Marian Uglow

Stuart Bull and Susan Vinson

Gail Waldman

Geoffrey Walker

Claudis Kenyatta and Greg Walsh

Pauline Wearden

Matthew Webber

Richard Webber

Catharine Wells

Vanessa Whinney

Anon

Cara and Philip Williams

Mary Williams

John Wise and Roger Harris

Elizabeth Woodman

Jenny Wright

*For organisational sponsors, see pages 82-85

INTRODUCTION

With over 1,000 groups, the Civic Amenity Society movement is a unique feature of British society and a model for civic engagement in the planning of our cities, towns, villages and countryside. It is admired and envied worldwide. With over 1,300 members, the Highgate Society, founded in 1966, is one of the largest of these societies.

What makes people join the Society? And why do they renew their annual subscription? There is no single answer. As with many other amenity societies, some do so to participate in cultural activities, to paint, listen to live music or go on a historical guided tour. Newcomers to the area may be looking to make new friends, perhaps at a social or over Saturday morning coffee. Membership provides the public-spirited with a platform for engaging in community and voluntary work, such as conducting a planning surgery or setting up a play group. People passionate about the environment find the Society a rallying point from which to apply pressure on central and local government. A number of members engage in many or all of these different activities.

It is not uncommon for non-members to perceive the Highgate Society principally as a group concerned with planning issues. This is understandable when it is its environmental campaigns which receive most press coverage. Indeed, as must be the case with many other amenity societies, the catalyst for its formation was the anger generated by a proposed threat to the local environment. In practice though, however visible and important they are, environmental and planning campaigning is just a part of what the Society does.

So just what are the activities that have engaged its members over the years? How have these activities changed and why? How have they advanced the core mission of the Society, to make the community it serves a better place in which to live and work? And what sorts of people have made this happen?

The Buzz archive

We are fortunate that, for fifty years, the day-to-day activities of the Society have been recorded in the issues of Buzz, the quarterly magazine it distributes free to members. To commemorate its fiftieth anniversary, the Society decided to draw on the contents of back issues of Buzz to compile a comprehensive account of the activities into which its members have thrown their energies during the five decades since its formation in 1966.

From this initial intention the scope of the project has expanded. The Society's archive of early press cuttings has been used to piece together an account of some of the environmental disputes that predate its existence and led to its formation. The Society's photographic archive has also been re-researched. These press cuttings and photographs, only a few of which can be included in this book, can be viewed at www.highgatesociety.com/50/. Finally, we have contributed colour and context to the historical account by tapping the memories of members of the Society who were active in its earliest years.

This story is therefore not just one of the environmental campaigns and of the social and cultural activities in which the Society's members have been involved. It is also one of notable people with vision and commitment to public service. It is their energy that has been critical for the success of the Society. Many of them have gone on to found and build other successful voluntary organisations in Highgate. The achievements of these organisations are described in chapter 10.

This book has many purposes. One of them is to produce an account which refreshes the fading memories of the older members of the Society. Others are to energise younger members and to provide new members with a clearer understanding of how its various groups came into being. For those of us with long memories it also an opportunity to honour the contributions of former giants of the Society, many of whose names and contributions are otherwise at risk of being forgotten.

Fifty years of change

At first glance an account of the craft activities that were once popular with children, and of how particular anniversaries were celebrated, may appear to have little relevance to today's very different world. On reflection we hope that readers will realise that the archival material we draw on provides an unusually rich resource for contributing to the English tradition of community studies, in this case the seemingly paradoxical phenomenon of a London "village". The material is equally relevant to cultural studies. The social, economic and cultural changes that have occurred over the past fifty years have radically reshaped the pattern of people's daily lives. How have they affected what people choose to do when they come together in a community organisation?

It is hard to credit that when the Society was founded only fifty years ago post-war reconstruction involved the adoption of a utopian utilitarianism that destroyed much of Britain's urban heritage; that urban planners could countenance the demolition of half

a historic High Street to accommodate a one-way lorry route and that a motorway could be planned across the southern edge of Hampstead Heath. In the early 1960s the threats to the heritage of Highgate and other historic communities were, if anything, even more serious than they are today.

Fifty years ago, when few mothers worked and before the advent of television affected how we spent our leisure time, the sorts of activities in which children liked to be engaged were very much less sophisticated than they are today. For a young mother, discouraged by social convention from returning to the labour market, the Society's Social Services Committee offered an outlet for her energies which fitted a lifestyle very different to that of her counterparts today.

Just as they have altered the Society's social activities, fifty years have altered the issues which are the focus of planning campaigns. In 1966, when residents were searching for alternative uses to which Highgate's grandest mansions could be put, none imagined that one day the pockets of the global rich would be deep enough to finance their restoration. At a time when homes were acquired for their owners to live in, not as investments or seasonal accommodation, householders were not kept awake at night by the prospect of neighbours digging basements. When only a minority of households owned a car, a campaign for the introduction of a pedestrian crossing engendered greater public agitation than the review of parking controls, today's bug-bear. It was not that long ago when, at least in the opinion of Margaret Thatcher, it was only the unsuccessful who travelled to work by bus. Now almost all classes do, at least in London.

These fifty years have also witnessed profound changes in the political landscape. In the early days of the Society, local authorities' freedom to

Borough of Haringey

Technical Services

Borough Planning Officer
D.W. Frith DipTP(Lond) FRTPI FRICS

Hornsey Town Hall
The Broadway Crouch End N8 9JJ
01 - 340 3220 ext

Please quote BPO/YL

1 October 1973

Mr D Budgett-Meakin,
83 Highgate West Hill,
LONDON N6

Dear Mr Budgett-Meakin,

I have just heard from Mr Hughes that he has resigned as Chairman of
the Highgate Society Environment Committee and that you have taken
his place. I would like to congratulate you on your appointment and
assure you of our continued co-operation in the future.

Should you require any assistance on planning matters, please do not
hesitate to contact the appropriate member of my staff.

Yours sincerely,

BOROUGH PLANNING OFFICER

0.01 Letter from Borough Planning Officer to newly elected Chairman of the Environment Committee

respond to local needs was relatively unfettered by the well-meaning but often ill-informed interventions of central government, or by the imposition of straitjacket legislation which more recently has resulted in developers being allowed to pay little regard to the needs or character of the local area. Today it would be exceptional if Haringey's Planning Officer had the time to write, as his predecessor did in 1973, to congratulate a newly-elected Chairman of the Society's Environment Committee and to assure him of Haringey's commitment to work with the Society.

Today the focus has shifted to different issues. The prospect of climate change is a source of

huge concern to many. So too is the impact of the internet on the viability of the High Street. Less acknowledged, but nonetheless of great importance, is how social media and email threaten to render face-to-face contact an outdated form of personal interaction. That Highgate, surrounded by London suburbs, will continue to remain a close-knit local community should not be taken for granted.

What implications does all this have for the future? This account of the Society's history presents material which must surely be relevant to decisions every organisation has to face. What are the core activities which give it its identity and which provide continuity of purpose? And how, in the face of deep-seated social, political and technological changes, can an organisation adapt in such a way that it remains vibrant, fresh and relevant to the community it serves?

Chapters 1 and 2 provide a brief account of the historical development of Highgate as a residential community and a summary of the environmental battles which engaged its residents during the years before the Society was founded. Chapters 3-7 give a chronological account, decade by decade, of the fifty years of the Society's history. Because some subjects crop up many times over these five decades, these chapters are followed with three others which address issues that have been on-going throughout the period. Chapter 11 seeks to place the changes in the Society within the context of wider social change.

The Society hopes that community associations in other parts of Britain may find interest, and even encouragement, in this record of voluntary action by a London community. We believe the implications of this story are as relevant to planners and other local government officials and to politicians and their think-thanks as they are to volunteers.

Sheep in North Road, 1924

Setting the scene

CHAPTER 1:
HIGHGATE AND HIGHGATE VILLAGE

Highgate's early years

Highgate is one of a number of London settlements which, until the encroachment of suburban development ended their physical separation from the capital, were once self-standing country villages. It owes its existence to its position on the coaching route from London to the Midlands and the North. Situated 400 feet above sea level and five miles from what was then the City of London, it was here that a testing climb necessitated the first change of horses. Drovers of cattle and sheep travelled in the opposite direction and it was in Highgate's butchers' shops that livestock was prepared for onward delivery to London's retail markets. Travellers sought entertainment in local taverns and overnight accommodation in local inns[i]. Today the physical presence of these inns and taverns and in particular the distinctive canopies over former butchers'

shops, act as important visual reminders of Highgate's historic past.

Coach connections to the city, fresh water and clean air attracted wealthy Londoners to Highgate as early as the sixteenth century. Its artisans and traders were then joined by a new class who built for themselves small

1.01 Canopy, legacy of butcher's shop, Highgate High Street

1.02 Prickett & Ellis, Underhill

country houses set in extensive grounds. It is no accident that what is believed to be the oldest continuously serving estate agent in the world, Prickett & Ellis, now Prickett & Ellis, Underhill, operates from an office in Highgate High Street. It has been serving customers since 1767.

Professional practice was a more common source of the wealth of these new owners than land or trade. For example, it was a former Lord Chief Justice, Sir Roger Cholmeley, who in 1565 founded Highgate School, an important reason why families today choose Highgate as a place to buy a family home[ii].

1.03 Chapel, Highgate School, 1867

Despite its wealth, Highgate has from its earliest years possessed a liberal - even a radical - edge. In 1655, when it was forbidden within five miles of central London to preach other than according to the liturgy of the Church of England, a wave of non-conformists settled in Highgate. Cromwell House, built in

the seventeenth century, was the first home in England to be owned by a Jew after their expulsion in the thirteenth century. In the eighteenth century it was in nearby Kenwood House that the legal basis of slavery was first challenged and in Heath House, between Highgate and Hampstead, where campaigners later led the campaign which resulted in the abolition of the slave trade.

In the nineteenth century residents on both sides of Hampstead Heath united in a thirty-year campaign to preserve the original core of Hampstead Heath from residential development. In the first decade of the twentieth century, from her summer cottage beside The Spaniards Inn, Dame Henrietta Barnett employed Raymond Unwin to mastermind her vision of one of Britain's largest and most successful experiments in garden city living, Hampstead Garden Suburb.

The campaign to save Hampstead Heath from development drew inspiration from local memories of early Romantic artists and poets such as Constable, Morland, Keats and Coleridge, the last renting rooms at The Grove, one of London's finest early eighteenth-century residential rows. Many long-established residents believe that the memory of these social reformers and artists has left an indelible mark on the character and ethos of the neighbourhood[iii].

1.04 Commemoration of Samuel Taylor Coleridge, 3 The Grove

Between 1867, when a new railway linked Highgate to the City, and the outbreak of war in 1914, a settlement of small seventeenth and eighteenth-century country estates was increasingly overtaken by a denser pattern of streets of speculative, two and three-storey terraced houses suited to the needs of the more affluent members of the middle classes.

From 1880 a new form of housing started to be built on land previously belonging to the Ecclesiastical Commissioners. This consisted of roads of very large detached houses, many in an Arts and Crafts style and each of a unique design. Merchants, industrialists, lawyers, doctors and partners in professional practices acquired houses on these roads. John Sainsbury, the founder of the supermarket business, and a Mr Tavener, who built a confectionery business bearing his name, were early occupants[iv].

The grand mansions

The residential locations which were most sought after during this period were those on the mostly gravel ridge linking Highgate and Hampstead villages. These sites enjoy uninterrupted views over Hampstead Heath and the Thames Valley. Here former farmland was sub-divided first into large estates and then into what became the grounds of some of London's most spectacular private residences.

Parkfield was acquired in 1912 by soap magnate Sir Arthur Crosfield, MP who led the campaign to preserve the grounds of the Kenwood Estate from development. During the 1920s he built a new mansion, Witanhurst, in its grounds. That it is the largest residential property in London after Buckingham Palace is a better known fact than the name of the Russian oligarch[v] who currently owns it.

Beechwood was built in 1839 by architect George Basevi for his brother Nathaniel Basevi on land

obtained from the break-up of the Fitzroy Estate. In 1910 it was acquired by Edward Perronet Sells, the owner of a coal distribution company. By 1929 it had been acquired by Oswald Lewis, son of John, the founder of the John Lewis Partnership. In 2016 it is owned by an Uzbek billionaire.

Athlone House was constructed in 1870-2 by Mancunian architect Edward Salomons of behalf of the industrialist Roger Brooke who had made his fortune from the manufacture of aniline dyes. His business was acquired by Francis Reckitt, son of the founder of the Reckitt family business. In 1909 it passed to the ownership of Arthur Cory-Wright, a coal merchant, and in 1929 to Sir Robert Waley-Cohen, Managing Director of Shell. Until 2016 the mansion was owned by an off-shore company, unoccupied and in a state of disrepair.

1.05 Athlone House, Hampstead Lane, c 1880[vi]

Kenwood House overlooks perhaps the finest country estate in London. William Murray, a Lord Chief Justice, who subsequently became the Earl of Mansfield, bought the original seventeenth-century house. In the 1790s he entrusted its redesign to Robert Adam and the landscaping of its estate to Humphry Repton. By 1925 the house had been acquired by Lord Iveagh, heir to the Irish family fortune based on the Guinness brewery, who in 1927 donated it to the nation. Today it is managed by English Heritage.

1.06 Kenwood House

The presence of these mansions gives a certain cachet to Highgate. However their vicissitudes, the aspirations of their seemingly ever-changing owners and the uses proposed for them have been an ongoing source of contention since the Society's inception. As is explained in detail in chapter 9 they have been the objects of many of the Society's most high-profile campaigns.

The development of the Highgate community

It might seem odd to a foreign observer that, before starting his engine in Moorgate in the City of London, a driver resets the indicator board of his single-decker bus to "Highgate Village". Why, in the very heart of the world's most vibrant financial centre, would a small bus be setting off for a "village"? Understanding this aspect of Highgate's identity provides useful insights into the distinctive character of the Highgate community and of the Highgate Society.

We associate a number of very distinctive images with the word "village". In the village

1.07 Route 214 bus at Liverpool Street

of our imagination each building is different from its neighbour, perhaps built in a different period or a different style. We picture a village as a place encircled by greenery and open land. In an archetypal village residents invariably encounter and chat to friends whenever they walk to their "local" pub or corner shop, whose owners they often know by name.

Many might therefore consider it a pretentious misuse of language to apply the epithet "village" to a London dormitory suburb where speculative developers have concreted over fields and nursery gardens with streets of

1.08 Original road sign outside The Flask pub[vii]

1.10 Signifiers of Highgate's rural origins

houses of uniform appearance in whatever style was in vogue at the time they were built.

However, not least by virtue of various accidents of history, both Highgate Village and its immediate surrounds have, to varying degrees, succeeded in retaining each of these three hallmark features of a quintessentially English village - a legacy of unique and historic buildings, an encirclement of open spaces and a vibrant mesh of community organisations[viii].

1.09 Rus in urbe, Hampstead Heath

Highgate's inns and taverns would still be easily recognised by the travellers they served over two hundred years ago. So too would street names such as Hampstead Lane, Hornsey Lane, Swain's Lane and Southwood Lane which reflect its rural past.

Thanks to a series of some of the world's earliest mass environmental campaigns, much of the

countryside which has surrounded Highgate since medieval times, such as Hampstead Heath and the woodlands that once lay within the Bishop of London's hunting estate, is still freely accessible to local people. Highgate's principal traffic arteries may now be choked by cars rather than horse-drawn carriages, but they are still overlooked by the homes that London's wealthy merchant and professional classes built in the eighteenth and nineteenth centuries when clear air, fresh water and distant views attracted them to Highgate.

It is from physical manifestations of this sort that places acquire distinctiveness. From this distinctiveness arises a shared sense of belonging which forms an important element in identity many residents feel their community possesses - or "place-making" to use current jargon. And though it does not necessarily follow that such a sense of place results in strong community networks, or "social capital"[ix] to use another piece of political jargon, it certainly makes it easier for them to flourish.

Much to the chagrin of its many local estate agents, Highgate retirees so value their access to London's cultural riches, an attractive environment and a wealth of community organisations that they are relatively resistant to the economic temptation to downsize to a rural cottage or seaside bungalow. This is pertinent to the fortunes of Highgate's voluntary organisations, since the combination of leisure time and professional skills with which this group is endowed provides the leadership on which so many of them depend.

But even in an age where personal interaction is challenged by the impact of globalisation, digitalisation and the spread of social media, there are nonetheless distinct sections of London's younger liberal intelligentsia which are attracted by proximity to these village-like features, heritage buildings, greenery and a dense network of face-to-face social contacts. Many of them currently live in Highgate and many others aspire to do so if and when their finances permit.

Not all of these busy, younger residents live in homes that lie physically within Highgate's historic core, the part that by convention is referred to as "Highgate Village" and in which approximately half of the Society's members live. There is no doubt though that the presence of heritage buildings, shops, schools, churches and community organisations on their doorstep does give this group a much sought after sense of distinction and identity. Many members of the Society belong to this group even though they do not have the time to engage actively in many of its activities. For many, membership of the Society is a symbolic token of the lifestyle choice of living in "Highgate", the term used to describe the combination of Highgate Village and its surrounding nineteenth and twentieth century accretions.

1.11 Southwood Lane, Highgate Village

Some critics complain that Highgate residents and community groups are too removed from modern life, living in a hermetic heritage bubble detached from the excitements and opportunity made possible by social, technological and political changes. No doubt some are. But as we have already noted Highgate, like its neighbour Hampstead, has for many centuries been a great centre for intellectual and social reform and most members of the Society would vigorously refute any imputation of "nimbyism". Notwithstanding the recent invasion of city bankers, this philanthropic and intellectual tradition is still evident from the size of the audience that specialists in their particular subjects draw to evening lectures at the Highgate Literary and Scientific Institution (HLSI) and the numbers that sing Christmas Carols in Pond Square.

Where the Society opposes development, it claims that its target is not what is modern in itself but architectural designs which are pastiche, shallow and ephemeral, ones which, if built, future generations would not consider contributed to Highgate either as a "heritage asset" or as a community.

2.01 Highpoint I, when newly built, c 1935

CHAPTER 2:
EARLY PROTESTS (1930 - 1966)

Londoners flex their muscles

In London, opposition to development is nothing new. In the early seventeenth century, Londoners commented none too favourably on Inigo Jones' new development in Covent Garden, with its fancy continental ornaments. It was the protests of country people living near fields owned by the Earl of Leicester that preserved Leicester Square from development. The Regency architecture of John Nash we so admire was at the time described as "monstrous", the author Maria Edgeworth "indignant at plaister statues and horrid useless domes and pediments crowded with mock sculpture figures which damp and smoke must destroy in a season or two". Of what we now regard as fine Victorian suburbs, Disraeli said It is impossible to conceive of anything more insipid, more uniform. Pancras is like Marylebone, Marylebone is like Paddington.

Formal systems which gave communities a say in what should and what should not be built originated with the Housing and Town Planning Acts of 1909, 1919, 1925 and 1932. During the 1930s many of the most vociferous complaints about new development occurred in Hampstead which at that time was a popular location for "modernist" architecture. That the planning system was under the control of the London County Council (LCC), which could overrule objections by the local Borough of Hampstead, prompted particular outrage. Appeals against refusal were heard by the Minister of Health, whose responsibilities included local government. Only in the late 1930s did the Town and Country Planning Act give councils control over the scale of proposed new developments and, to a limited extent, their appearance.

Though the earliest reaction to the impact of modernism on urban heritage came from Hampstead, Highgate was quick to follow.

On 2nd November 1935 the *Hampstead and Highgate Express*, commonly known as the *Ham and High*, reported a public meeting against "unsightly and unwanted building development" protesting against "certain forms of modern building development, especially large blocks of flats". It was regretted that when the LCC determined planning applications, as it did at the time, it paid "scant regard… for the views of the people most closely affected by building proposals", and demands were made to devolve decision-making to local councils.

In the same month there were reports that a "… movement to preserve the… historic and picturesque parts of Highgate is taking shape and is likely to become an effective force". Local newspapers highlighted the threat to the "amenities of Highgate", and featured protests against Highpoint II, the apartments at the crest of North Hill: "North Hill used to be a thing of beauty", but the new building was "a mass of ugliness". In April 1936 protesters flagged "the need for constant vigilance … to safeguard … the district from undesirable developments…", and that "close co-operation is desirable between the Hampstead Heath & Old Hampstead Protection Society (HOHPS) and the newly-formed Highgate Preservation Society" (HPS).

The Highgate Preservation Society

These conflicts led to the founding of the HPS in 1935, to oppose the "vandalism" of flat-building which threatened Highgate's large old houses and gardens, many of which, at a time when servants were virtually impossible to find, were no longer suitable for single family occupation.

The catalyst was Highpoint. It could not be ignored in the same way that the smaller

1920s blocks of neo-Tudor and neo-Georgian flats had been. The Highpoint complex, now Grade I listed and regarded as a major example of 1930's architecture, was built in reinforced concrete by Lubetkin & Tecton for the duplicating machine tycoon Sigmund Gestetner. The nine-storey Highpoint I was built in 1935 on a double cruciform plan, with concealed plumbing and a basement garage. It originally had a winter-garden hall, tea room, maids' rooms and a public terrace on the eighth floor. It even had laundry chutes and centrally-operated refrigerators. Its lifts opened directly into the entrance hall of every flat. Highpoint II was built shortly after.

2.02 Highpoint I

The construction of Highpoint brought Highgate face to face with the problems of the large-scale planning needed to accommodate the expanding demand for housing in the metropolis. While the small blocks of flats disguised as Tudor or Georgian mansions did not raise objections, the emerging trend towards the construction of larger blocks, and the infra-structure works necessary to meet the increased pressure on public services, did. The principal motivation for the founding of the HPS was to oppose this new form of development rather than promote or control it.

Its officers were drawn from the apex of Highgate society. Its President was Sir Percy Hurd, MP and its Vice Presidents included Sir

Robert Waley-Cohen, owner of Athlone House, Sir Arthur Crosfield, owner of Witanhurst, and the influential Admiral Sir Herbert Purey-Cust. The Chairman was Sir Gilbert Upcott, KCB, and its object was to be "the preservation of the old or historic buildings in Highgate, and its roads, ways, passages and open spaces, and generally the protection of Highgate from undesirable development." Interestingly, the proposed area of coverage was far more extensive than the Village and broadly similar to the area the Highgate Society covers today. The annual subscription was two shillings and six pence, the equivalent of £6 in 2016.

2.03 Membership application form, Highgate Preservation Society

The Society's inaugural public meeting was held in March 1936 in the Hall of Channing School. It was addressed by two eminent guest speakers, George Pepler, President of the International Federation of Housing and Town Planning and Chief Town Planning Inspector to the Ministry of Health[x] and Sir Raymond Unwin, Chief Adviser to the Greater London Town Planning Committee, a social housing expert and the renowned designer of Hampstead Garden Suburb. The debate would resonate with audiences today. One reads the summary with a distinct feeling of déjà vu, including Sir Arthur Crosfield's view that "what has happened in certain places does make me wish that the HPS had come into existence a lot sooner".

In May the Society issued a five-page position statement, starting with the warning that "in recent years, building development in Highgate has been upon a very considerable scale, and there is a great danger that new buildings unsuited to the general character and physical characteristics of Highgate may lead to the destruction of many of the amenities of the neighbourhood", and itemising a string of threats and dangers across the area, including "an immense block of flats of seven storeys, which overshadows the whole of the neighbourhood" at the top of North Hill, and objecting not to its architecture but its scale. This, of course, was Highpoint.

The first annual report, for 1936, expanded on the Society's objective to "keep a vigilant eye upon attempts to change the character of the district by the destruction or alteration of old buildings or erection of unsightly structures, by felling trees, or encroachment on open spaces". It explained that the HPS owed its existence to an action taken by the Committee of the HLSI in October 1935, and reported that it had taken part in opposing the proposal of the LCC to rename the High Street by merging it into Highgate Hill, but noted that a compromise had been reached, and that what until then was officially named "High Street, Highgate" would become "Highgate High Street". In due course objections were also lodged against the LCC's proposal to change the name of Highgate West Hill to West Hill Drive.

The second annual report, for 1937, noted that the London Passenger Transport Board had proposed to run a trolley-bus route either along

North Road, down North Hill to the Wellington Inn, now the site of an Esso filling station, or via North Road, Castle Yard and Southwood Lane[xi] – a proposal opposed by the Hornsey Borough Council[xii] . The Society had protested against the new Hornsey Town Planning scheme – particularly new regulations allowing great building heights, zoning for shops, destruction of trees, and plans for road widening. At the public inquiry the Society, represented by a barrister, got its way on all its objections, and particularly on the maximum height for buildings, which was reduced from 65 feet to 40 feet. It also fought proposals to widen Hampstead Lane and fell many of its trees.

The Society's third annual report, for 1938, announced that the trams which linked Highgate Village to the tube at Archway would be replaced the following year by trolley buses, which would turn at the corner of Pond Square and the High Street; the new stand for the buses would involve the demolition of the nineteenth century building occupying the site. The Society had prevented the demolition of numbers 3, 4 and 5 Pond Square.

Reconstruction

Civic activity of this sort was inevitably halted for the duration of World War II, and the only subsequent annual report to survive, the sixth for 1948, reported that the HPS had secured the permanent opening of the path through the Ken Wood Orchard, and announced plans to open up the graveyard next to the chapel of Highgate School as a public open space. These were never realised.

Many bombs were dropped on Hampstead and Highgate during World War II and the early post-war rush to repair war damage produced dreary utilitarian buildings, whilst the period from the 1950s to the 1970s saw the arrival

and triumph first of minimalism and then the proudly flaunted brutalism considered by some to be unsurpassed in ugliness and bleakness. This contributed to the founding in 1957 of the Civic Trust, whose aim was to arrest the destruction of Britain's town centres and to promote an appreciation that planning was for people and that Britain's heritage was an asset worth preserving. To underline how seriously the issue of responsible town planning was taken at all levels, the original Trustees of the Civic Trust included a spectrum of opinion ranging from the Archbishop of Canterbury to the Secretary of the Trades Union Congress.

There is insufficient information from the 1950s to provide a coherent account of the HPS's activities, but the sudden onslaught of multiple threats from the early 1960s has left the Society with an *embarras de richesse* of material, particularly in the form of newspaper cuttings, carefully preserved by Lady Susan Cox, one of its early stalwarts, and her colleagues. There are so many of these, and they give such a vivid and dramatic account of the almost daily threats assailing Highgate from all directions, that they have been reproduced in full at www.highgatesociety.com/50/

Among the 1962 list of members of the HPS were the renowned architect Ove Arup, who lived in Fitzroy Park; Lady Crosfield, the widow of Sir Arthur Crosfield of Witanhurst; the actor Michael Hordern who lived in The Grove; Lt.-Col. Sebag-Montefiore, whose daughter Henrietta had married Sir Robert Waley-Cohen, former owner of Athlone House, and who was also related by marriage to the Gestetner family, for whom Highpoint had been built; Sir Bernard Waley-Cohen, who had donated Athlone House to the National Health Service and part of the gardens, today called Cohen's Field, to Hampstead Heath; future Highgate Society founder Ronald (Ronnie) Bernstein QC, and others who were to be involved in founding the Society, such as Sir James Brown,

Denzil Budgett-Meakin, Quentin Edwards, John Lacey and David Lowe-Watson, and the Heads of Channing and Highgate Schools.

The Archway Road Campaign

In June 1961 a large-scale scheme was announced by the Ministry of Transport (MoT) for a London lorry route designed to relieve traffic between the newly built M1 and London's markets and docks. Archway Road was to be widened to 100 feet with two 30-foot carriageways, on the railway side north of the intersection with Shepherds Hill and on the west side south of it. Planning blight immediately hit householders along Archway Road, house prices dropped and homes became unsellable. In November Hornsey Borough Council told Transport Minister Ernest Marples[xiii] that the upgrading of Archway Road to a motorway was a priority. One of its councillors stated: "Archway Road should be returned to its original purpose, to provide London with an entry and exit."

In December the HPS, HOHPS and Hampstead Garden Suburb Residents Association (HGSRA) wrote to Marples claiming that it would be "disastrous for our communities… Long-established communities are being sacrificed in favour of vehicles… The problem of through traffic must not be solved at the expense of people living in these communities" and, a little surprisingly, "The congestion at the so-called bottlenecks is all that saves our communities from being cut to pieces by fast moving traffic."

Combatting the threat of a lorry route

The first news bulletin, for November 1962, majored on the threat presented by the lorry route scheme of the MoT. The HPS and the newly formed Save Highgate Committee

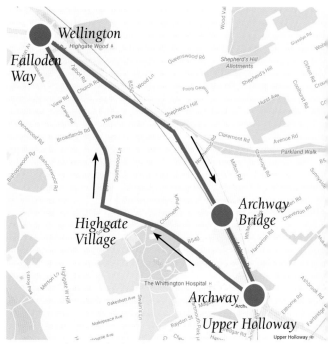

Map Two: The Marples battleground, 1962-65

(SHC) attended a public meeting organised by the Kensington Society, also threatened by major road works, to discuss the motorway box being proposed for London[xiv]. The route proposed for this motorway between Swiss Cottage and Camden Town was to pass along the southern edge of Hampstead Heath and to involve extensive demolition of housing. It was clear that the problems of those two societies were shared by communities across the whole of London and that Highgate was merely the first to face them. "If the battle is lost, the rest of London is at risk. The SHC will fight the proposals as a national issue…." Traffic measures, they stated, cannot be looked at in isolation from social considerations; good government must also promote safe living conditions.

The meeting passed a resolution deploring the proposed one-way scheme. The meeting then urged Hornsey Council to proceed with the widening of Archway Road as soon as possible – a move which immediately led to dissent between residents of Highgate Village and those living along its route.

By late 1962 opposition had ballooned; but divisions between communities became increasingly apparent, with the newly-formed Archway Road Association (ARA) accusing the HPS of wanting to see homes and shops destroyed to preserve amenities and property values in Highgate Village, despite the HPS arguing that the scheme would be disastrous for both.

The MoT's solution, which would have destroyed both communities, was to make a widened Archway Road one-way southbound and Highgate Hill and High Street, North Road and North Hill one-way northbound, with one side of Highgate High Street demolished to accommodate the 600 lorries a day which it was predicted would use the route from London's docks and markets to the newly built M1. Cholmeley Park, Dartmouth Park Hill and Hornsey Lane would also be made one-way. In February 1962 the announcement that the Archway Road "will be widened – but not yet", caused even worse planning blight. The Minister was adamant that London's transport problems could only be solved by demolishing thousands of homes and supported the LCC's plans to make Finchley Road, Aylmer Road, Lyttelton Road and Falloden Way six-lane highways.

Alfred Doulton, Headmaster of Highgate School, was appointed Chairman of the Save Highgate Committee (SHC) which would coordinate the campaign, and on which the HPS was represented, and 6,000 campaign leaflets were distributed. David Lowe-Watson was elected Treasurer and Ronnie Bernstein was asked to act as legal advisor.

Opposition grew dramatically as the extent of the motorway proposals, and the resulting destruction of communities they entailed, became apparent. Objectors included the LCC, Middlesex County Council[xv], eight Borough Councils, the Royal Institute of British Architects, the Society for the Protection of Ancient Buildings and the Pedestrians Association, as well as the Transport and General Workers' Union and the London Transport Executive.

There then followed an extraordinarily high-profile campaign, spanning the last days of the HPS and the early days of the Highgate Society, which culminated in the defeat of the government's plans to build a motorway network across London. This campaign set a benchmark for community action in opposition to insensitive centralised planning systems.

In March 1963 Sir James Brown, of the HPS, proposed a cheaper option, but in April the Road Hauliers Association welcomed the London lorry route, and so began the avalanche of letters which was to fill the correspondence pages of The Times and other national and local newspapers in the following years.

On May 1st, 800 Highgate residents met to launch their fight against the Village one-way scheme, and 6,000 leaflets were distributed. The Hornsey Journal noted the chaos that an experimental one-way system in Highgate had caused in February, and that the ARA were pleased that Highgate High Street was to become one-way – "the best solution". "Perhaps it will be", the Journal cynically noted, "when the amenities of the Village have been destroyed and there is nothing worth preserving. In fact, widening and reconstruction are likely to improve Archway Road out of all recognition," and successive editorials deplored the destructive effect the proposals would have on the Village.

The fight goes national

The Minister announced that the proposals were "only an experiment" but, by the end of May, what Alfred Doulton called "The Battle of Highgate" had started, with warnings that 650 three-ton lorries would pass through Highgate each day. Such was the effectiveness of campaigners that the conflict went national. It was supported by twenty-two MPs and three peers, and the HOHPS called for a Royal Commission to investigate London's traffic problems properly, even supporting such a radical solution as a tunnel under Hampstead Heath.

But the dispute between the Archway Road and the Village also intensified, each trying to defend its patch at the expense of the other, and each accusing the other of being indifferent to its fate. In June, it was Islington's turn to wake up to the potential disaster when it realised that Upper Holloway would become part of the lorry route. The newly formed Upper Holloway Residents' Association joined the fight, proposing a tunnel under the Archway Road, and the row became national news, with contributions to the SHC's fighting fund coming in from across the country, quickly reaching £858 – around £13,000 in today's money. On 28th June, the London Evening News and *The Spectator* reported huge opposition, and a petition against the proposal was even signed by 2,000 London busmen. The Middlesex County Council supported the Minister and pressed for widening.

MPs started to question the Minister in the House. Islington MP Eric Fletcher called sending lorries up through Highgate Village "ludicrous", a group of MPs agreed to fight the scheme and a petition with 13,000 signatures was presented to the Minister by Lady Gammans, the Conservative MP for Hornsey.

In July, the campaign was taken up by the *London Evening News* in a series of features entitled "The Great Road Row" which conducted a detailed analysis into the impact of the whole route between dockland and Highgate. This concluded that the proposals were unnecessary and proposed that disused railway lines should be converted into roads. Unexpected support came from David Eccles, Minister for Education, who sided with the campaigners. The next community to realise the likely impact on their lives was London's East End, where it was declared "It would be hard to think of a less appropriate district through which to send all the heavy traffic bound from the docks and markets of London to the Midlands and North." Such heavy traffic, it was demanded, must be kept away from shopping streets, commercial centres and residential communities.

On July 12th, a deputation from the SHC, including Alfred Doulton, Ronnie Bernstein and two MPs, met minister Ernest Marples to urge him to look at alternatives. "There must come a position at which the social considerations involved outweighed the traffic gains." The LCC came out in support of the eight councils along the route now opposing it, and MPs wrote to The Times.

On July 20th, the *Hornsey Journal* observed that "The protests have grown from a local to a national affair. The protest can be said to have arrived to full stature with last week's article in The Times supporting it." But unsubstantiated reports were circulating that the Minister had decided to reject all protests and introduce the scheme on a six-month experimental period. As St. Pancras Councillor Eric Fisher told his colleagues, "he is in love with transport. He can't see the people for lorries." Unexpected support came in August from the Automobile Association and the Royal Automobile Club, though the

ARA, unable to see the value of concerted action, continued to assert that Highgate Hill was well able to take the lorry traffic proposed.

The campaign even excited the attention of the music industry, with the release in August of a record featuring local schoolchildren singing two songs: "The Battle of Highgate Hill" on one side and "Pity the Poor Pedestrian" on the other. The BBC was promptly banned from broadcasting it for the unlikely reason (under orders from the Minister?) that it "deals with a current problem still under discussion". However, a second, long editorial from The Times came out strongly in favour of more holistic planning. "So long as [Marples'] measures merely afford temporary relief to traffic in pursuit of a policy which appears to regard cities as places in which to move but not to live and have your being, they cannot be expected to generate much enthusiasm," and Marples agreed to meet a twenty-five strong delegation from the HPS and SHC on September 25th – unfortunately, no news cuttings reporting it survive – while Hornsey Council affirmed that, in its view, the one-way through Highgate was unnecessary and the solution was a dual carriageway along Archway Road.

In early October the New Hampstead Society, formed to fight similar proposals for the Finchley Road, suggested two tunnels under Hampstead Heath, one to take through traffic to Central London, and the other as a Hampstead by-pass, turning the whole area from Hampstead Village through Whitestone Pond and Spaniards Road into a pedestrian precinct. Not before time, the Minister's Traffic Adviser, Alex Samuels, visited Highgate to look at the situation on the ground and to confer with Alfred Doulton.

Denouement

This intense and lengthy campaign did have an impact. At the end of January 1963, the *London Evening News* headlined "Mr Marples Agrees to Drop the Highgate Hill Lorry Route" – Sir Gilbert Upcott, Chairman of the HPS, remarking "We knew all along the original scheme was a crazy one" – but there was a sting in the tail, the headline continuing "But the Village one-way Remains", to the great concern of St Michael's School and Highgate Primary School, directly on the route. People in Islington now called Highgate Village "selfish" for the surely rather selfish reason that their own problems had not been solved and the lorry route would still go through Islington.

More was to come. In February, the MoT proposed the creation of a new gyratory which would divert northbound lorries from Archway Road along Church Road and then down North Hill. This generated a 1,000-signature petition from Highgate Primary School, which would have faced the full force of the diverted traffic. It was also pointed out that, if Archway Road was to be a dual carriageway, northbound traffic would no longer be able to turn right into Muswell Hill Road and would have to be diverted via Woodside Avenue, East Finchley. The HGSRA continued their fight, since the Minister still intended to drive a new road through the Garden

2.04 Church Road

Suburb, with Aylmer Road, Falloden Way and Lyttelton Road becoming a six-lane lorry route.

Was Highgate grateful? Alfred Doulton remarked that the Minister's decision was given in "such grudging terms" that the schools' petition had little chance of success, and suggested that their best recourse was through Hornsey Borough Council, which was preparing alternative proposals, including replacing the Church Road diversion with the more restricted mini-gyratory that now exists at Baker's Lane.

By March, it was clear that even the village one-way system would face a "gigantic revolt", for what was felt to be its sheer crass insensitivity to the community on which it would impact, and local anger was exacerbated when it was found that the ministry had been carrying out secret tests to send buses along Hillside Gardens, a most impractical route. The ARA called for the abolition of the lorry route proposals and, encouraged by the Minister's back-down over Highgate, protests and marches grew along its entire length.

The *Hornsey Journal* for April 19th opined that "There would be no need for all the protests from Highgate and Upper Holloway... if we had a sane traffic policy... Railways should be taking traffic off the roads, not the other way round", and attacked the Church Road lorry diversion for the danger it posed to schoolchildren. It was soon able to announce "A Victory for Common Sense" when the Church Road proposal was dropped in favour of Hornsey's preferred option, the use of Baker's Lane.

The Highgate Village one-way system

However, by July 1964, a more modest Highgate Village one-way system had been introduced. This involved reducing the block bounded by

2.05 Press cutting, Highgate one-way system

North Road, Castle Yard, Southwood Lane and the High Street, containing Highgate School with its 650 pupils, into an island cut off by traffic. When a Hornsey Councillor claimed that it seemed to be working, he was careful to add, "at least from the Minister's point of view"; but Hornsey Council claimed that it was a success, its sole concession to residents being that more barriers would be put up if it became permanent.

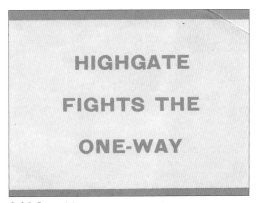

2.06 Opposition to one-way system

Residents, though, were not convinced, with faster traffic and danger for the many elderly residents in Castle Yard and the Pauncefort almshouses in Southwood Lane, and letters to the *Ham and High* in August made clear that conditions for pedestrians, especially when trying to cross the roads, were far from ideal. Conditions were good for motorists but inhuman for people, the danger and disturbance highlighted by an editorial in the *Hornsey Journal* of August 16th asking:

> What sort of victory was it? In defeating Mr Marples on one front, the village forgot that he could attack them on another. He has now given them one-way traffic, and the stresses and strains they thought they had avoided by beating off the lorry route are now with them. One-way is the terror which befalls residents in the sacred cause of keeping the traffic moving.

Indeed the view at the time, which has persisted ever since, was that the village one-way was Marples' "revenge" for the defeat of his lorry route.

2.07 The Highgate one-way system

On October 4th, the SHC announced that although the one-way experiment, due to last three months, was almost over, they had heard nothing from the MoT. The MoT eventually wrote assuring them that it would be reviewed "after a few months". Hornsey Council agreed that it should continue to the end of the year, though they were forced, as a result of residents' complaints, to withdraw a report intended for the Minister that the scheme was working satisfactorily. On October 11th, a Mr Phelps of New Southgate was foolhardy enough to write to the press to advise that his drive to town via Southwood Lane was now much easier – "Mr

Marples has done a worthy job in Highgate to solve the traffic problem."

By November, Castle Yard was being called "The Street of Fear". Five of the eleven cottages had been hit by skidding cars and houses damaged by traffic vibration, while eleven people had been injured on the one-way since July.

2.08 Accident, North Road

Castle Yard and Southwood Lane were now jammed with traffic during rush hours, while during the rest of the day traffic was speeding through at up to fifty miles per hour. Hornsey's Deputy Mayor Murray, who lived in Sheldon Avenue, claimed that, "in the main, this scheme is a ridiculous failure", and that although "outside the rush hour it is entirely successful... You just shift the problem..." The Ministry must "throw it out and look at it again", while Councillor Hugh Rossi, later to become MP for Hornsey, said, "The scheme has proved a disaster. There are holdups on North Hill sometimes extending from Castle Yard back to the Wellington... it must be absolutely appalling to live in [Castle Yard]." However the scheme persisted and it was not until 1993 that the experiment was abandoned.

Widening the Archway Road

In November the ministry confirmed that the Archway Road would form part of a five-year £212 million traffic scheme, being transformed into a six-lane "Gateway to London" and involving the demolition of dozens of shops and houses. The blight was to haunt the Archway Road for decades, and Hornsey's Borough Engineer tried to convince the public that Archway Road "will become a tree-lined avenue". If the Archway Road were to be widened, the MoT warned, the Archway Bridge would have to be demolished.

2.09 The section of Archway Road which was upgraded

Hornsey Council urged the MoT to delay another proposal – the widening of the Gate House junction at Hampstead Lane – until the effects of the Baker's Lane works were known.

During 1964, other development issues came to the fore, but the motorway threat remained, and continual vigilance was necessary to monitor the MoT's next move, and to prepare for the next round of protests should the wider lorry route proposals come forward again without further consultation. In February, concerns were flagged up in Islington about the dangers of increased traffic already evident in Archway Road, highlighted by a fatal accident at the junction with Highgate Hill, where the failure of a lorry's brakes killed two pedestrians.

Then, in March 1964, it was reported that Hampstead was to be the starting point for a "giant" ten-mile motorway across North London, mainly on or alongside railway lines, but running 100 feet beneath Hampstead, and connected by radial roads with the M1 and other major highways, commencing on a seventeen-acre railway land site at West Hampstead. Astonishingly for today's readers, Hampstead Councillor Michael Butterfield felt able to say that "Hampstead will benefit enormously by having a motorway to carry vast volumes of through traffic... [but] it will need to be very sensitively designed if it is not utterly to overwhelm its surroundings." To the relief of many, the £30 million scheme was rejected by the LCC. However, as we explain in chapter 8, the issue of the Archway Road was to resurface during the 1970s.

As if the Archway Road/Highgate Hill campaign were not enough, the HPS also fought two public inquiries in 1962. The first was an appeal by Pearl Garages against refusal of a six-storey block of flats on the Highgate Nursery, part of the land known now as The Highgate Bowl. To public relief the Minister dismissed the appeal. The second was the proposed construction of the Russian Trade Delegation building in West Hill. This was also opposed by the HOHPS, because of the impact it would have on views from Hampstead Heath. Though the appeal against refusal was also dismissed, the Minister overruled the inspector's decision, perhaps for political reasons, clearing the way for what many consider one of Highgate's ugliest buildings.

The legacy

Following the defeat of the MoT's proposals, a new alignment of hardened campaigners now appeared on the scene. When they met in the 1960's, John Lacey, President of the HPS, and Ronnie Bernstein, who had been closely involved with the lorry route campaign, discovered that they had known each other during World War II when they had both flown observation planes over enemy territory. Their friendship was the catalyst for the eventual amalgamation of the HPS and the SHC.

2.10 John Lacey, President, Highgate Preservation Society

Ronnie Bernstein was anxious lest the community spirit that had been built up during the campaign against the lorry route would be lost after their victory, particularly when the threats to Highgate were growing by the month. To this end, he had proposed that those residents who had formed the campaign team should form a new society to campaign for good development for the area. When, thirty-eight years later he wrote to the Highgate Society about the Saturday Farmers Market proposed in Pond Square, he recalled his own remarks at a meeting in Highgate School hall in 1966. "I said I would sooner

see the people of Highgate fighting each other in the streets than sitting at home watching television."

On December 28th 1965, John Lacey wrote to Bernstein, supporting "your proposed new Society", which "could well complement the work of this Society.... with your society concentrating more on the traffic aspects and ourselves... dealing with the physical development aspects," adding that the HPS was proposing to rename itself "The Highgate Society" to avoid being associated entirely with its preservation aspects. However, after further discussions, they agreed that they should unite to form a single group, to be called the Highgate Society, and that the HPS should become the new society's Planning Committee.

On April 14th, 1966 it was resolved, at a special general meeting of the HPS, "to support the proposal to form, jointly with the Save Highgate Committee, 'the Highgate Society'. The first public meeting will be held on May 3rd, 1966 at Highgate School Hall." Posters were put up all over Highgate, the Hall was filled to overflowing, and the meeting, one attendee recalled, "was quite rowdy at times, and was attacked by some left-wing elements as only for 'the nobs on the hill', and even 'for white people only'. The Minister was invited, but sent a representative, Andrew Mackintosh, who made some comment about the lorry scheme 'not being too exclusive for the village' and was booed for it, but in general the meeting was productive." In the months that followed, membership quickly climbed to 1,700.

CHAPTER 3:
THE FIRST DECADE (1966 - 1975)

The founding of the Highgate Society

During 1965 and 1966, a foundation working group under the leadership of Ronald Bernstein hammered out the purpose and shape of the new community association for the Highgate area. What was described as a "working group" of upwards of fifty people was formed. Around one half of them were younger people, many of whom had moved into Highgate comparatively recently. They held regular meetings to progress the detailed aspects of the project. The other half were mostly older, longer established residents who were not directly involved but who were eager to be kept informed and consulted as progress was made.

The name, objectives and structure were settled in a constitution drafted by Quentin Edwards. A memorandum was drawn up declaring that its signatories were members of the "Highgate Society". This paper was signed by those who happened to be present at a routine meeting of the working group on April 15th 1966 and the

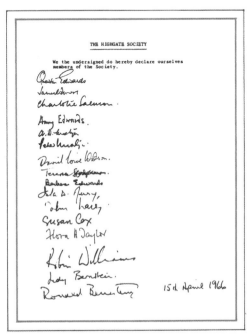

3.01 Declaration by early members of the Society

31

Society then came into existence. Only in a very technical sense were these signatories the founders.

Membership forms were printed and within days the working group joined together with other residents who had previously just kept in touch. Within the next two weeks the membership of the society had grown to around a hundred people. All these people could be said to be among the founder members of the Society. This founding group then selected from their number members to serve on a temporary basis as the Society's first officers and chairs of committees.

These appointments included Ronald Bernstein as Chairman and Yehudi Menuhin, who lived in The Grove, as President. The fifty-year-old Menuhin was at that time at the height of his career as a concert violinist and one of the best known residents of Highgate. The HPS' last President, John Lacey, was appointed a Vice- President of the Society and the Chairman of its Amenity and Planning Committee. With these and other appointments, the formation of the Society was complete.

It was also decided that elections would be held in July for positions on the Council of the Society. By then membership would have substantially increased. All the temporarily-appointed officers would then resign and tender themselves for re-election to a newly formed Council.

A large public meeting was held on May 3rd to present the Highgate Society to the residents at large. Leaflets were distributed showing the aims and structure of the Society, introducing its first officers and drawing attention to the July election of the first Council. These leaflets stated the aims of The Society which were:

THE HIGHGATE SOCIETY
make Highgate a better place
to live and work in

FIRST PUBLIC MEETING

Highgate School North Hill   8·15 Tuesday 3rd May 1966

ALL WELCOME

3.02 Inaugural public meeting of the Highgate Society

"To make Highgate and its neighbourhood a better place for people to live and work in, and in particular:

(a) to encourage a vigorous community life

(b) to promote schemes for protecting Highgate as a residential community from the evils of excessive traffic; for controlling the volume of traffic passing through residential areas to and from Central London; and for improving public transport

(c) to ensure that new buildings and other changes in the environment enhance the amenity of Highgate and maintain its scale and character; to encourage sound planning in future development; and to protect individual buildings and groups of buildings of architectural merit or historical interest.

At the May 3rd public meeting and in the weeks that followed, residents joined the Highgate Society in their hundreds.

It was the Society's founding Chairman, Ronnie Bernstein, who defined the character of the new organisation, as is evident from the following tribute written by Peter Mostyn and Quentin Edwards to celebrate his eightieth birthday.

Memories of Ronnie Bernstein[xvi]

"Ronald is neither unduly modest not given to hyperbole. When he describes himself in "Who's Who" as The Founder of the Highgate Society", he states the plain fact. Without him, there would never have been a Highgate Society. Ronald wanted – and he persuaded us all that we wanted – a Society that would help the old and the young, support the arts and enhance community life as well as defending the environment of Highgate.

For upwards of a year, there were endless councils of war in the drawing room at View Road, where Ronald and Judy then lived. What should be the aims of the nascent Highgate Society and how was it to be organised? What targets of culture, social purpose and environment should be its objects and functions? Ronald's genius for this process was widely and rightly seen as combining energy with patience and a sense of direction. He would typically cut off attempts endlessly to improve with: "we mustn't let the best be the enemy of the good." When he summarised a discussion, his summary was seen as the decisions we had all made.

But he had another more critical talent, of which only its subtle, even subversive deployment, prevents its description as prominent. It was an elusive combination of flexible persistence and crisp charm. Many saw (and some were rashly prepared to savour) a natural conflict between the ambitions for this new Highgate Society, the venerable Highgate Literary and Scientific Institution, and the Highgate Preservation Society. For Ronald they were never rivals, but allies to be won over. To achieve this, he had an unerring instinct for the identity of opinion leaders in the community.

Not only did he win the support of Sir James Brown, President of the Institution, John Lacey, Chairman of the Preservation Society and Alfred Doulton, Headmaster of Highgate School; but also of Denzil Budgett-Meakin, Edward Fowler and many others who long had their own agendas for the community. The Presidents of "rival" bodies were enlisted as founder members. They became his friends. And so he recruited their influence in the community to his own vision.

The Society needed its own premises. Ronald discovered a property in the heart of Highgate Village as the Institution gave the Society a tenancy of part of its own building complex at an absurdly low rent. Prospective rivalry with the Preservation Society disappeared when they acquiesced in their own demise to be subsumed as the Planning Committee of the Highgate Society, and its Chairman, John Lacey, one of the most respected citizens of Highgate, was pleased to become a Vice President of the new Society.

The master bridge builder was a master bridgehead builder too. As he recruited new allies and occupied new territory, one by one the then old guard of the Highgate Community surrendered to Ronald; but they would not see it this way - his eyes had become their eyes too. The final coup was to secure as titular head of the new society our most celebrated local citizen. Having succumbed, Menuhin was not left to bask in Community affection. From time to time Ronald would wheel him (and the redoubtable Diana Menuhin) out like a gun and fire him at a target of Ronald's choosing.

Perhaps Bernstein's greatest coup was to recruit Yehudi Menuhin as President. Menuhin did not consider this position merely an honorary one. The appeal for funds which he launched included a personal appeal in his own hand.

3.03 The Society's first President, Yehudi Menuhin

The objective of the HPS had been to conserve Highgate's visual appearance while the primary aim of the SHC had been to oppose the MoT's plans for handling the growth of traffic; a major new direction pioneered by the Highgate Society was the development of leisure and cultural activities that would enrich everyone's daily lives.

Its objectives

That the objectives of the new Society were more ambitious than either of its predecessors' is evident from the committees proposed by the founders, amenity and planning, traffic, social and entertainment, community services, arts and membership.

From its inception the Society published a monthly newsletter. By 1968 it had evolved into a quarterly magazine designed by member and graphic designer Richard Downer and edited by Ion Trewin. According to Peter Mostyn:

We convened a group of professional journalists to advise on a members' magazine. One of them was Harold Evans, of the Sunday Times, shortly to be its Editor. We tossed around Highgate Diary and every other generic. It was Harold who said: "Buzz" and Buzz it was.

From its first issue Buzz recorded social, cultural and community activities, with the aim of meeting the Society's declared objectives.

Editors of Buzz 1966-2016	
Ion Trewin	1966-1969
Richard Toeman	1969-1970
Peter & Cornelia Usborne	1970
David Lowe-Watson & Ion Trewin	1970-1971
David Lowe-Watson, Ion Trewin & Barbara Rogers	1972
Barbara Rogers	1972-1973
Linden Nicoll	1973-1975
Ron Field	1975-1979
Tim Ades	1979-1982
Fleur Bowers	1983-1984
Vanessa Whinney	1984-1986
Ruth Phillips	1986-1987
Leila Hodge	1988-1991
Margot Slater	1992-1997
Brendan Nolan	1997-2009
Tamar Karet	2010-

Just one month from its launch the Society had recruited 1,000 members. Later in the year membership neared 1,500 households[xvii], a number which has remained remarkably consistent for the following fifty years.

Ronald Bernstein's leadership continued to be vital during the fast-moving early growth period of the Society. He was able to attract energetic and talented people to work well together. "Let us not make the best the enemy of the good" was a typical comment by which he prevented a log jam from the torrent of ideas. His talent was to resolve the natural tension between creativity and common purpose and so lead everyone forward.

At a time when Council Social Services departments were in their infancy, the scope of the Society's activities was far more ambitious than those of other voluntary organisations that existed in Highgate. The community activities that it started included a Good Neighbours scheme to help the disabled and the housebound; a *Monday Club* for older people; a Registered Play Group for infants every weekday, run by a professional play leader; a Mothers and Babies Afternoon to help young mothers to make a wider circle of friends; and a pool of drivers who ferried patients between hospitals and convalescent homes and who brought elderly people to Bridge evenings. The Society was particularly mindful of the need to cater

3.04 Ronnie Bernstein, QC, the Society's founder and first chairman

'Highgate buildings must be cherished'

FIRST MEETING OF NEW SOCIETY

About 450 people packed into the hall of Highgate School, on Tuesday evening, for the first public meeting of the newly-formed Highgate Society, the organisation formed to "continue the work of the Highgate Preservation Society and the Save Highgate Committee, and to do many other things as well."

The first president of the new society, Mr. Yehudi Menuhin, said there were a number of old buildings in Highgate which should be cherished. He hoped the society would continue to enlist the help its predecessors had.

Object of the meeting was to tell people of Highgate what the new society would be doing for them. The chairman, Mr. Ronald Bernstein, said that on July 4 elections would be held. Until then acting officers had been appointed.

He asked the committee chairmen to explain what they intended to do in their field.

'CHANGING'

Mr. John Lacey, former chairman of the Preservation Society, now in charge of amenities and planning, said Highgate is a beautiful but changing place. The committee want to make sure the changes do not destroy Highgate.

Chairman of the traffic committee, Mr. David Lowe-Watson, warned that commuter traffic through Highgate would increase. The objects of his committee are to study the problems of this increase, to look into parking problems and the needs of pedestrian traffic, to put forward constructive plans to the authorities and to look at the situation of public transport and, if necessary, make suggestions to the London Passenger Transport Board.

The community services under Mrs. Barbara Edwards will aim, she said, at doing two things first—finding out what is already going on and being a central bureau, and starting a good neighbour scheme to help one another. She, like Mrs. Isla Merry, in charge of social activities and entertainments, would welcome suggestions.

ARTS

The last committee chairman, Mrs. Charlotte Salmon, for the arts, said it was possible for Highgate to become a vital centre of the arts. She believed there were many people in Highgate who would enjoy showing their work.

When the meeting was thrown "open," Cllr. A. McIntosh, vice-chairman of the town planning committee of Haringey Council, said he hoped the voice of the Highgate Society would be there to tell the council what they should be doing for them.

Other speakers brought up points which met with shouts of approval: questions of getting rid of street litter; organising an annual Highgate Festival; preserving "Beechwood" now that Mr. Oswald Lewis has died; and providing a wet fish shop in Highgate High Street.

3.05 Hornsey Journal, 6 May 1966

3.06 Poster protesting at the plans to build a "motorway" through Highgate Village

for younger members: a children's chess club, a children's theatre group, a children's orchestra. *Buzz* even included a children's crossword.

Traffic and transport of course remained an important focus of the Society's activities, as it has continued to be for the fifty years since. Chapter 8 describes the transport issues that were to dominate its thinking during its earliest years.

Notwithstanding all the energy that had been put into opposing the MoT's traffic proposals immediately before its formation, during the Society's first years planning and environmental issues tended to take second place to social, cultural and community activities. By 1967 it had already organised a Highgate Week, 3-10 June which, as is explained in chapter 6, was the precursor of the current Fair in the Square.

Its first year

Early meetings were mostly held in the Bernsteins' home in View Road. But once committees had been established their members tended to meet in the homes of their chairmen. The result was a hectic programme of events at the rate of two a week. The range of activities is evident from the following report on its first year, 1966-67, contained in a special issue of *Buzz*.

3.07 Pedestrian crossing installed in 1966 at junction of Southwood Lane and High Street, 2016

The Arts Group began a series of drawing room recitals [which continue to this day as Music in Highgate Homes], Community Services held the first of a number of talks and the Social and Entertainment Group began a quarterly Luncheon Club with invited speakers, the first being Baroness Summerskill, former Government Minister and ardent feminist. The Amenity Planning and Traffic Groups organised watchdog teams to ensure that new buildings, planning developments and traffic schemes were in the interests of Highgate as a community.

The highlight of the autumn was undoubtedly the Children's Art Exhibition…Everyone hopes that a children's exhibition of this kind will become an annual event.

There was almost a complete sell-out when members crowded in to buy their Christmas presents from the Craft Fair early in December. The products of hitherto unsuspected cottage industries were on display.

A calendar of social events reached a climax with hot sausages and carol singing in front of the first ever Christmas Tree in Pond Square – a village-style Christmas for everyone that should come round every year. The Bridge Club held a grand slam of a first evening in January.

The Traffic Group had a triumph when the Greater London Council's (GLC's) Highways Committee decided that parking restrictions should be relaxed in part of Highgate High Street. At the same time the GLC has agreed to our request for the extension of the pedestrian crossing from the central island where Southwood Lane meets the High Street, to the south side of the street.

As to Amenity Planning, we are beginning to be regarded as the natural voice of the community by the various planning authorities. We are engaged in a number of broad studies of Highgate, which will enable us to develop a policy against which future planning projects can be examined.

The ordinary good relations of Highgate residents have been harnessed under our Good Neighbour Scheme.

What is in the future? With new premises we shall take a great leap forward. The next major date in the calendar is "The Highgate Week", a village festival with music, exhibitions, drama, dancing and other events still to be conjured up.

By today's standards the early years of the Society were marked by a lack of formality: a sense that anyone who had the drive to make something happen could set up a group and just get going. A new team might be set up as a working group within an existing committee or it might operate independently and, if successful, morph into a new committee in its own right.

Finding a permanent home

Initially there was an assumption that active members of the Society would gain a special vitality by meeting in each other's homes. This would fit in well to more relaxed social arrangements which were popular with professionals in the new creative industries many of whom at that time were moving into Highgate. Ronald Bernstein said he was comfortable with this but Barbara Edwards, wife of the drafter of the constitution, Quentin Edwards, expressed a different opinion. Barbara was the first Chairman of the Community Services Committee and it was she who first proposed that the Society should have its own headquarters. Everyone demurred. It took six months to find it.

The HLSI had been the centre of cultural life in Highgate since its foundation in 1839 and is one of only four surviving examples of these once great Victorian institutions. Its support and cooperation has always been of paramount importance to the Society and eventually the HLSI came up with a solution: the lease of 10A South Grove, a small building adjacent to their main building at No 11 South Grove on the south side of Pond Square.

3.08 Highgate Literary and Scientific Institution

10A South Grove

Built in 1840, 10A had been used by a stonemasonry business which serviced the demand for tombstones and monuments to commemorate those buried in nearby Highgate Cemetery. The business closed in 1918 when its last stonemason died. Between the wars the building was put to a variety of uses. During World War II, it was bought by the HLSI.

The family of the artist Margaret Thomas was the first to lease 10A from the HLSI. In 1944 its distinctive curved front window was blown in by a V2 flying bomb that landed on the tennis courts of Waterlow Park. Mr and Mrs Thomas and their daughter Margaret had the foresight to collect the shattered fragments and organise them in such a way that sufficient details could be recorded for a replacement to be made.

The Thomas family were followed by Leslie Skippon, a Highgate resident, who used 10A to replace his London warehouse which had been destroyed during the war. His retirement in 1964 left the HLSI looking for a new tenant.

At that time and for many years to come the HLSI had no need of extra space. However, Sir James Brown did not welcome the prospect of another warehouse on his doorstep. Nor was he in a hurry to lease the space. This was helpful for the emerging Highgate Society because the acquisition of premises was not on its agenda.

Ronald Bernstein's skills included keeping his finger on the pulse of Highgate. He knew of Leslie Skippon; that Skippon's wife had recently died; that he had then married his secretary; that he had decided to retire and no longer needed 10A. It did not take long for Bernstein and Brown to do the deal: the HLSI would clear out the place and the Highgate Society would refurbish it, the Society paying a peppercorn rent.

Refurbishment

A highly professional team of Richard Downer, Geoffrey Salmon, Brian Palmer and David Whitby launched an appeal for the £5,000 needed to do the place up, equivalent to £85,000 in 2016. In the words of one early member, "collectively, they were part of the booster rocket which put the Society in orbit". As a team they gave the Society access to skills of the highest quality and their story deserves to be told.

Geoffrey was a partner in a prestigious West End firm of architects, the Austin Smith, Salmon, Lord Partnership. His wife Charly was a professional sculptor of some standing who became Chairman of the Arts Committee. Geoffrey drew up a detailed specification for the conversion of 10A into the headquarters and meeting house of the Society.

Richard Downer ran his own graphic design studio and had already produced a widely acclaimed logo for the Society which was to be

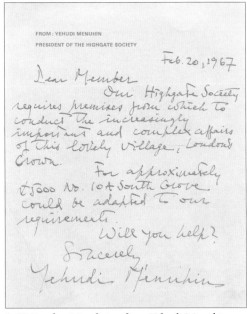

3.09 Fund-raising letter from Yehudi Menuhin

used for over forty years. He now drew up a visualisation of Geoffrey's plan for the finished conversion. Brian Palmer needed this for the appeal package he was designing.

Brian was a partner in Kingsley, Manton and Palmer, newly-formed advertising agency. Brian knew that the Society had to go well beyond the routine "Dear Member" letter which would be glanced at and tossed aside. So he designed a colourful folder to contain various items which, he claimed, members would spread on their kitchen table and talk about. These included a brochure by Ronald Bernstein setting out the proposal for the premises, a facsimile of a hand written letter from Yehudi Menuhin, Richard Downer's sketch and donation forms. Instead of a stamped and addressed envelope, Brian included a postage stamp for each member to stick on the envelope addressed to the Society Treasurer. "They won't want to keep the stamp for themselves; and when they have stuck it on the envelope their cheque will be in it." said Brian. The appeal was a great success and the financial target was exceeded.

David Whitby was the chairman of a city discount bank, the Society having elected a banker rather than an accountant as Treasurer. Each day, literally as the cash came in, David invested its receipts in a growth fund. In the few months of the fund's accumulation and before the date for paying the builders, David had virtually doubled it. The £5,000 target was reached within a few months.

Geoffrey Salmon redesigned 10A so that it would cater for recitals or lectures for an audience of up to 100 people, with a dais which could be dismantled to form coffee tables. It provided for the preparation of food in a kitchen area and for exhibitions to be mounted on the walls.

3.10 10A South Grove

How 10A *came to be – memories of Geoffrey Salmon*[xviii]

Members with relevant skills rallied round to help in the financing and conversion of 10a into a practical and pleasant environment for the new society, and in October 1966, it fell to me to advise on the structure and interior design aspects. I was at the time engaged upon several pretty large projects in my Architectural Practice, but I confess that the '10a Project' proved far more daunting than any of them!

A small Design Advisory Committee was formed 1 November 1966. The interior was a pretty dismal place, with no heating save an ancient and inefficient gas fire - I think the workers simply added another layer of clothes in winter. The lighting was minimal: a few naked light bulbs hung above the aisles between high wooden racking which reached almost to the ceiling. I needed plans and sections of the building upon which to work out a design, but none could be found; so I set about measuring the place. The racking proved useful, and by climbing up it while it swayed alarmingly (brushing the cobwebs away in the process), I could drop a measuring tape to someone below. I used a ladder to get through the ceiling trap door and thence on to the roof – and pretty dirty it all was.

There were structural defects. They were not serious, but the roof, gutters and brickwork needed attention. I met John Lacey, Architect to the HLSI, to have friendly negotiations and settle an appropriate division of costs. The rear lavatories were, at the time, shared with the Institution, but needed considerable refurbishment. All this meant that money had to be spread pretty thinly and we estimated that over £2,000 was needed to achieve our intentions. These included repairs and redecoration, a simple but practical kitchen, acres of pin-up board, heating, new lighting, and spotlights for exhibition display.

My design and report were presented to the Committee; happily, the proposals were accepted and they were approved in January 1967. My drawings were translated by Richard Downer into attractive illustrations which became part of a "Premises Appeal Fund" brochure prepared by Brian Palmer. By April, that fund had reached £2,014. The Society's minutes of the time recorded: "We have been careful not to cut down on basic essentials... but until more money is raised there can be no refinements; no chairs, no floor covering and no screens or lighting for exhibitions."

This did not deter Barbara Edwards and Isla Merry from campaigning vigorously for a "jolly good kitchen". In pursuance of this, they dragooned me into visiting half the kitchen suppliers of the West End until we had settled the equipment to their satisfaction.

I wanted the interior to be "jolly". To this end, the ceiling and upper walls were painted bright orange, with large but inexpensive Japanese paper lanterns providing lighting. Richard Downer designed the clever and iconic logo which recorded in graphic form the dastardly intentions of the then Government to make Highgate part of a destructive one-way lorry route. This was emblazoned at high level on the old chimney breast and used on our notepaper to remind us how we had all begun.

3.11 10A prior to refurbishment

Adjoining this was a framed plaque recording the names of the founder members of the Society. Ventilation was a problem because the end windows did not open. By good fortune, the plaster plaque high up above the front window was just large enough to take the proud inscription "THE HIGHGATE SOCIETY", set out by Richard Downer in that distinguished font 'Clarendon Bold'. Our funds did eventually stretch to chairs, screens and display lighting, but not to the paving of the

3.12 Design for refurbishment of 10A

forecourt, which was dealt with by a group of hard working volunteers, and this gave the final welcoming touch to the Society's new home.

By spring 1967, everything was completed and the Society opened for business. What a relief! Back to my drawing board, to more large, impersonal and comparatively boring projects.

The price of a family subscription was initially set at £1 but the appeal that was circulated proposed an initial donation of between £5 and £10. Members were then invited to devise a suitable name for the Society's new headquarters; after much debate, it was simply called the Highgate Society, though it has ever since been known as 10A.

As a result, the Society became one of the few amenity societies in Britain which has permanent access to its own premises – an asset which has been instrumental in forging a particularly strong feeling of community. 10A became the venue for an expanding number of Society activities such as the Monday Club, bridge evenings, talks and exhibitions. In due course the room assumed the role of a village hall, providing an additional source of income when booked by outside organisations or private individuals for events such as a recital, lecture or children's party. It is important to recognise that the Society does not "own" these premises, it merely rents them and if ever the HLSI wanted to recover the space for its own needs, the current lease might not be renewed.

Social activities

Activities that flourished throughout this period were:

Bridge evenings
Theatre groups for adults and children
Cordon Bleu Cookery demonstrations
Supper evenings focused on the cuisine of a single nation

Art exhibitions, and an art lending library
Craft evenings, with talks, and an annual Craft Fair
Food Fares
The Highgate Chamber Orchestra with concerts by local or invited performers

Supper evenings included ones with Swedish, Swiss, French, Hungarian and Russian food. Members enjoyed a Burns Night with bagpipes, an American Thanksgiving dinner and classical guitar music for the Spanish evening. After the Russian evening the wives of members of the Russian Trade Delegation, located close by on Highgate West Hill, offered their recipes for publication in *Buzz*. The head of the Trade Delegation himself delivered them the day before press day, only for the Editor to discover they were in Russian. Not a problem for Highgate: a quick translation secured their inclusion in *Buzz*.

A theatre group was formed. This made bookings and organised transport for visits to West End theatres, opera and ballet as well as the Wembley Ice Show, Epsom on Derby Day. The Kenwood Lakeside Concerts were not overlooked. A children's theatre group followed.

Some proposed activities were over-ambitious. Among these were an Italian language course and a group formed under the direction of a distinguished actress and Highgate resident Nancy Nevinson to read plays, but which had difficulty recruiting people to read male parts. A short-lived programme of films included a showing by another Highgate resident, Dmitri Tiomkin, of his film *Tchaikovsky*. The viewing took place in Highgate School's Dyne House in the presence of Madame von Meck, wife of a descendant of Tchaikovsky's famous patron Madame Meck. In later years the HLSI has proved to be a more successful operator of a film club than the Society.

As 1971 was the year when Britons had to vote on whether they wanted the country to remain

THE HIGHGATE SOCIETY

THE COMMON MARKET
—A BRAINS' TRUST

Rt Hon Douglas Jay MP
Patrick Jenkin MP
Rt Hon Harold Lever MP
Sir Robin Williams Bt

Chairman: Sir Mark Turner

This critical decision for Britain is imminent. The Highgate Society has therefore organised a Brains Trust, whose members are not only distinguished but are authorities on this issue, and who represent views both for and against.

Questions to be put to the panel may be submitted in advance to Mr. Ronald Bernstein at 10A South Grove.

Questions (but not speeches!) from the floor will also be welcome, and will be answered as far as time permits.

MONDAY, 20th SEPTEMBER, 1971 at 8.0 p.m.
in HIGHGATE LITERARY AND SCIENTIFIC INSTITUTION
(unless otherwise advertised)

The Highgate Society has arranged this meeting because of the widespread interest among its members. It will however be an open meeting for all to attend.
We shall be taking a '10p collection' during the meeting to help defray expenses.

3.13 Debating the Common Market, 1971

in the Common Market, the Society organised a Brains Trust of experts to whom members could submit questions.

Cultural programme

The Society was particular effective in meeting the interest of its members in cultural activities and events. Among the many artists living or working in Highgate, was John Gay, who generously contributed many of the front covers of *Buzz*. The photographs he took in Highgate Cemetery in particular are internationally famous. An Art Lending Library was launched in 1967, changing its title in 1972 to the Highgate Picture Lending Exhibition. This allowed members to borrow works that local artists exhibited in 10A for a modest monthly fee or to buy them if they preferred. Richard Downer took responsibility for organising evenings in Highgate pubs where poets read their poems.

3.14 John Gay, photographer

A series of talks was held on the topic of *My Living: the Arts*. These included one on being a writer by local historian Gillian Tindall, whose novel *Fly Away Home* had won the Somerset Maugham Award in 1972, one by the journalist Gerard Isaaman, who was appointed Editor of the *Ham and High* in 1973, and one by John Herbert, then the PR director of Christie's. A Life Class met briefly, and fell into abeyance until revived in 1992 as the Life Drawing Group.

For many years Marie Gay, wife of John Gay, was the driving force behind the regular, and very popular, Craft Fairs. Her husband John, besides being a photographer, was also a potter and assisted Marie with the organisation of the Fairs. The Society hosted them and took twenty per cent of the profits. Children's Craft Afternoons were held on Saturdays. Two professional artists judged competitions and the winning entries were displayed on the front cover of *Buzz*.

In these years there was much interest in craft activity of all sorts, for children and adults, and special craft evenings were held on the widest variety of topics. In today's world, dominated by electronic entertainment and social media, it is difficult to imagine craft events of this sort would attract many children.

Whether the success or failure of these events depended on the energy of the organiser or the level of interest from members is difficult to tell.

MUSIC IN 🎵 HIGHGATE

1971-72

8 pm. SUNDAY JANUARY 23rd 1972

at

DYNE HOUSE, SOUTHWOOD LANE, HIGHGATE, N.6

'MEET THE COHEN FAMILY'

RAYMOND COHEN (violin)

his wife ANTHYA RAEL (piano)

and their son ROBERT COHEN (cello)

PROGRAMME

BRAHMS   SONATA No.1 IN E MINOR FOR CELLO AND PIANO, Op.38
            Allegro non troppo — Allegretto quasi minuetto — Trio — Allegro

PROKOFIEV   SONATA No.2 IN D MAJOR FOR VIOLIN AND PIANO, Op.94
            Moderato — Scherzo (Presto) — Andante — Allegro con brio

——— INTERVAL ———

MENDELSSOHN PIANO TRIO No.1 IN D MINOR, Op.49
            Molto allegro ed agitato — Andante con moto tranquillo —
            Scherzo (leggiero e vivace) — Allegro assai appassionato

OUR ARTISTS

RAYMOND COHEN was born in Manchester of musical parents. His father gave him his first violin lessons, and he later took lessons with Lionel Falkman. On leaving Manchester Grammar School, at which point he decided to make music his career, he won the Adolph Brodsky scholarship to the Royal Manchester College of Music where he studied for five years, and, in particular, the violin with Henry Holst.

During this period he became the youngest-ever member of the Hallé Orchestra and, at the same time, was heard frequently as a soloist.

The war cut short what promised to be an outstanding career, but soon after the war, still in Army uniform, he became the first winner of the Carl Flesch international violin competition; in the following year Sir John Barbirolli invited him to give several performances with the Hallé Orchestra, which led to engagements with every major symphony orchestra in Britain.

(cont.)

3.15 Invitation to meet the Cohen family, 1972

1968 saw the foundation of the Highgate Society Chamber Orchestra. Later the word "Society" was dropped from its title; it thus became the first of many groups which had been started within the Society which in due course took on an independent life. Some of these are described in more detail in chapter 10. The orchestra performed most often in Highgate School, and played with such soloists as Tamas Vasary (piano) and Anthony Pleeth (cello). "Music in Highgate" was the name given to a series of subscription concerts, featuring Dmitri Tiomkin, the Finchley Children's Music Group, and Robert Cohen (cello), then only twelve years old, with his parents Anthya and Raymond. So small was the audience for the last of these – a performance by the Concert Brass Ensemble of London - that the series was discontinued. Lack of success was attributed to Highgate's proximity to London's many concert halls.

Community Services

Community service was an important part of the Society's mission in these days and the Community Services Committee distributed leaflets asking both for volunteer helpers and those in need of its services. The Good Neighbour Scheme then organised regular visits to those needing support. Children were driven to special schools and patients to and from hospitals and convalescent homes in a programme closely coordinated with the local Councils' social workers. The *Monday Club* provided tea for the over 60s, for a while accompanied by whist, and those who could not get to 10A under their own steam were driven there by volunteers.

From 1968 the National Blood Transfusion Service set up a regular blood donor station outside 10A.

Children's Services

An energetic organiser of the Society's children's services at that time was Nicky Gavron. How her campaigning skills were to result in the establishment of a community and arts centre in the former Methodist church at the junction of Archway Road and Jacksons Lane is told in chapter 10.

Playgroups for pre-School Children were run in the United Reformed Church Hall in South Grove. There were sessions on Monday to Friday afternoons for two and a half year olds upwards, at a cost of five shillings per session. These playgroups provided vital pre-school provision at a time when Highgate was not as well provided with nursery schools as it is today. Mother and Baby Afternoons were introduced on Tuesday afternoons to enable young mothers to meet others and to make new friends.

Children's Chess events, for older children, were first organised in 1969 on Saturday afternoons. Also that year Highgate Week included an exhibition of children's pottery and a children's concert at the HLSI. In 1971 children between the ages of 8 and 10 were encouraged to enter a poetry competition. A cookery course for children was organised during school holidays.

The back page of the April-May issue of *Buzz* was devoted to Junior *Buzz*, with a join-the-dots puzzle of the head of Karl Marx, and a junior crossword. The same issue advertised a children's book mart at 10A. Meanwhile a Children's Theatre Group was organised alongside the one for adults. A block booking was made for the Ernest Read's Children's Concerts at the Royal Festival Hall. It was estimated at this time that more than 500 children were Highgate Society members by virtue of their parents' family membership.

Planning and Traffic

In 1967 a decision was made to consolidate the Traffic Committee and the Amenity & Planning Committee into a single committee, named – and still called – the Environment Committee. Its remit was to monitor planning applications, development proposals and traffic issues. Its role was enhanced by the designation of the Highgate Conservation Area in 1968, under the Civic Amenities Act (1967). This gave recognition to the importance of conservation as well as preservation. A further step towards the support for the environment was the introduction of Tree Preservation Orders in 1969. The Committee's interest in trees had been evident some time before when it had asked the residents of Cholmeley Crescent if they would like a tree to be planted on the pavement in front of their house; Haringey Council planted those that were requested. The trees, now fully mature, give distinction to the Crescent.

A fundamental part of the Environment Committee's work involves working closely with local Councils. Highgate, unlike most other identifiable village communities, suffers from its High Street acting as a borough boundary, in this case between Camden and Haringey, two of the new London Boroughs formed as a result of the reorganisation of London government in 1968. A third London Borough, Islington, also contains a number of residents who feel they belong to Highgate. Indeed the Society's area of interest even includes a small part of Barnet. The reorganisation of London local government led in future years to many difficulties in achieving consistent policies on traffic and planning which would often vary from one side of the High Street to the other.

There was always a feeling in the community that both boroughs considered Highgate issues as of low importance given its location on the outer edge of their jurisdictions. The feeling still remains. A celebrated example of this occurred during the 1990s when a Haringey case officer recommended giving permission for conversion of yet another premises into an estate agency on the grounds that there were only six in the village. An irate Highgate Society pointed out that there were actually twelve – he had not counted the ones on the Camden side. To the Society's disappointment approval was nevertheless granted.

In the summer 1971 issue of *Buzz* reference is made to what is known as the Highgate Bowl, an area of historic significance since it was the place where cattle were grazed prior to slaughter in Highgate butchers' shops after their long journey from the north. What would be an appropriate use for this land would be disputed for the following forty-five years, a saga which is described in chapter 9.

The huge range of issues covered by the Environment Committee is clear from the planning and transport topics covered in *Buzz*:

Public transport

Radio interference from masts

The need to discuss the condition of Highgate Cemetery with the company that owned it

Planning applications

The Greater London Plan, the GLC's Development Plan and the opportunity to submit comment on its implications for Highgate

Finding a use for Lauderdale House

Protecting the appearance of the Village from inappropriate development

The conversion of the disused railway track between Finsbury Park and Highgate Wood into a Parkland Walk.

The term "indefatigable" could be applied to any of the members of the Environment Committee and is still used to describe two of its legendary stalwarts of this time, Susan (Lady) Cox and her colleague Joan (Lady) Neale, Secretary to the Environment Committee for more than twenty years. Of them it was said:

"Lady Cox and Lady Neale

Wield the rod developers feel

Councils too endure the shocks

Of Lady Neale and Lady Cox"

The four Borough Councils were by no means the only public bodies that the Society needed to liaise with. The list included the then *Inner London Education Authority*, the GLC and two Government departments.

3.16 Joan Neale (l) and Susan Cox (r)

On the death in November 1974 of Denzil Budgett-Meakin, Chairman of the Environment Committee, *Buzz* carried personal tributes from the Society's President Yehudi Menuhin, other Society colleagues and representatives from the HLSI, Heath & Old Hampstead Society and Camden Council. A copse on Hampstead Heath was planted in his memory.

3.17 Denzil Budgett-Meakin, with wife Kathleen and daughter Catherine

Buzz

After Ion Trewin had relinquished the editorship of *Buzz* in 1970, a long-term replacement proved hard to find. The team under Diana Toeman, Chairman of the Membership Committee which had taken over the task of communicating with members of the Society, decided that a more soberly-titled quarterly newsletter and diary should replace *Buzz*. Instead of the typed entries being assembled by

3.18 Contest for the Merry Mug[XIX]

a printer, it would now be desktop published enabling it to be produced more quickly and thus be more up to date. There were only four pages in the first issue.

The first issue, in March 1975, reported the death of Isla Merry, Ion's mother-in-law, just a month before. A woman of boundless energy and wide interests, she was one of the Society's founding members, a former Chairman of the Society and the inspiration and instigator of many of the activities of the Social and Entertainment Committee. She had also donated a silver tankard, known as the *Merry Mug*, to be awarded to the winners of an annual quiz competition which the Society and the HLSI still contest.

Isla Merry owned a shop and as a trader she was very much the voice of the Village. When she died the corner shop that she ran was let by her estate to "Raj". A constant refrain during the foundation years was that without the High Street there is no Village. The Society was keen from the start to work to sustain the High Street and to unite residents and retailers, in 1966 almost all "business" being retail trade.

Kenwood House, 1860

4.01 Christina Nolan with Mayor and Lady Mayor of Camden, Burns Night 1976

CHAPTER 4:
THE SECOND DECADE (1976 - 1985)

The tenth anniversary

Christina Nolan, who had been elected Chairman in 1975, decided that the tenth anniversary of the Society should be celebrated in style. The activities of the Social and Entertainment Committee had been faltering but in 1975 things picked up when Marjorie Wilson and then Lilian Buss took over its leadership and when the anniversary provided justification for fresh celebrations.

The January 1976 *Buzz* announced the following programme of events which would take place between the 7th and the 15th of May:

Friday 7th, a concert in St Michael's given by Yehudi Menuhin as President, accompanied by a star pupil from the Menuhin School, pianist Yitkin Seow, a Highgate resident

Saturday 8th from 10:30, the second Highgate Society Fair in the Square

Saturday at 8:30 pm, People on the Hill, "a scrapbook of Highgate through the ages in words and pictures, with wine and music", compiled by Brendan Nolan[xx].

Sunday afternoon, two walks: Old Highgate, led by Sir James Brown, and New Highgate, led by Gordon Shelley

Sunday evening, a Festal Service at St Michael's, with contributions from all the Highgate churches

Tuesday evening, a literary discussion Book Shop at HLSI

Wednesday 10:30, a demonstration of Cordon Bleu cookery by Rosemary Morris, followed by a three-course lunchtime dinner in 10A

Wednesday evening, a Gala Bridge evening in 10A

Thursday, late morning, a fashion show followed by lunch, in HLSI

Thursday 7:30 pm, an Old English Supper Party in 10A

Thursday 9 pm, A Partial Eye, John Gay's photographs of Highgate, with commentary by playwright and local resident Christopher Hampton

Friday, 8:30 pm, Wine tasting of after-dinner wines

Saturday, 2:30, local Craftsmen at work, with sale of their products

Saturday 15th, 7:30 for 8: coaches leave for Anniversary Ball at Alexandra Palace

And in addition to these one-off events, there were:

An Anniversary Competition for writers under 12 and aged 12-16 years for an essay, poem or story entitled *Highgate*

A competition for children to make a mobile incorporating the letters H and S

A children's art exhibition at the Centaur Gallery in the High Street

An exhibition by the Environment Committee throughout the week at 10A.

Review of the Society's progress

Ion Trewin returned to edit the May 1976 *Buzz*, an *Anniversary Souvenir* edition, which began with a discussion of the following questions:

What had been achieved?

What had failed?

What were the continuing problems?

What were the changes of direction not envisaged by the founders of the Society?

Taking part in a debate on these questions, hosted by Sue and Ion Trewin, were the first Chairman Ronald Bernstein, the current Chairman Christina Nolan, past Editors of *Buzz*, Cornelia and Peter Usborne, and the Editor of the *Ham and High*, Gerard Isaaman, who had supported the Society from its early days.

4.02 Wine tasting pre-decimalisation, 1969

Ronald Bernstein noted that he had expected the Community Services Committee to monitor the services provided by Borough Councils that covered Highgate. In the event, its members decided that they would act instead as a Community *Service* Committee, i.e. one which would itself provide needed services to the community directly. He said that, while he saw this shift of emphasis as a failure to deliver one of the original purposes of the Society, he felt the provision of community services was an excellent additional activity which had helped to bring the community together.

It was agreed that it might appear somewhat paradoxical that a Society, founded to campaign on transport issues, should have placed such emphasis on social and community activities. But it was these activities that had enabled the Society to knit the community together and hence to speak with a more powerful voice on environmental and planning issues. Bernstein attributed the success of these activities to Barbara Edwards' determination that the Society should have its own premises; the lease of 10A had made possible a panoply of events, such as art exhibitions, craft evenings, food fares, bridge evenings, play groups, mother and baby afternoons and blood donor sessions.

Bernstein paid tribute to Sir James Brown, President of the HLSI, for enabling the Society to take a short lease on 10A at a modest rent, despite the high market value that its central position in the village would command. He added that Sir James had helped the Society in many ways, contributing articles on historical events and personalities in Highgate and leading many walks around Highgate to educate visitors in its history.

The fact that the Society's membership had, by this time, reached over 1,700 had given increased authority to the representations of its environmental and transport spokesmen. Bernstein added that:

now that the Community Land Act is law the balance of power between the developer and local authority and the people of the amenity

societies has been revolutionised – you used to have the developer and the planning authority fighting and the residents' association watching in the wings and sometimes intervening, usually on the side of the local authority. From now on all development is going to be carried on, in effect, by the local authority and the developer as partners, so that that balance has gone and the only check on the council – which after all is meant to be doing what is best for the community – will be the amenity societies.

Sue Trewin cautioned, however, that the Society's social and entertainment activities were too middle-class to engage residents in social housing such as Highgate New Town and Hillcrest[XXii], who certainly considered themselves Highgate residents. *Buzz*, having reported this debate, published four pages of photographs from the first ten years, including the mobiles made in the children's craft sessions, incorporating the letters H and S. Would these have engaged children from Highgate's areas of social housing?

The Society's original constitution had made provision for a Council of thirty, a third

4.03 *Peggy Jay chairing the Witanhurst committee*[XXi]

of whom were elected each year, serving a term of three years: no retiring member of Council could be immediately re-elected. The purpose of the three-year limit was to counter the formation of cliques and to encourage newcomers. However this rule did not apply to Chairmen of committees or to committee members, and it had become evident that the Society's continuing vigour was as much attributable to the long and dedicated service of many of these individuals as to the overall direction given by the Chairman or by Council.

The broadening of activities

During this decade the Society, or more particularly its members, became more deeply involved in the development of Highgate's voluntary organisations. Among the most far-reaching of these developments was the formation of Friends of Highgate Society (FOHC), the

4.04 Yehudi Menuhin opening the Highgate Art Fair[xxiii]

Harington Scheme, the Lauderdale House Society, Jacksons Lane Community Centre, the North London Hospice Group and the Highgate Decorative and Fine Arts Society, many of which are described in more detail in chapter 10.

A feature in *Buzz* explored the role of members in supporting Hill Homes, the charity described in more detail in chapter 6 which was founded by Mrs Margaret Hill to provide apartments for the elderly. Its Chairman, John Samuel, later served as President of the Society. In 1968 *Buzz* published a letter from Joan Schwitzer, wife of a subsequent Chairman Mat Schwitzer, which was critical of its failure to report the activities of other Highgate societies such as the Highgate Horticultural Society. Joan was to become a founder member of the Hornsey Historical Society and, between 1974 and 1985, its Chairman.

In February 1978 *Buzz* ran a piece on the Friends of Whittington Hospital and issued a request for gifts to provide amenities for staff and patients. In April of the same year an article appeared about the Highgate Council of Churches, which includes St Anne's, St Augustine's, St Michael's, All Saints and the United Reformed Church.

Existing activities evolved. Though competition between the Society and the HLSI for the *Merry Mug* continued unabated, the rules were changed so that all members of the two organisations who attended the event were involved, not just a selected team of specialist quiz-answerers. The programme of theatre evenings and craft fairs was expanded with a Poetry in Pubs or Gardens and a programme of Live Music Now instituted by Yehudi Menuhin. A

4.05 Sara Kaye

4.06 The first advertisement in Buzz

Jazz Ball was held at the Gatehouse in 1981 with two local groups, the Crouch End All-Stars and the Highgate Choral Society's Barbershop Quartet. Music in Highgate Homes continued under the inspired management of its founder, Sara Kaye.

During the 1970s the Decorative and Fine Arts Society was spun off from the Arts Committee and some years later affiliated itself to the national body NADFAS. It arranged for eminent art historians to give lectures to its members and formed a number of specialist study groups. The Society offered its members guided tours of country houses and museums in the UK and overseas.

In September 1985, under the editorship of Vanessa Whinney, paid advertisements appeared in *Buzz* for the first time. One of the first advertised the products of Marie Lecko, a dress designer in the High Street. Ruth Phillips volunteered to act as Advertising Rep and sold two whole pages of advertisements for the Christmas '85 issue and many more

in subsequent issues. There were some within the Society who considered that such advertisements cheapened *Buzz*. Others welcomed the exposure which *Buzz* could now give to the local business community, and there is no doubt that income from this source enabled the magazine to be produced in a more professional manner than it otherwise would have been.

The Editor of *Buzz* successfully showcased the lesser known skills of the Society's multi-talented members, including reviews of books they had written. Michael Hammerson contributed a series of early photographs on Highgate As It Was, showing local landmarks in the late nineteenth and early twentieth centuries, and John Lacey, a former Chairman of the Planning and Amenity Committee and then a Vice President, a watercolour of St Joseph's Church which was used on one of its covers.

Yehudi Menuhin was the most inspirational example of a multi-tasker: besides being a world-renowned violinist, founder of an internationally recognised school in Switzerland for young musicians and an organiser of prestigious music festivals, he found time as

51

4.07 *Yehudi Menuhin marks twentieth anniversary of the Highgate Society, 1986*

President of the Highgate Society to perform in concerts in aid of the Society, to set up Live Music Now and to plant a tree to mark the Society's twentieth anniversary with the help of trainees of the Harington Scheme, of which he also became President. He was prevailed upon to write an introduction for the publication *Portrait of Highgate* which contained drawings by Ann Usborne with text by Tim Ades.

John Gay supplied several cover pictures for *Buzz* and many others which are reproduced in this book. He illustrated *Highgate Cemetery, a Victorian Valhalla*, published by the Friends of Highgate Cemetery, and provided ninety-six views of Highgate for a competition in which members were challenged to identify each view's location. His wife Marie served as Chairman of the Arts Committee.

4.09 *Bernard Miles at Wedding Day Whoopee, 1981*

Commemorations

The 1980 Olympics were the inspiration for what, in June 1980, *Buzz* recorded as the Highgate Society Olympicnics, a kind of huge picnic with sports or "family-food-and-fun" day, held at the Aylmer Road playing fields. It raised £450 for the Environment Committee. The wedding of the Prince of Wales and Lady Diana Spencer in 1981 was celebrated by a "Wedding Day Whoopee".

In 1983 the Society organised a ceremony to celebrate Yehudi Menuhin's new position of "Patron". Earlier in the year he had announced that he and his wife were planning to leave Highgate, necessitating resignation from his position as President. At the ceremony he declared that the happiest years of his and Diana's lives were the twenty-five they had spent in Highgate. Ronald Bernstein, who had been the Society's first Chairman, took over as President.

4.08 *Poster promoting the Olympicnics, 1980*

Fund-raising

Lauderdale House on Highgate Hill is perhaps the oldest surviving "grand house" in Highgate. In 1889 its owner, Sir Sydney Waterlow, donated it to the LCC together with its grounds, which became known as Waterlow Park, one of a chain of green spaces that encircle Highgate. The house was restored in 1893 but a disastrous fire in 1964 severely damaged its upper floors. Encouraged by the Society, the Friends of Lauderdale House was formed. It registered as a charity in 1976 and negotiated a five-year lease from Camden Council, which by that time had inherited the property from the LCC via the GLC.

A campaign raised sufficient funds to enable the house to be partially restored, and it was re-opened by Yehudi Menuhin in 1978. More fund-raising followed; the Society held its playgroups there when building work started in the United Reformed Church, and used it for such large events as the Burns Supper in 1979. The Society's Watercolour Group still uses it for its annual summer show. By February 1984 the main staircase was restored, and the Trust was appealing in *Buzz* for £120,000 to restore the Long Gallery.

In 1982 a North London Hospice Group was formed in response to the lack of any hospice facility in North London. It set out to buy the disused Whittington Hospital Geriatric Annexe in Broadlands Road which it wanted to convert into a hospice. From March 1983 onwards the Highgate Society was deeply involved in fund-raising for the hospice. Proceeds from Carols in Pond Square, an annual event run by the Society, from a Grand Ball, and from a watercolourists' sale at Lauderdale House were donated to this project.

Fund-raising continued for years. In December 1985 Marion Judd instituted a series of dinner parties intended to raise £16,000 by Easter 1986. Until the hospice could be established home care was delivered from a shop premises in Crouch End. Eventually, after much effort from the Society and other supporters, an in-patient hospice was opened in Woodside Avenue on a site bought in 1987. This was supplemented from 2016 by a Day Centre in Enfield catering for residents in Barnet, Enfield and Haringey.

Planning

In 1976, under the chairmanship of Michael Wright, the Environment Committee was active on several fronts: monitoring of the weight restriction on lorries in the Village, sustaining the campaign against development of the Bowl and working on the proposed Parkland Walk. There was disappointment over the decision to give permission for Highgate's first example of a new phenomenon, a gated housing development, on the lower part of the historic landscaped gardens of Witanhurst.

In 1985 Michael Hammerson took over as Chairman, a role which he held for the following twenty-five years.

4.10 Michael Hammerson

During the Society's second decade, the work of the Environment Committee continued to grow in volume and to expand in scope. The workload intensified, if in the best possible way, when in 1977 the Conservation Area was enlarged as far as the bottom of Highgate West Hill, now taking in Holly Village and the East Cemetery and, on the other side of the Archway Road, the Miltons.

4.12 York stone paving, Pond Square

Alarmed at Camden's proposals for higher housing densities, the Society urged the Council that housing density on the fringes of the Heath Area of Special Character should not exceed seventy habitable rooms per acre.

Opposition to the proposals to widen the Archway Road not only persisted throughout the decade but also hardened. As is described in chapter 8, there seemed no obvious way to resolve the conflict.

The Society was one of a number of local groups that had been considering the future of the disused railway track between Finsbury Park and Muswell Hill. The common preference was that it should become a woodland walk, open to the public, a use to which many other derelict railway lines were being put. Such was the level of opposition to Haringey's proposal to build housing on the former track that a Public Inquiry was held in 1978.

4.11 The Parkland Walk

In October 1979 the Inspector's dismissal of the proposals was celebrated as a major success. However, the same year, undeterred, Haringey tried again to build on two sites along the line, and in 1980 the Society had to flag up concerns about the removal of an old railway bridge over the walk, and of rubbish dumping outside one of its disused stations. Fortunately, yet another public inquiry into Haringey's latest proposals was not necessary: the local authority gave in to public pressure, and the abandoned railway line, today familiar to locals as the Parkland Walk, is both a popular local amenity and a valued, and vital, part of a local ecological corridor.

Comments on local authorities were not always negative. The April 1979 *Buzz* records, "We are delighted with the new York stone paving recently laid by Camden Council in South Grove. It is one of a number of environmental improvements originally suggested by the Society." The extent of this paving was substantially increased some twenty years later as part of a wider refurbishment of Pond Square.

The Society also succeeded in persuading Camden Council to restore rather than demolish and rebuild the seventeenth-century wall of Waterlow Park which by then was in a state of some disrepair. In December 1983 the Committee scored another success, the conversion into flats of the former Presbyterian Church at the junction where Highgate Hill meets Hornsey Lane and Cromwell Avenue. This conversion almost certainly saved the building from demolition.

The December 1981 *Buzz* explained the Society's role with respect to Highgate Wood: that the wood was managed by the City of London, but the Society sometimes got involved in management issues such as the refurbishment of its children's playground. Soon the Society was to become a member of the City of London's Highgate Wood Consultative Committee and would thereafter play a more formal role in the management of the wood.

In 1981 Camden proposed the closure of Dartmouth Park Hill at its junction with Highgate Hill, Hornsey Lane and Cromwell Avenue. This followed complaints about the congestion caused by traffic wishing to turn right into it from Highgate Hill. After a trial closure period, the level of congestion in Magdala Road became so intolerable that Dartmouth Park Hill was re-opened in December 1984. The introduction of phased "all-red" traffic lights at the junction, as the Society had originally proposed, made it much safer to cross the five roads which meet at this intersection.

Highgate's historic houses

The spring 1983 *Buzz* announced that four of Highgate's historic houses were up for sale. One was The Old Hall, immediately east of St Michael's Church, which contains traces of the seventeenth century Arundel House. It was here that Sir Francis Bacon, who was already very ill at the time, died after catching a chill during his experiment in refrigeration: he wished to find out whether a chicken would stay fresh longer if it was stuffed with snow. Two houses on The Bank, Highgate Hill, were also for sale: the seven-bayed, Grade I listed Cromwell House, built in 1638 but with no connection to Oliver Cromwell, and its Grade II* listed neighbour, Ireton House, which was not named in memory of Cromwell's general but of William Ireton, its owner from 1895 to 1905. The fourth was Hillside, a fine eighteenth and nineteenth-century house on Jacksons Lane.

The Society was not entirely pleased by the proposal to convert Cromwell House into offices, and endeavoured to interest the National Trust in acquiring it as a natural partner for Fenton House in Hampstead. In 1985, when this overture proved unsuccessful, the Society worked with the new owners to preserve its fine features having been reassured that its magnificent seventeenth-century staircase, with its newels depicting Cromwellian soldiers, its fine panelling and its splendid Jacobean plaster ceilings would be restored. Suddenly, however, the owners backed out, apparently baulking at the cost of restoration, and the house was sold once again, this time to developers who proposed to convert it into seven apartments. Their proposals were rejected by Haringey, but there were to be further developments in the next decade, as revealed in chapter 5. Hillside, too, faced inappropriate development, but was eventually sold and today continues to remain in private occupation.

4.13 Lillian Buss

The stable buildings of Angel Yard, one of Highgate's last coaching inn yards to survive in anything like its old form, were threatened with an extension to the Angel pub next door. After a determined campaign, the Society succeeded in persuading Camden to insist on the restoration of the stable yard buildings. The buildings were sensitively restored for residential use, but, to the Society's regret, it failed in its attempt to persuade Camden to apply a condition requiring that no gate should be put across the yard entrance. As a result, Highgate's best-surviving old coaching inn yard is today a gated development and the public are unable to gain access to this historic and atmospheric part of the village.

Community Services

The Society's playgroup, set up in 1968 against some opposition, had by 1970 become so popular that afternoon sessions were added to the morning ones. In 1980 primary schools started to open nursery classes, so the afternoon session was discontinued, but the morning sessions continued, together with a Mothers' Support Group.

Fund-raising activities for these playgroups included a Jumble Sale in 1977 and a Jazz Ball in 1984. In 1979 the playgroup joined the Pre-School Playgroup Association and received a grant from Camden Council. In 1982 it had to vacate the United Reformed Church, which was being refurbished. After a spell in the house of the headmaster of St Michael's School it moved into its current location in Lauderdale House.

In 1980 the Community Services Committee produced a list of babysitters. This was followed in 1986 by the publication by Sandy Graham of a Good Tradesmen Guide to plumbers, decorators and other craftsmen that members of the Society had found trustworthy, the plan being to update the list annually.

Classes in children's Scottish Country Dancing were introduced in 1982 and in 1985 a class for Beginners and Improvers Bridge on Wednesday mornings. In 1986 Isabel Jardine retired after eighteen years of running the Bridge Evenings.

4.14 Calendar page drawn by Caitlin Egen, then aged 10, Hillway, N6

Eating and Drinking

During this decade the Social and Entertainment Committee held a Brazilian luncheon, a Burns Night Supper, a celebration of Bastille Day at Lauderdale House, a Harvest Supper and a Halloween party. Cookery was also on the Committee's agenda. Cordon Bleu cookery classes were run by members, more than one of whom had won awards in national competitions. Lillian Buss, now Chairman of this committee, was among those who contributed a seasonal recipe to each issue of *Buzz*.

Besides fulfilling statutory obligations, the Wine Committee advised on and purchased the wines that were enjoyed at Society events. Its members organised wine and cheese parties, whose profits went to the Society, and contributed a regular column in *Buzz* on the varieties of wine suitable for seasonal celebrations.

In July 1977 *Buzz* published a review of the numerous pubs in Highgate and followed this up with reviews of various Highgate eating places with the aim of promoting local businesses.

Arts and Crafts

The Art Lending Library continued to prove popular, with an annual exhibition in January 1977 drawing record numbers. Members lent sculptures for a well-attended exhibition and Kaia Mayer initiated a series of *Sunday Salons* which exhibited cartoons, ethnic sculpture, and historic maps. Poetry in Highgate held readings of their own works by Highgate poets, including Danny Abse, and also readings of Andrew Marvell. In 1978 the Society's first poetry anthology was published, price 50p.

In 1978 the Arts Committee also held a "Thackeray Vanity Fair" in the Centaur Gallery in the High Street, now no more, including part of J. M. Barrie's *Quality Street*, and ending with a ball in The Gatehouse to the band of the Duke of Cambridge's Hussars who appeared in full uniform. The Fair raised £650 for new spotlighting and curtains in 10A, which were installed in early 1979 for an exhibition of works by local artists. The committee also organised Stage Craft sessions on Fridays for aspiring actors and Drama Workshops for children between 7 and 10.

In 1977 the Crafts Committee introduced classes in patchwork, cane seating, creative embroidery, upholstery, dressmaking alterations, make-do-and-mend, script writing and lettering, and simple crochet. Children's craft sessions were held on Saturday afternoons, with sessions on puppet making, cushion collage, pin-art, paper sculpture and finally a puppet show using the puppets made in the first session.

Midway through this decade a *Highgate Calendar* was published, to which Ann Usborne contributed drawings of local beauty spots. Calendars continued to be published for some years afterwards, though on a sporadic basis.

Pond Square in the 1840s

THE PONDS, HIGHGATE.

5.01 Yehudi Menuhin and quartet, 1986

CHAPTER 5:
THE THIRD DECADE (1986 - 1995)

Further anniversary celebrations

In 1986 the Society celebrated the twentieth anniversary of its foundation. Celebrations were, if anything, even more elaborate than those held ten years earlier. Sir Yehudi Menuhin, in his role of Patron, sent a long message of congratulation. So too did founder of the Society, Ronald Bernstein, its first Chairman and Menuhin's successor as President.

The celebrations involved all sections of the Society. In the spring the Community Group staged a Valentine's Day Concert which they followed up in the summer with a Jazz Band Ball. Yehudi Menuhin took the opportunity to organise a performance featuring students from his school. Another performance involved a quintet drawn from the members the Waterhouse family. A Reflections on Highgate event incorporated material put forward by the Society's membership in a variety of art forms.

Anniversaries, whilst backward-looking to a degree, can often encourage organisations to confront the future with renewed vigour and confidence and this seemed to be the case from 1987. With Ruth Phillips[xxiv] as Editor, a decision was made to give *Buzz* a more professional appearance, not least in order to make it more attractive to its advertisers. Ruth expanded the spring 1987 issue to thirty-two pages. Some pages were now printed in colour and where they remained in black and white their legibility was improved. The improvements had the desired effect as, from 1987 onwards, most issues of *Buzz* had as many pages of advertisements as they did of text.

Swearing on the Horns

Some people consider the ceremony of *Swearing on the Horns* at one or other of Highgate's pubs to be an ancient ceremony, others that it more likely originated in the eighteenth century. The colourful ceremony is described by John Oakes in the summer 1986 *Buzz* as follows.

As part of the June 28th Fair in the Square, and in celebration of twenty years' existence, the Highgate Society will hold special sessions at The Flask of a custom unique to Highgate, the *Swearing on the Horns*. For this, we will be combining with the current custodians of the mystery, the Hornsey Round Table.

Following hallowed tradition a pair of horns is set on a pole supported by a frock-coated beadle. A 'court' is then convened by an impressive judge in wig and robes, and visitors are invited to step forward, grasp the horns, and subscribe to what one historian called 'ye merrie conceit yclept ye Highgate oath'.

Having sworn to eat white bread and drink strong beer, unless he prefer anything else, and to kiss the serving maid, the swearer then pays a fee and becomes a Freeman of Highgate, with a certificate to prove it. The Freedom carries one inestimable benefit: 'If at any time you are going through Highgate and want to rest yourself, and you see a pig lying in a ditch, you have the liberty to kick the animal and take its place'.

It seems likely that the ceremony was always a catchpenny attraction for travellers, and one nineteenth century illustration shows a landlord administering the oath. Nowadays, local charities are the sole beneficiaries, and on June 18th, the Hornsey Centre for Handicapped Children will receive all fees and court fines for smiling, frowning, bad jokes, and other misdemeanours!

The Swearing was already centuries old when Byron recorded it in *Childe Harold's Pilgrimage*:

'Many to the steep of Highgate hie;

Ask ye Boeotian Shades! The reason why?

'Tis to the worship of the solemn Horn

Grasped in the holy hand of Mystery

To whose dread name both men and maids are sworn

And consecrate the oath with draught and dance – till dawn.'

'Dawn' seems a bit optimistic…but there may be the odd extension on licensed premises.

5.02 The Flask public house

The strikingly awful piece of doggerel from Byron's usually inspired pen has served to give the ceremony a certain cult status.

The Fair in Pond Square was bigger and better than ever, with children's games organised by the Highgate In 1987 the Fair in the Square was bigger and better than ever. As ever there were a number of events to entertain children. Face painting, fairground rides and sticky sweets are evergreen regulars whose popularity has survived over the subsequent thirty years. But at the twentieth anniversary fair in 1986 there were many events which would probably be less familiar to today's children than to their parents: Morris Dancers, fortune telling and a Fantastic

Hat competition. The main sponsor was Wheeler's, a chain of seafood restaurants more popular in those days than it is now. Based in the West End, it had recently opened a branch in South Grove. The mock ceremony of Swearing on the Horns was timed to coincide with the anniversary fair. The ceremony was celebrated at The Flask tavern.

In the last twenty years the policy of the Editor of *Buzz* has been not to publish letters to the Editor. However thirty years ago correspondence to the Editor was more common and, in such a letter, Marie Gay expressed her concern that, whilst the quality of musical performances had maintained the standards set during the first decade, activity in the visual arts and crafts had deteriorated. This was notwithstanding a Buy or Borrow Works of Art exhibition proposed for the anniversary programme, a repeat of an innovation which had proved successful in the past.

Members of the Society's various committees decided that the programme should include a multi-faith thanksgiving service, several Highgate Walks, a fashion show, a food fair and an exhibition of members' photographs. The programme included an Anniversary Ball in the main hall of Highgate School.

A watercolour exhibition is an event that many societies would include in their anniversary programmes but a public poetry reading is one which could succeed in few communities other than those in London's Northern Heights. It was repeated in 2016. Fleur Bowers, a member, was the inspiration behind the workshop group, Highgate Poets which at this time met monthly in its members' homes for them to read their latest poems and obtain constructive criticism of their work. In 1992 they launched their fifteenth anthology of poems, *Kites 15*.

One lasting legacy of the anniversary was the purchase of the large aerial photograph of Highgate, taken in 1966, which since 1986 has hung on the east wall of 10A.

To commemorate the anniversary and to embellish South Grove, it was decided that Yehudi Menuhin should plant a horse chestnut tree at the junction of South Grove and Highgate High Street on ground prepared by graduates of the Harington Scheme. Alas, notwithstanding the species' reputation for longevity, honey fungus was discovered in the tree in 2014 and a decision was taken to replace it with the fastigiate beech which President Stephen Panke planted in March 2015.

The lease of 10A

The party mood which had characterised the rest of the year was somewhat dampened in autumn 1986 when the HLSI issued three years notice of its intention to terminate the lease. Apparently the growth in the size of the HLSI library was such that it needed additional space to store its books. This notice concentrated the mind of the Society not just on securing a new home but on finding the money to ensure that 10A was redecorated under the terms of its lease.

Discussions over the lease of 10A had been ongoing with the HLSI for more than two years. The yearly rent for 10A had been increased from £500 to £1,250 three years before. The Society suggested £1,750 would now be appropriate but the HLSI, whose finances at that time were not as strong as they were before or have been since, considered that £3,500 would be a fairer amount. Eventually, in late 1988, it was agreed that the HLSI would undertake the structural repairs that were by then urgently needed, with a contribution of £2,000 from the Society, and that afterwards the Society would be granted a nine-year repairing lease. The rent during that lease was yet to be agreed.

Arguments over what would constitute a fair rent had by 1990 not only strained relations between landlord and lessee but had resulted in quite serious friction between the members of the two organisations. Indeed so serious had the rift become that a decision was made to reconstitute a Joint Committee which had previously existed between the Society and the HLSI "to promote and maintain good will and understanding between the Highgate Society and the HLSI". Incoming Society Chairman Gavin Doyle publicly acknowledged that there had been a rift, declaring in an interview in 1991 that in his term of office he hoped that "the breach between the Society and the Institution should be healed at once and forever".

Long-standing members of the two bodies, many of whom were members of both organisations, worked hard in the background to improve relations. In 1995 it was announced that there would be cross-representation of members of the Highgate Society Council and the HLSI Management Committee for the first time. It seems remarkable that this had not been decided in 1966, when the HLSI had so warmly encouraged the Society into being.

The spring 1991 issue of *Buzz* reported that the roof of 10A had been repaired and that the entirety of the building would soon be refurbished at a cost of £13,000 plus VAT, of which £10,000 was to be raised by special events. The first of these was the 25th Anniversary Concert in April. Refurbishment was completed in July 1991, £3,000 over budget.

Social activities

The social activities of the Society had changed very little over the years. Most were reliant on the continuing dedication of a particular individual. In the case of the *Monday Club* for the over 60s, that was Elizabeth Caddy its organiser for over thirty years. During this period it success relied on a proven formula of card games and tea. By tradition this format was punctuated twice a year with a summer and a Christmas party, the high points of which was the singing by the Highgate School Choir. Perhaps this was a particularly popular period for bridge, as it was played not just on Monday afternoons but also on Wednesday evenings, with or without instruction as preferred, and on Wednesday mornings with sessions for "Beginners and Improvers".

5.03 Elizabeth Caddy

Earlier on a Monday Mothers and Toddlers took over 10A. The playgroups, which the Society had been instrumental in setting up for slightly older children and which had for many years been held in the crypt below the United Reformed Church, had by this time been relocated to Lauderdale House. Funding now came by way of grants from Camden Council who from time to time complained that their largesse was benefitting parents who lived in neighbouring Haringey.

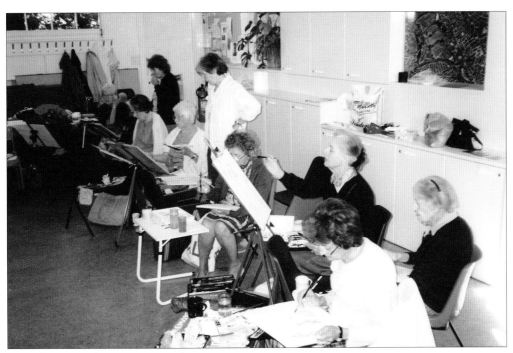

5.04 The Watercolour Group at work

Another activity whose format never seemed to need revision has been the Saturday morning coffee at 10A. It is not often that combining seemingly competing objectives in a single event proves a formula for long term success, but the format of this event is an exception. At one end of the room old friends come together to discuss plays, trips and grandchildren. At the other end of the room visitors arrive with the hope, usually fulfilled, of obtaining some useful advice on a planning dispute which is bothering them. In between the two, both physically and metaphorically, the more active members mix ad hoc discussions on forthcoming activities and campaigns with social chat or engage in discussion with new members or potential new members keen enough to join the throng.

That it was not only residents who turn to the Society for planning advice is evident from the following letter, received from a developer in August 2005.

"In the course of one's working life, there are encounters that begin with difficulties and result in worthwhile relationships. When the issues are sensitive, but negotiated by manifestly decent people like you and those of the groups you represented, good things result, and not only am I grateful, to you for all your courtesy and support, I still acknowledge that a better scheme evolved directly from your inputs and our discussions… It has been a pleasure to know you and your colleagues, to whom you might convey this letter."

The Arts

The cultural activities of the Society continued to flourish. Places on the Thursday morning meetings of the Watercolour Group had become so over-subscribed that serious consideration was given to forming a second group. Such was the standard of its output that, when its work was exhibited at Burgh House, Hampstead, as it was during the winter, and at Lauderdale House during the summer, purchasers were found for a number of the exhibits.

Complementing these weekly slots in the Society calendar were the monthly meetings of the French Circle. The group welcomed members irrespective of whether their knowledge of French was elementary or fluent. Its sole requirement was that members should speak French throughout the evening. It was Mat Schwitzer who conceived the idea of the Group, led from its inception in 1988 by David Weight, the French master at Highgate School and an accomplished watercolourist. Beginning with informal conversation over coffee the evening might progress to a quiz, a video, a film or board games – in French. At first fewer than a dozen turned up but as the reputation of the Group expanded numbers increased. For much of its twenty-five year existence it has been led by Elizabeth Woodman who joined the Circle soon after it was formed.

In October 1992 the French Circle and the Arts Committee decided to collaborate to produce a French Fortnight. A number of the Arts Committee's members exhibited paintings of the areas of France where they took their holidays; opportunities arose to taste French wines from the Loire region when a French arts evening was held. After a surprisingly varied programme of talks, slideshows, musical evenings and a general knowledge quiz, the fortnight concluded with a grand finale dinner at the Café Rouge, which by then had replaced Wheeler's in South Grove.

Wining and dining

The knowledge of the Wine Committee has always been a boon to the organisers of social events, for which it could always be relied upon to suggest a suitable wine. It added greatly to the success of the French Fortnight which then encouraged

the events committee in 1990 to hold a Spanish Fiesta with Spanish food, wine and music. This raised £200 for the 10A refurbishment fund. The proposed Oktoberfest with German wines proved a bridge too far, but the following February a Mardi Gras party was a success.

The impending proclamation of the European Union in December 1992 provided an excuse for the Committee to hold a Fête Européenne or Soirée sans Frontières with food and drinks and a medley of music from the twelve member countries. A Balkan Bacchanalia followed in 1995. Despite this and a wine tasting of "affordable and available wines", the Committee reported that 1995 had been a relatively quiet year notwithstanding its contribution of £150 to Society's funds.

Highlights of the *Italian Week* organised in 1993 were an exhibition of members' paintings of Italian scenes, an evening of Neapolitan songs, a talk entitled "Giotto in Padua" by an expert from the V&A, another talk on contemporary Italian film and a competitive exhibition of members' photographs of Italy. The final dinner took place at Mr G's, a well-known Italian restaurant in the High Street, with a menu specially put together by the owner's wife, Mrs Guselli.

In 1995 the Society attempted a *Chinese Festival*. It featured a lecture by Donald Barron "Chinese civilisation adapting to change", and a rather ambitious Fun Day, during which an authentic lion dance careered along a startled High Street and ended in the Victoria Hall of the HLSI, where there were demonstrations of Chinese calligraphy and of decorative paper cutting. There then followed a talk by a British Museum curator on Chinese sculpture and a demonstration of Chinese medicine and acupuncture. An auctioneer from Christie's who had handled the famous sale of Nanking export pottery gave a talk on Chinese art in

Western interiors after which he offered to value any Chinese objects brought by members. The event ended with a banquet at the Dragon Seed Chinese restaurant which at that time added to the diversity of the High Street.

Despite this abundance of offerings, the *Chinese Festival* proved a failure. Other than for the Fun Day, attendance was disappointingly low and the festival resulted in a financial loss. Whether this was due to poor advance publicity, or there being too many events, or that China was at that time too remote from most members' interest or experience, is hard to tell.

From this time on the range of entertainment activities began to decline due to the lack of a Chairman of the Social and Entertainments Committee and, in due course, a committee with this name or function. However, the Society's inclination to use anniversaries as an excuse for a party was given full rein during this decade. The Silver Anniversary in 1991 was celebrated with a ball organised by Leila Hodge, who had at one time acted as co-editor of *Buzz* with Sue Vinson and who was a stalwart supporter of the annual craft fair. The occasion was also celebrated by a special exhibition of members' paintings, drawings and photographs displaying views of Highgate.

After an opening Bubbly and Birthday Cake Party the programme for the thirtieth anniversary in 1996 included yet another Grand Ball, this one at Channing School, an exhibition Highgate and Beyond and a short-story competition. Once again, Chairman Stephen Panke invoked Ronald Bernstein's phrase about the spirit that infused the beginning of the Society, "a blast of energy released by the anti-Marples campaign".

Debating

In 1966 the year the Society was formed, a Sainsbury's store was opened in Muswell Hill, on the site of the former Athenaeum building in Fortis Green Road. The Athenaeum had since 1902 hosted the Muswell Hill Parliament, a debating society. Given the number of cabinet ministers who at various times have lived in Highgate, it may seem strange how infrequently the Society has hosted debates.

Three were held in 1992, the year of the Society's only systematic effort to organise debates. The first one, somewhat in advance of its time, was on green issues. Perhaps because one of the speakers was the actress Glenda Jackson, who had recently been elected Labour MP for Hampstead and Highgate, the debate was quite well attended. The opposing speaker, in due course to become Conservative MP and policy guru, Oliver Letwin, stressed the need to curb the use of the private car by imposing a heavier tax on petrol.

The Society seemed to have a knack for inviting aspiring politicians as the second debate featured the future MP, but at that time still leader of Islington Council, Margaret Hodge.

5.05 Glenda Jackson and Oliver Letwin debating under the chairmanship of Ronald Bernstein

The subject of her debate with Andrew Mitchell, Conservative leader on Haringey Council, was the role and funding of local government. Hot topics at that time were the Poll Tax and the extent to which responsibility for London-wide planning should be vested in the Greater London Council, the revival of an issue that, as was noted in chapter 2, had been a subject of extensive debate during the 1930s (p19).

So disappointing was the turn-out for the third debate, on ethics and television, that the recently formed Current Affairs Committee decided not to organise any further political debates for the foreseeable future.

Serving the community

During this period those who the Society had relied on to organise community service activities were finding it difficult to recruit new members. One activity to suffer was the blood donor sessions which had been organised by the Community Services Committee for a number of years. *Buzz* accounted for the decline in the number of donors to the Blood Transfusion Service to their scheduling sessions during summer holidays. But the 1990 Gulf War increased demand for blood and generated awareness of the need for donors. Numbers rose to 134 and, by 1996, three sessions were held in the United Reformed Church each year.

The Good Neighbour Scheme was also disbanded for want of volunteers, though members of Council still shopped for the residents of the Mary Feilding Guild. The activities for young people, which had been such a successful feature of the Society in its first decade, had by now virtually ceased. That the Good Tradesmen Guide, rebranded the Trusted Trader Scheme, was kept going was, like many other Society activities, due to the commitment of a single individual, in this case Sandy Graham.

The reputation of the Environment Committee

In the Society's early days its principal role in planning and transport was as a campaigning group, typically contesting what were felt to be inappropriate planning applications or lobbying for particular enhancements of the environment. True to the initial intention of Ronnie Bernstein and John Lacey, the Society acted as a vehicle through which experts in particular fields could offer their services for the benefit of the community by helping it engage more professionally with public bodies. Over time the nature of this relationship began to change as public bodies came to respect the expertise of the Society's planning specialists and the contribution they could make, and not just on Highgate planning issues. As a result the Society's specialists increasingly became viewed as potential partners as well as reliable channels for communicating local opinion.

This had resulted by 1990 in an impressive list of organisations on which the Society had a representative, these including:

Archway Study Group

Camden Environmental Open Forum

Defending Parkland Walk

Hampstead Heath Consultative Committee

Highgate Cemetery Trust

Highgate Conservation Area Advisory Committee

Highgate Woods Joint Consultative Committee

Islington Conservation Area Advisory Committee

Kentish Town Crime Prevention Committee

Lauderdale House Society

London Amenity and Transport Association

London Forum of Amenity and Civic Societies

Membership of these bodies did more than add to the Society's credibility. It exposed members to wider discussion on planning issues. This in turn enabled it to put forward proposals better in line with the policy objectives and procedural constraints of local councils. Links established with other campaigning groups, many of which shared similar problems, allowed the Society to speak with a more authoritative voice and from time to time to support neighbourhoods in Camden and Haringey, less well endowed with technical expertise than Highgate was, with valuable advice.

To remind members of the Society's objects, *Buzz* introduced in 1988 the practice of printing the mission of the Highgate Society in a prominent position:

We aim to make Highgate and its neighbourhood a better place in which to live and work; to ensure that any changes made in the environment enhance the amenity of the area; to encourage sound planning and to improve public transport.

These core goals and aims are the concerns of the Society's Environment Committee in particular. The Committee had gained a new Chairman in the person of Michael Hammerson in 1987. From that date to the present, each Environment report in *Buzz* has been written by him, its length and detail depending on the discretion of the editor. In the belief that members needed to understand the degree to which the Committee's objectives were constrained by local and national legislation, these reports increasingly included background commentary on the national planning situation. To criticisms that the Society "always objects to everything", the riposte was that the vast majority of applications vetted by the Committee were allowed to pass without comment.

5.06 Joan, Lady Neale

By the end of Michael Hammerson's first year at its helm, there were twenty-three members of the Environment Committee and it had testified before a House of Lords Select Committee as well as presented its case in dozens of planning appeals. At its heart were its hard-working officers, many of whom would dedicate long years of service to its efforts. All were sad to see Joan Neale, later Lady Neale, stand down as Secretary to the Committee near the end of 1990 after twenty years in that position.

Cromwell House

One of the more encouraging trends during this period was that Borough planning departments were giving greater consideration to the recommendations of the Society. Cromwell House was a good example. Having

5.07 Cromwell House, 2014

refused an application for its conversion into seven apartments, Haringey Council consulted with the Society on the revised plans that ensued. However, the applicants then asserted that redevelopment of the property was not financially viable unless they could obtain permission to construct an additional eight flats in the rear garden, so the entire venture was scrapped. A plan for the restoration of the original main staircase met with the Society's support in 1988, and there was further positive movement when, in 1991, Haringey declared its intention to issue an enforcement order to restore the building to its previous condition. Given the context, the Society was surprised to hear that Cromwell House had been sold, *Buzz* revealing that it would now serve as the Ghanaian Embassy and that the Society was a member of a working group advising Haringey about the proposed alterations.

The Embassy still owns Cromwell House but, notwithstanding the work involved in restoring it, the house and its magnificent staircase can only be seen by visitors by prior arrangement.

Relations with Camden

There was a general deterioration at this time in the relationship between local voluntary organisations and Camden Council. This deterioration was not specific to the Society. Other groups criticised Council officers for "treating local groups with contempt; handling was confrontational where cooperation would be far more fruitful".

Whether in a spirit of reconciliation or out of desperation, Camden decided to appoint consultants to produce a report on how engagement with stakeholders might be improved. When this report was published in early spring 1996 the view of the Planning

Group was that it "accurately reflects locals' views; we will now see whether they will be adopted".

Meanwhile, taking note of the recommendations being put forward by the London Forum of Amenity and Civic Societies, which had been formed in 1990 and of which the Society was a member, the Society joined forces with other local groups to form the Camden Amenity Forum, whose purpose was to provide a more coherent, powerful voice in communications with the Council. The Forum was chaired by Helen Marcus, a formidable and effective member of the Heath & Hampstead Society.

Hampstead Heath and Kenwood

In 1986 the GLC was dissolved, leaving the Society and others wondering who would take over the running of Hampstead Heath. The government's decision was to set up a London Residuary Body which would manage instances of this and other legacy assets throughout the London region. Unconvinced by the merits of this approach, both the Highgate Society and the Heath & Hampstead Society lobbied for the establishment of an organisation which would be exclusively dedicated to the Heath's upkeep and administration, and that appointees to the board which would run this body should include members of the local communities and relevant organisations which were already involved with its care. In 1988 the London Residuary Body finally decided to place the Heath under the control of the City of London, on the grounds that they had over a hundred years' experience of running several other open spaces, such as Queen's and West Ham Parks and Epping Forest.

Although the Society did not oppose this decision, it did have concerns over the lack of clarity in the proposals, particularly regarding how various wooded areas forming part of the Kenwood Estate would be managed, as well as the sites of special scientific interest on Hampstead Heath. The Government's response was to place the Kenwood Estate under the care of English Heritage, a move opposed locally on the grounds that local people viewed the Heath and Kenwood as two parts of a single open space.

One positive outcome of the transfer of the Heath to the City of London was the establishment, by statute, of a Hampstead Heath Consultative Committee incorporating representatives of relevant local groups. The Highgate Society has been a member of the Committee since its inception; each year it meets three times and makes three other Heath visits accompanied by City of London staff. It has not only made local groups more aware of the complexity of managing a space such as the Heath, but has also brought to the City a fund of useful local knowledge.

One valuable effect of the Consultative Committee on the City's management of the Heath arose in 1990. Plans for a new staff building near the foot of Parliament Hill put forward by the City were opposed by the Society on grounds of both design and situation. The Consultative Committee then worked with a City team to produce a more acceptable and less obtrusive scheme, successfully completed in 1992. In contrast it proved impossible to prevent British Gas installing a large mains pipe across Heath lands, despite intense opposition from numerous local groups; the impact this project has had on the Heath is still clearly visible.

Heath Litter Picking Day was a successful joint initiative of the Highgate Society and Heath & Hampstead Society. In due course this was transferred to a new volunteer group, Heath Hands, founded by Heath & Hampstead

5.08 Heath Hands at work, 2016

Society member Bobby de Joia and operating on behalf of the City. Heath Hands now forms an integral and thriving part of the Heath's management. It takes on major ecological management projects both on the Heath and at Highgate Wood.

Originally the Kenwood Estate was managed without the involvement of a consultative committee. As a result, when in 1990 English Heritage published a series of controversial proposals for reorganising its management, only a well-intentioned but generally ill-informed public was invited to comment, not an active group with experience of the management of the Estate. The main focus of the Society's response was English Heritage's plan to fell a number of mature trees in order to open up "views of London from the house as they were in the eighteenth century". Phrases such as "clearance of scrub" were strongly objected to, concealing, as was probably intended, an extensive programme of tree removal. A consultative committee was mooted, but this proposal was rejected by English Heritage, at least initially.

In 1995 *Buzz* published a summary of the public consultation which the City of London had undertaken regarding the management of Hampstead Heath. The most significant findings were that most respondents wanted the Heath to remain in its current natural state, but that, if active management were necessary to preserve its current state, actions such as coppicing, thinning and mowing should be performed section by section, not all at the same time.

Relations with English Heritage reached a low point in 1996 when, despite the objections of the Society and other groups, Kenwood House and its grounds were closed for a number of days when they were let out to foreign royalty as a venue for wedding celebrations.

In response to the widespread criticism of the seemingly autocratic manner in which it ran the estate, English Heritage decided to set up the Kenwood Landscape Forum, described in more detail in chapter 6. Made up of representatives from the Highgate Society and other local organisations, it meets twice a year, with two further site walks with the Head Gardener. Although it lacks the statutory status of the Heath's Consultative Committee, it remains a useful channel of communication between English Heritage and the local community and for conveying local concerns and suggestions to Kenwood's management team.

Equally anxious to maintain and protect green and open space, the Society has always sought to preserve not just public open spaces but also the many extensive private gardens which make such a valuable and irreplaceable contribution to the appearance of the locality and to its ecology.

Hence there was jubilation when the rear gardens of numbers 78 and 79 Highgate West Hill were officially designated by Camden Council as Private Open Space. These extensive grounds, along with a stretch of private garden between West Hill and the Heath, were long known to local residents from occasionally being open to the public, and it was assumed that Camden's actions would significantly constrain further development in the neighbourhood. The protection, however, subsequently proved to be rather weaker than the Society had anticipated when Camden approved an application to construct a large pastiche mock-Gothic house on the garden behind numbers 78 and 79 Highgate West Hill.

Trees and woods

Following the hurricane of 1987, which felled 3,000 trees in Haringey and left another 2,000 in need of far-reaching reparative works, the Society contributed to the restoration funds for all three of the Boroughs that cover Highgate.

In 1992 Camden Council initiated a programme for training local residents to become tree wardens. Meanwhile, under Haringey's direction, a group of volunteers was recruited to work with Friends of the Earth to review the current list of Tree Preservation Orders with a view to recommending suitable additions. This enabled the Society to point out that a number of trees in North Hill had been lopped out of season in early May; acknowledging its error, Haringey assured the Society that all future pruning would be carried out only during the early winter period.

One of the many positive results of the Society's involvement in Highgate Wood was the City of London's award-winning refurbishment of the popular children's play area and the creation of a Wildlife Information Hut, showcasing exhibits on the wood's history and ecology. Both were undertaken at the Society's suggestion.

A more contentious issue was the future of land owned by London Underground running round the north-west edge of the Wood. Until 1957 this land formed part of the railway line between Finsbury Park and Alexandra Palace. It provides an important screen to the park and a valuable woodland habitat. Following pressure from the Society, the City of London

5.09 Veteran oak in Denewood Road, relic of old hedgerow

offered to take over the land and incorporate it into the wood. However London Underground showed no interest in the offer, arguing that they might want to take back the land at any time for operational reasons. This rebuff was contested by the City, and despite further representations from the Society and local MPs, the land remains unmanaged and at risk from vandals.

In 1995, Haringey published plans to demolish the attractive but neglected Edwardian lodge in Queen's Wood rather than fund the programme of repair and restoration which had repeatedly been advocated by the Society. With the help of local councillors Haringey were persuaded to change their mind and to allow the building to be used as a café.

Keeping Highgate Tidy

In 1989, a number of members of the Environment Committee decided it was time to take direct action to combat the growing problem of litter. "Keep Highgate Tidy" was the slogan they adopted. To assess the situation they decided to walk round N6 and to photograph the most serious instances of dumping that they found. Supported with this evidence they then met with officers responsible for waste management services in the three Boroughs between which Highgate is split, reporting in *Buzz*:

The three authorities have been very cooperative and at our request have cleared away several refuse dumps we have found on our walkabouts.

The team reminded Society members of the need to place refuse that was left for collection in a closed container and that foxes in particular were likely to scavenge anything left in a plastic bag. The group followed up its efforts with visits to local schools as a result of which it produced a guide to the use of refuse services in the area. Not content to leave it at that the group then investigated rubbish problems in the area's principal shopping areas and managed to persuade Haringey's refuse department to clear the worst examples of dumping that they found.

With surprising persistence the group then went on in 1991 to organise a Litter Picking Day. Though the intention was that this should be the first of an annual series, it was not repeated in 1992. Clifford Wearden, who formed and chaired the group, stood down and Christina Nolan took over. Her team met with Camden to discuss business refuse collection in 1993, but with "no entirely satisfactory outcome".

Rubbish and litter seemingly then ceased to be an issue. Did citizens become more litter conscious? Did measures to fine litter louts have an impact? Were local authorities more assiduous in keeping streets clean? Or by tackling the worst excesses did the group unwittingly demonstrate the effectiveness of "zero tolerance"?

Waterlow Park

In the early 1990s complaints about the state of Waterlow Park resulted in the formation of a new charity, the Friends of Waterlow Park, of which the Society became an active participant.

Initial discussions between the Friends and Camden proved 'encouraging'. Successive bids to raise some much-needed income focused on plans to sell or lease the two Park lodges. They required significant restoration first. Perhaps with good reason, Camden considered the costs incurred by the refurbishment of Dartmouth Park Lodge were too great to justify, although *The Friends* believed these costs were overstated. People were more optimistic in 1995 when the *Landmark Trust* considered taking on the Swain's Lane Lodge as one of the portfolio of properties it makes available for short lets. Camden consented to undertake only the most basic repairs and full restoration was not completed until 2016. The restoration of the Dartmouth Park Lodge was completed in 1995 when it became home to the newly appointed Head of Parks and Open Spaces.

Weakening of planning controls

The cause of heritage conservation suffered major setbacks in 1987 when the Government argued that planning regulations were hindering economic growth. Controls were relaxed and a directive issued to planning departments requiring them when assessing planning applications to presume in favour of development. Exceptions to this directive were to apply only in cases where an application was deemed to cause considerable harm to a recognised site of major cultural significance. The construction in the gardens of Nos 78-79 West Hill was an early example of how this policy would have damaging consequences for local heritage.

In direct response to the central government mandate all three local authorities responsible

for Highgate instigated reviews of their planning policies in 1989. The Society was encouraged by being invited to comment on each of their draft proposals. The Society also contributed to the widespread view that a far more coordinated and unified approach was needed for planning across the whole of London.

In 1992 the Society broadly welcomed the publication of Haringey's Draft Unitary Development Plan not least on account of its firm measures for protecting and promoting the conservation of the environment. Unfortunately, the Borough's own Director of Property Services was hostile to any such strengthening of policies and its provisions were watered down.

The East London Assessment Study

The 1988 East London Assessment Study (ELAS) was another government initiative that sent shockwaves through the city's amenity and environmental groups. It was positioned merely as a discussion document. But the expansion of the road network that it proposed as the preferred means of tackling traffic congestion was met with universal condemnation, particularly in the face of long-running and well-supported campaigns to solve traffic issues by the provision of better public transport and the removal of tax breaks for company cars. Locally the Society was alarmed to learn that there were seven plans for the construction of a highway on the Parkland Walk.

During the year that followed evidence from traffic counts contributed to widespread opposition to the study. People objected to the disjointed nature of the proposal and called for a unified metropolitan proposal. It was to the great relief of many that the ELAS was discreetly discarded.

5.10 Surveying lorries in the High Street[xxv]

Yet another new and rather expensive solution to London's traffic problems, this time advocated by the new Secretary of State for Transport, Paul Channon, was to increase London's road capacity by building a series of underground road tunnels. The view of the Society was that while this might superficially appear attractive, the effect would merely be to shift environmental problems onto those who lived at the entrance to each tunnel.

The Archway Road

The summer 1996 *Buzz* reminded Highgate that "The Archway Road problem is still with us". Though the threat of widening had been removed, twenty years of uncertainly had resulted in extensive blight along the entire length of the road. This *Buzz* issue also featured a piece honouring the late Simon Wolff, a leading anti-pollution activist who had at one point chaired the Archway Road Residents and Business Association (ARRBA). Residents planned to dedicate the work they planned for monitoring the road's air quality to his memory.

St Columba's Lodge

The Society found itself facing a new challenge in 1995 from St Columba's Lodge, just off Spaniards Road, one of the surviving great

houses with their own grounds on the fringes of Hampstead Heath. Originally built as The Elms, this mansion was transformed with a range of Jacobean revival details in the 1870s, remaining a private residence until 1953 when it became a new home to St Columba's Hospital which until then had been located in Swiss Cottage.

When the hospital closed in 1981 the house and grounds were sold for redevelopment. Ten years later, permission was granted, despite great opposition, for the construction of a four-storey block of flats on the site. This permission expiring before the works could be commenced, the owners applied for a renewal, to which the Highgate Society and the Heath & Hampstead Society both vigorously objected on the grounds that it would destroy a significant and much-valued view across the Heath. In response Camden asked that a four-storey scaffold should be constructed on the proposed site to help them assess its likely impact. This was not to end satisfactorily.

Around this same time, a trial installation of a new radio tower was proposed for St Columba's Lodge, where it was considered it would be less obtrusive than the location adjacent to Whitestone Pond which had originally been proposed. The test found that reception was better at the site near the pond, but to the dismay of both Societies and to the detriment of the view from the Kenwood House terrace, it was decided that not only should the St Columba's mast be erected, but that the one at Whitestone Pond should remain as well.

Some planning failures

At this mid-point of the Society's history, it's illuminating to consider to what extent the Society was succeeding or failing in its struggles with borough planners and with developers.

73

We have already recorded the approval of the controversial development in the rear gardens of numbers 78 and 79 Highgate West Hill, notwithstanding Camden having designated the site as Private Open Space. The Council's sale of Holly Court School, a pioneering open air design from 1960 by prominent local architect Stephen Gardiner and situated in Merton Lane, also breached the policy it had adopted on management of the fringes of the Heath. Despite furious opposition from the Society the site was subsequently redeveloped for luxury housing.

In Haringey, the Society was unable to prevent the demolition of many of the large Edwardian and inter-war family dwellings with spacious gardens in the prestigious streets laid out in the former Bishop's Hunting Park to the north of Kenwood. The vast and, to many, tasteless luxury villas that replaced them were criticised for their crudely derivative details, stripped bare of their greenery and set atop enormous basement complexes, all testifying to the unequal struggle in which the Society was engaged against the government's guidance favouring development at the expense of the maintenance of local heritage and Haringey's seeming unwillingness to defend their own policies for the Conservation Area.

Dating from late-Victorian times, the ornate Royal Mail Sorting Office is a long-established feature on the route between the Village and the tube. As part of its streamlining programme, Royal Mail announced in 1995 that the activity of the sorting office was to be moved to its Holloway sorting office, and that the Highgate building would be put up for sale. The Society was quick to act and appealed to Barbara Roche, MP for Hornsey & Wood Green, in the hope that her intervention could preserve the building. Though she was unable to prevent the relocation of the sorting activities, the building was successfully converted into studio workshops soon afterwards.

5.11 Demolition of the Wellington Inn

Even when a local authority and the Society agreed on how a planning application should be responded to, there remained a danger of an appeal placing the decision in the hands of the Planning Inspectorate and hence removing from the decision any influence of those with the most experience and understanding of local circumstances. This is what happened in 1988, when the popular early nineteenth-century Wellington Inn, situated at the junction of Archway Road and North Hill, was demolished to make way for a new petrol station. Opposition was fierce – "No way am I going to drink petrol!" wrote one angry objector – and although Haringey rightly refused the application, it was upheld on appeal.

Some planning successes

From the perspective of the Society the story was not all bad news. Among the positive outcomes during this third decade was greater collaboration with other local community groups such as the Heath & Hampstead Society. Improved dialogues between the Society and the Borough planning departments began to bear results. The Society stimulated and coordinated the community's response to changes to the management strategy for Kenwood put forward by English Heritage and generated public interest in tree maintenance work in Highgate Wood, in Queen's Wood and

5.12 The Gatehouse, 2012

in local streets. As is explained in more detail in chapter 10 members of the Society were closely involved in the first of what proved to be a long series of endeavours to rectify the poor condition of Waterlow Park through the formation of the Friends of Waterlow Park.

The Society's determined but reasoned opposition to Government policy diktats insisting that development take precedence over conservation did contribute to the emergence of a new sentiment, "localism", which promoted the right of residents to participate in and to contest planning decisions affecting their local areas. In due course this emerging policy resulted in the formation of statutory body also described in more detail in chapter 10.

In 1989 the corner shop at the junction of the High Street and Southwood Lane was at risk of closure due to a proposed increase in its rent. A letter from the Chairman of the Environment Committee to the arbitrator helped save the shop, at least until 2016. The landmark Gatehouse public house was another premises where Society efforts paid off. Having been closed for some time, it was eventually given a major makeover in 1991 following a concerted drive by the Environment Committee to inform its management of the numerous complaints it had received about the condition of its exterior. This had not only become dilapidated but was also regularly plastered with unsightly fly-posting. The interior was also redecorated at this time.

Fortunately the new owners, Wetherspoon's, had a policy of preserving the historic details and ambience of their pubs; they worked with the Society to incorporate within the building a range of historical displays about Highgate, and after an anxious period when they proposed re-naming it "Ye Olde Gate House", were persuaded to call it simply by its original name, The Gatehouse. In 1995 the Society welcomed the revival on its upper floor of the Gatehouse Theatre. After a dispute with the management of a theatre of the same

5.13 Upstairs at the Gatehouse: "Singing in the Rain", 2014

name, which now performed at Jacksons Lane, it was renamed "Upstairs at the Gatehouse". Its managers, John and Katie Plews, were soon to become active members of the Society.

The Society was also successful in its efforts to persuade Camden Council to introduce Pay-and-Display parking at various points on Highgate Hill and South Grove.

The award of a Millennium Grant for restoration work in the Village was used to renew the historic listed railings bounding the reservoir along Highgate West Hill and to place bollards around the small grassy space adjacent to the Flask in order to prevent cars being parked there. The bollards themselves were later replaced by railings. When in 1996 English Heritage encouraged the Society to apply for Heritage Lottery Funding to extend these improvements, it formed a Pond Square Working Group to draw up the proposals for enhancing the Square that are described in Chapter 6.

However disheartening the loss of the Wellington Inn, the Society was pleased with most of the changes proposed for The Wrestlers in North Road, so named since 1548 and one of the oldest

pub names in the country. However on the sudden appearance of new branding, "The Slug and Lettuce", Michael Hammerson launched a campaign which resulted in the reinstatement of the old name in little more than a fortnight.

Another of the Society's battles in the early 1990s was to prevent the approval of inappropriate large scale building works at the significant corner plot, number 67 High Street, which was occupied by the Village flower stall. In 1996 debate over the future of this site was as yet unresolved, and this remained the position until 2014 when what was felt to be a grossly insensitive four-storey redevelopment scheme was granted permission on appeal, to the dismay of local people, Camden and English Heritage (see Chapter 7).

Inevitably the Society's planning team achieved rather less than they would have liked but more than they might have feared. The decade was one where it was difficult to forecast the outcome of any planning application and where success arose from keeping a keen eye on developments, understanding the interests of different parties and adopting a pragmatic and flexible approach.

Caen Wood Towers, 1889

6.01 Mat Schwitzer giving lecture at 10A

CHAPTER 6:
THE FOURTH DECADE (1996 - 2005)

A *period of transition*

The contents of *Buzz* during the years which followed the Society's thirtieth anniversary do give the impression that it had in some ways lost its initial vigour. Maybe this was an inevitable consequence of the maturity of the organisation, the fact that many members of the cohort that had so enthusiastically founded the Society were growing old. Maybe the character of British social life was changing too.

The late 1990s saw the deaths of three members who had made particularly important contributions to running of the Society. The first of these, in 1997, was that of Margot Slater. Margot had edited *Buzz* between 1991 and 1997, sometimes on her own, at other times as co-editor with Leila Hodge and Vanessa Whinney. From her hospital bed Margot spent many hours discussing the handover to her successor, Brendan Nolan.

The second death, in 1999, was that of Walter Bor, an internationally-renowned urban planner. He was a member of the Environment Committee for over thirty years and he founded and was the first Chairman of the London Forum of Amenity and Civic Societies. The third, also in 1999, was that of John Gay, the eminent photographer and ardent Friend of Highgate Cemetery. The Society's photography competition for children in 2000 was held in his memory, and his name commemorated by a conservation centre in Highgate Cemetery. Like Mat Schwitzer (Slovakia) and Walter Bor (Austria), John Gay (Germany) was one of a large group of foreign-born émigrés who, after fleeing the Nazis, were to contribute so much to their adopted communities.

In the early 2000s five more Society stalwarts died: Elizabeth Caddy, who ran the *Monday Club* for over thirty years; John Samuel JP, who was the Society's President between 1993 and 2001; Lady Joan Neale, who was struck and killed by a lorry while investigating the safety of the pedestrian crossing at the junction of Broadlands Road and North Hill; her architect colleague Lady Susan Cox; and John Lacey, architect, artist and former Chairman of the Environment Committee, whose witty drawing on the cover of the winter 1998 issue of *Buzz* made mischievous reference to a mythical visit of Pieter Breughel to Kenwood.

2004 marked the close of an era, with the death of the Society's founder, Ronnie Bernstein, its first Chairman and the driving force of many of its early years. He was its President from 1983 to 1993, then Past President throughout John Samuel's presidency and into Ivor Burt's. A memorial service took place at the HLSI, of which he was also an active member, and he was awarded the rare distinction of being buried in the West Cemetery of Highgate Cemetery.

To a degree the Society was suffering from the increased remoteness of Council planning departments, many of whose officers appeared less willing than they had been to consult with local residents. Planning decisions seemed to be more capricious and members of the Planning Group became fatigued and increasingly disheartened by officers who seemed reluctant to pay any regard to what were mostly well informed and carefully argued recommendations. Where once officers and councillors had been considered as allies in a common cause, the Society increasingly found itself battling against what appeared to be a new philistinism among Councillors as well as officers.

Any loss of vigour did not seem to affect either the social activities that had become embedded in the Society's calendar or its involvement in worthy causes. The *Monday Club* continued to meet on Mondays. Donors continued to give blood. The young disabled continued to be

trained, and with ever greater professionalism, by the Harington Scheme. The experience of visitors to Highgate Cemetery continued to benefit from the work of its many volunteers.

Hill Homes

The Hill Homes charity was not in any way an offshoot of the Highgate Society but it was an important object of voluntary activity by the Society's Community Services Committee, led by Marion Uglow. It was founded by Mrs Margaret Hill in 1944 to house elderly women whose homes had been destroyed during the war. As several Hill Homes were situated in Highgate, many local people mistakenly supposed that its name originated from the location of its homes rather than, as was the case, from the surname of its founder. The committee of which Marion was Chairman had provided many services to the residents since the 1960s – visiting them, shopping for them and driving them to the meetings of the Monday Club. It continued to support them right through to Hill Homes' 60th birthday in 2004 by donations from parties such as that on Mardi Gras in 2000, from the Spring Ball in 2001 and from wine tastings.

During this period the trustees of Hill Homes were obliged to review the manner in which

6.02 Marion Uglow

they provided services to their beneficiaries. Thus the autumn 1999 *Buzz* published a feature on the opening in 1999 of Hill Homes' first new facility outside Highgate – situated beside the canal close to King's Cross. It reported a description by one of the older beneficiaries of being rescued from her bombed-out home. Referring to the ball of wool from which she was knitting when the bomb struck, her initial comment was, "It's terribly difficult to get that shade of wool nowadays, wasn't I lucky?"

With the death of its original beneficiaries, the charity increasingly found itself catering for elderly people nominated by local authority social services departments. From this source of income alone Hill Homes were unable to find the investment needed to meet the cost of improvement required by new legislation. In 2005 the charity's trustees decided to sell to housing associations all except the two of their homes that provided extra-care facilities.

Cultural activities

Cultural activities also continued to flourish. In 2002 the Craft Fair was successfully revived, "after a lamentable absence". Mat Schwitzer and Ruth Hazeldine continued to organise activities which were conducted in French, the watercolourists and life drawers continued

6.03 *Harley Atkinson thanking the Albany Piano Trio, Music in Highgate Homes, October 2015*[xxvi]

to develop their skills at 10A each week and Music in Highgate Homes was revived, the programme introducing outstanding young performers to a knowledgeable and appreciative audience.

Though operating under a Highgate Society banner, many of these groups ran themselves with minimal involvement from the Society's Council, as is evident from the following description by Ed Gordon of the Life Drawing Group.

6.04 *The Life Drawing Group at work*

Figure drawing is considered by many as the most challenging area of graphic art. Drawing from life has long been regarded as the soundest basis for the practice of figurative art.

The Highgate Society Life Drawing Group was founded in 1992. It stemmed from a life drawing class run by a Society member. She and other Society members attending the class agreed they were of a standard beyond which tuition had any point. Their main need was opportunity to draw from life regularly, to allow them to maintain the facility of observation and hand-eye co-ordination that constant practice confers.

The group was initially led by Jeanne Dodd. She was succeeded by Michael Read. Edmund Gordon took over from him. Ulla Mead currently leads the Group.

Sessions have taken place on Tuesdays in 10A since the group's foundation. Easter and summer breaks used to be observed but the group now meets every Tuesday except at Christmas and New Year, following demand from members, so forms a significant element in the Highgate Society's activities.

The tradition of no teaching has been maintained. A reasonable standard of graphic ability has therefore been a consistent requirement for membership. Though all work takes place in silence, a convivial coffee break is a much enjoyed part of each session. The limited space in 10A and the tendency for those who join The Highgate Society Life Drawing Group to remain members indefinitely often results in waiting lists for membership.

Contacts among members with the wider London art world has led to the group enjoying a succession of good models. Many models now have lengthy and mutually rewarding relationships with the group, though new models continue to be introduced at intervals.

A noted artist once described life drawing as one of the most civilised activities he knew. This comment will have resonance for many who have or have had involvement in life drawing, not least Highgate Society Life Drawing Group members.

Whilst the Society proved equal to the challenge of organising life drawing, watercolour painting and music, it could hardly be expected to put on theatrical performances which is why it has been so supportive of the theatre *Upstairs at the Gatehouse* located above the Gatehouse public house. The directors of this small but widely acclaimed theatre gain particular pleasure from performances of short runs of plays, musicals and performances, written or directed by up and coming local artists. For many years issues of *Buzz* have carried reviews of their productions.

Thanks to a bequest made by Dame Geraldine Aves, one of the leading members of Highgate's various voluntary associations, the Society was able to arrange an annual visit by elderly residents to a West End Theatre. In 1997 *Buzz* recorded that a coach took them to the National Theatre to see *Guys and Dolls*.

An ability to appreciate different wines is, for many people, a critical attribute of a cultured person. Other perhaps than Oxbridge colleges, it is difficult to imagine that there are many institutions, in the UK at least, where a Wine Committee plays a more important a role than in the Highgate Society. The Committee's choices contribute significantly to the success of the annual New Members' Parties and the refreshments which follow Carols in Pond Square. It was also closely involved in the Society's supper parties featuring food of different nations. Wines would often be served to transform a talk into a social occasion, as when Walter Bor gave a talk on political developments in Prague or the event at which the Highgate Poets launched a new anthology. From time to time the Committee, under Marguerite Clark, arranged wine-tasting evenings. Features on wine by Cornelis van Vessem appeared regularly in *Buzz*, each focussing on a particular country of origin, variety of grape or price range.

Walter Bor's talk was one in an annual series of winter talks. These were designed to complement a series of summer walks.

"Sean O'Meara", one of many *noms-de-plume* of the Editor, guided *Buzz* readers on gentle excursions through Highgate introducing them to useful shops in the Archway Road which they might never otherwise have discovered for themselves, or making acid comments on the security grilles with which mansions near Kenwood would guard themselves against burglars.

Engaging more widely

During this period there was a concerted effort to engage more proactively with the local business community and the local press. In the early days of the Society local business owners such as Isla Merry played a much more prominent role than in later years. The Society had to make a conscious effort to engage with local traders, particularly those in retail trades which suffered from the opening of Brent Cross shopping centre in 1966 and the expansion of national supermarket chains.*

About twenty of the seventy members of the newly formed Highgate Society Business Circle would meet for lunch on the first and third Tuesday of the month as well as at 10A on one evening each month. Local MP Barbara Roche was one of their speakers. The Circle included the managers of local branches of banks and estate agents, many of whom were candidates for sponsorship of the Fair in the Square or the once-in-a-decade Anniversary Ball. The Circle found it easier to recruit members than to retain chairmen, the independent traders sometimes appearing to finding it a challenge to reach a collectively agreed decision.

The Society also felt that there was a demand from the increasing number of people now working from home for some form of association to provide companionship as well as networking opportunities, but this idea never got off the ground.

6.05 Brendan Nolan, Editor, Buzz, 1997-2009

Success in engaging with the press was in no small part the result of the appointment in 1997 of Brendan Nolan as the Society's Public Relations Officer. Brendan, husband of former Chairman Christina Nolan, also accepted the invitation to assume the editorship of Buzz, a responsibility he exercised with panache for the next twelve years.

Under Brendan's editorship Buzz became an important channel through which local traders could advertise themselves to the community. By 2000 Robin Fairlie, who had volunteered his services to increasing the income from advertising, had become so successful that advertisements had to be restricted to 40% of the pages. As the quality of the publication improved, the four issues of Buzz that were distributed free to members each year were increasingly seen as one of the principal benefits of membership. This did much to persuade families to renew their annual family subscription of £18, individuals paying £12 and those aged over sixty-three £8.

*For this reason we have included on pages 82-85 the faces of people well known in the community for heading organisations that over the years have contributed so greatly to Highgate being such a pleasant place in which to live.

ORGANISATIONAL SPONSORS

MICHAEL MARKHAM
Director, A.M. Accountants, High Street
18 years in Highgate

A.M Accountants Limited stands out in Highgate; the office with the yellow sign at the top of the High Street. We also stand out with our high standards of efficiency and service.

VASO LOUCA
Owner, BBC3 Hair Studios, High Street
30 years in Highgate

I love being in the heart of Highgate Village and my team and I would like to say a huge thank you to the local community for their amazing friendship and support over thirty years.

SEYHO KURT (MARIO)
Owner, Brooksby's Newsagents, High Street

It's a great place to do business: the schools, the workers and the people who live here make the Village what it is. I'm looking forward to organising the catering for the launch.

MITCHEL ADAMS
General Manager, The Bull, North Hill
5 years in Highgate

We love being part of the rich history of pubs & inns in Highgate. Reviving this 400 year old pub to brew ales and to serve great beer and food to has been a real privilege. We hope the pub will still be serving locals for another 400 years!

MRS BARBARA ELLIOTT
Headmistress, Channing School
Head since 2005, school founded in 1885

Channing is proud to be part of such a vibrant, welcoming community. We support our local shops and businesses and much of our pupils' community service takes place in Highgate itself.

STEVE DAY
Director, Day Morris Estate Agents, High Street
29 years in Highgate

Having lived and worked in Highgate since 1987 I still find myself enthusing about the area and what it has to offer. This certainly makes my job easier.

MALCOLM HEAP
Owner, The Gatehouse Pub
Highgate resident for two years

Highgate is such a wonderful place to live and run a pub for the local community. Big thanks to the Highgate Society for all the fantastic work they do for the people and businesses of Highgate.

ROB GRANT
Owner, Highgate Autos, Broadbent Close

The property has been a working garage since the 1930s and up to the early 80s had its own petrol station in the forecourt and car accessory shop where the hairdresser now is. I look after the cars of two of the four authors of this book.

MICHAEL GOODWIN
Owner, Highgate Bookshop, High Street
26 years trading in Highgate

I could not imagine a more friendly part of London. Over the years I feel I can identify the books that our customers will want to read and I make recommendations to my regulars.

HUGO HAGEN
Owner, Highgate Dental Practice, High Street
19 years in business

I joined the Dental Practice in 1997 and took ownership in August 2000. My wife's family were associated with the original Holly Lodge before it was developed. Our motto "let's make the wonderful Highgate Community smile!"

WILLIAM DEAN
Head, Highgate Primary School, North Hill
8 years as Head

Highgate is our outside classroom. Whether it's Forest Schools, the architecture of North Hill, growing on the allotment or a walk through Highgate Cemetery, our children are blessed to have such riches on their doorstep.

ADAM PETTITT
Headmaster, Highgate School
Head since 2006. School founded 1565

In addition to being at the heart of Highgate village life for 400 years our school has developed partnerships with Haringey schools, and, this year, the London Academy of Excellence in partnership with Tottenham Hotspur Football Club.

TAHA GULAMHUSEIN AND AMMAR CHOMOKO
Owners, Highgate Stationers, High Street
40 years in business

Our father, Tim, and our uncle and aunt ran the Post Office until 2008. It's a great Village to work in as our regular customers are so friendly and always walk in with a smile. We've photocopied many draft versions of this book.

STEPHEN WORSWICK
Owner, Highgate Travel, High Street
Operating for 89 years (not all under me)

I have been organising Highgate residents' travel plans for 42 years, from the tours of the Highgate Society's first president, Yehudi Menuhin, in 1974, to those of its current president, Stephen Panke, in 2016. And I have loved every minute of it.

DR RICHARD AND KATE SHADWELL
Owners, Highgate Wood Dental Practice, Aylmer Parade
30 years practicing in Highgate

Richard, Kate and family continue to enjoy the wonderful welcoming community. We also especially appreciate Waterlow Park, Kenwood, and the marvellous Buzz magazine which, with this book, visitors find in our waiting area.

OZGUR ALPER ALTUNCEVAHIR
Director, London Print Centre, Archway Road

London Print Centre has done all kind of work for the Highgate Society during its 50th anniversary year: the 15 panels for the exhibition on the grand houses, the invitations to the launch party for this book, a banner for use in the "Fair in the Square" and the campaign material opposing TfI's proposed changes to the Archway gyratory.

CHRIS UNDERHILL
Managing Director, Prickett & Ellis, Underhill, High Street
Highgate's oldest business, established 1767

A local lad born and bred and an agent in Highgate for almost 40 years. The firm is now entering its 250th year of trading in Highgate. We are passionate about Highgate, the Village and our community.

PATRICK FITZGERALD
Parish priest, St Joseph's Catholic Church, Highgate Hill
8 years in Highgate

Ours is a busy parish community in Highgate with a warm and lively atmosphere. The Parish was established in 1858 by the Passionist Congregation, a semi-monastic community whose commitment to preaching and proclaiming the Gospel of Jesus Christ continues today.

REV DR JONATHAN TRIGG
Vicar of St Michael's Church, South Grove
Vicar for 21 years

Many current and past members of the Highgate Society have been much involved in the life of St Michael's. Among their number are founder members, Quentin Edwards (Church Reader), Edward Fowler (Churchwarden) and Katherine Hetherington (Church Embroidery).

JOHN AND KATIE PLEWS
Managers, Upstairs at the Gatehouse
19 years producing musicals and drama

Upstairs at the Gatehouse, Highgate's very own theatre, opened in 1997. Situated in the former Victorian Music Hall above The Gatehouse pub, this family-run venue presents a year-round programme of musicals and drama.

JAMES WILKINSON
Manager, Winkworths, High Street
26 years living and working in Highgate

I have seen many changes in the property world but what never changes is that Highgate is special, a wonderful place for my customers to lay down some roots.

The Archway Bridge centenary

For a Society occasionally accused of being overly focused on celebrating the heritage of Highgate Village, July 2000 provided a welcome opportunity for it to work with residents living near the Archway Bridge who had planned an event to commemorate the centenary of the opening of the current bridge. Jacksons Lane Community Centre hosted an exhibition featuring the history of the bridge and promoted a book which had been written for the occasion by Simon Morris and Towyn Mason.

The mayors of Islington and Haringey contrived to introduce humour to the staging of a ceremony on the bridge itself, the Mayor of Islington shouting "Welcome to MY bridge" with the Mayor of Haringey responding by bellowing an identical welcome. It had been discovered that the intention had been for Princess Alice, Duchess of Argyll, to open the original bridge but that she had not been able to. So, on the principle of better late than never, a lookalike of the Duchess was driven to the bridge in an Austin 7 to undertake the opening it had been hoped she would perform a hundred years before.

6.06 Centenary celebrations, Archway Bridge

The assembled group then proceeded along Hornsey Lane, reconvening in Waterlow Park to listen to the princess's speech, then up Highgate Hill and along South Grove to St Michael's Church where tea was taken. To complete the occasion Upstairs at the Gatehouse enacted a play first performed in 1812 when the proposal to construct the Archway Road had caused such worry among Highgate's publicans who feared they would lose business.

Celebrating the millennium

Another indication of the Society's desire to engage more actively with the wider community was the Highgate Village Millennium Party which was held on 31 December 1999. This was organised jointly by the President, Ivor Burt, and by Jan Morgan whose first term as the Society's Chairman began in 1997.

The programme of events leading up to the welcoming-in of the new millennium began three hours beforehand with a display of fireworks at St Michael's School. Party-goers then walked to the steps of the United Reformed Church where a barbecue had been laid on beside Pond Square which, with its adjoining streets, Camden had closed to traffic to enable the crowds to move more freely between one venue and another. The more energetic then danced to a jazz band in the crypt of the United Reformed Church. From there they had the choice of returning to St Michael's school for a dinner dance or of repairing to 10A where Raj, the owner of the village store, had laid on refreshments to the accompaniment of background music.

6.07 Ivor Burt, President 2001-2010

The event culminated at St Michael's Church where, after desserts and a disco, the new millennium was ushered in by an ecumenical service. To the surprise and pleasure of Pond Square residents, Camden Council had anticipated the need for extra waste bins and for a crew to clear the rubbish - so the Village welcomed in the new millennium in pristine condition.

Pond Square

To lay credible claims to being a "village", a settlement should have a village "green" where the community gathers together on special occasions. Pond Square fulfils that role in Highgate. Though it has no grass, its two former ponds, now filled in, were where drovers and travellers would congregate to allow their animals to drink. A natural location for a fair, these are known to have been held in Pond Square since as long ago as 1744[xxvii]. The Square's history, position and configuration justifies its choice as the location for Highgate's two annual expressions of community spirit. In the weeks before Christmas the community

gathers in the Square to sing carols, after which many resort to 10A for seasonal refreshments. Close to midsummer the closure of a number of roads around Pond Square heralds what since 1971 has been called the Fair in the Square or the Highgate Festival. Katie Plews, of Upstairs at the Gatehouse, explains its more recent history:

Until 1996 there hadn't been a 'fair' in Pond Square for a number of years. Jenny Wright used to organise the fairs but I have no knowledge of when they stopped. I first became involved in 1996 when Lloyds Private Banking wanted to invest some money and attract new banking customers. A committee was formed from The Highgate Society and the HLSI. Lloyds Private Banking donated £10,000 and Lloyds a further £2,500. The week-long event was called The Highgate Festival. We had several events lasting a week - a classical concert with buffet, a Magic Evening, The Festival Fair, a choral concert and an evening of Betjeman.

In 1997 there was to be only one event, a fair in Pond Square, but it was still called The Highgate Festival. Unfortunately this was due to take place on the same day as Princess Diana's funeral so it was felt necessary to cancel. Lloyds Bank's support continued for a

6.08 Rock House, Pond Square in spring

further two years after which no further funding was given.

The 'Festival' then continued each year until 2007 with Rex Price, Sandra Stagg and myself being the main organisers. It was still called The Highgate Festival. In 2008 Christina Nolan took over as Chair. A larger committee was formed, no longer restricted to members of the Highgate Society, and the name was changed to Fair in the Square.

6.09 Carols in Pond Square, 2015

Setting up and dismantling the dozens of stalls which are set out around Pond Square and in recent years as far as St Michaels Church, providing for road closures, security and subsequent street cleaning requires a high degree of organisational planning and a significant financial outlay. This is recovered through sponsorship and by charges to the booth-holders. In a good year the surplus is sufficient to allow the organisers to make donations to local charities.

The Society is one of the Fair's leading sponsors, together with others including at various times St Michael's Church and School, the HLSI, the United Reformed Church, Jacksons Lane Community Centre, Highgate School and Camden Council.

Like the Fair in the Square, Carols in Pond Square affords opportunities for sponsorship by local businesses, among them the seemingly ever growing number of estate agents who operate from the High Street; in 2004, thanks to their sponsorship, the carol singing was illuminated by Christmas lights. So generous were the sponsors in 2004 that the organisers were able to repeat the event in 2005 without the need for any further financial contributions.

One of the reasons why Gavin Doyle and Derek Hall were such successful compères of the Carols in Pond Square was their ability to persuade the carol singers to give generously to charitable causes. Whilst Chairman of the Society, Gavin was instrumental in the formation of the 50/50 Club, a raffle whereby, in return for a £10 annual donation, a player's name would be included in a twice yearly draw for four money prizes. Half of the money raised was returned in the form of prizes, the rest added to the Society's funds. £245 was raised from the 50/50 club in 1997, £400 in 1999.

For many years, the Society had hoped to see Pond Square returned to its original function, as a space for community activities. These hopes were bolstered by English Heritage's proposal for the Square's redesign, following the collapse of a more extensive project encompassing the whole of Hampstead Lane and Spaniards Road. The Society decided to set up a Pond Square Working Group, including not just members of its own Environment Committee but also members of the Pond Square Residents Association, local traders and the HLSI. A number of improvements were considered, among them parking and road layout, the relocation of the 271 bus terminus to allow safer use by pedestrians, the public toilets, new paving and a range of tree works, from both the perspectives of wanting more light and that of wanting more shade.

In response to enthusiasm for a number of these options a public consultation was held during the next year, accompanied by sketch plan contests at nearby schools, an exhibit in 10A of some of the proposals developed by Adrian Betham, and a number of public meetings. Frustratingly, however, and without giving an explanation, English Heritage abruptly withdrew its funding for the project and simply gave Camden a grant of £16,000 with which, as the Square's owners, they were free to do as they wished.

Subsequently, at the recommendation of the Pond Square Residents Association but taking no account of the Working Group's overall views, Camden Council opted to renew the toilets and to partially resurface the Square. *Buzz* tartly observed that this served only to supplant a grim stretch of grey asphalt with one of sandy grit which would quickly spread into the surrounding streets. This comment was badly received by the Pond Square residents who felt their efforts to research and recommend a suitable surface had gone unrecognised.

The absence of a formal process of dialogue and consultation regarding the uses to which Pond Square should be put had the potential to become a source of conflict between its Residents Association and the Society. The understandable preference of Association members was for a quiet outlook with a minimum of intrusive activity. Many members of the Society, and more recently the Highgate Neighbourhood Forum, see Pond Square as a natural venue for community-based activities.

The planning surgery

By far the heaviest demand on the Environment Committee's time was its study and analysis of small scale planning applications within the Conservation Area. It is salutary to remember that in practice very few of these were ever objected to, and Society opinion remained favourable in general toward the principles of contemporary architecture so long as its scale and design complemented and enhanced the Conservation Area.

A practice emerged at this time for a handful of Environment Committee members to be available during the Saturday morning coffee gatherings at 10A as an informal planning surgery for members. *Buzz* enthusiastically encouraged its readers to take advantage of this new service, particularly in advance of submitting any new planning application so the Committee might improve their chances of a successful application. Occasionally the outcome was not what had been hoped for – three comprehensive revisions made to proposals for 5 Hampstead Lane under Society guidance were still insufficient to obtain approval from Camden. Fortunately, most efforts enjoyed more satisfactory results.

6.10 Saturday planning surgery, 10A

Although the surgery was publicised only in *Buzz*, word got around that non-members of the Society would be welcome. The Committee's best estimate is that, since its formation, around two thousand different individuals or groups have sought its advice on planning issues. The service continues to this day.

In the late 1990s, in an effort to tackle its ever-increasing workload, the Society's Environment Committee was split for a while into separate sub-committees: Michael Hammerson chaired the new Planning Applications Group while first David Shelbourn and later Robin Fairlie took charge of Traffic and Transport. In addition there was a handful of individually driven initiatives born of the Environment Committee, such as Open Spaces, again represented by Michael Hammerson, and Keep Highgate Tidy with Marguerite Clark and Jan Morgan at the helm. In fact, of the sixty Society members now identified in each issue of *Buzz* as having special roles or responsibilities, nearly half were in some way attached to the Environment Committee, a clear and strong indication of how much the increasing pressures of development had caused the Society's focus to shift toward campaigning on planning and environment concerns. It is hardly surprising that the Highgate Society was described by the *Evening Standard on 8th October 1997* as one of the UK's "Big Five" local amenity organisations. The others were the Heath & Hampstead, Blackheath, Greenwich and Putney Societies.

In 1999, the Local Government Bill was enacted. This required Councils to implement a "cabinet" method of legislation whereby small committees of Councillors would decide matters confidentially rather than in public meetings. Haringey adopted this procedure almost immediately, much to the Society's dismay. It reinforced the impression that the Council was largely uninterested in the concerns of Highgate residents, which could reasonably be considered relatively trivial by comparison with the more demanding issues facing Council services in Tottenham and Wood Green in the east of the Borough. To compound the problem, Haringey's only Conservation Officer, the highly respected Stephen Gould, was made redundant, leaving the aims of the Conservation Area and the efforts of the Environment Committee in grave peril as the millennium dawned.

Witanhurst

During the Society's fourth decade two proposals were put forward for the transformation of Witanhurst: one simply for a conference centre, the other more extensive, incorporating a hotel and restaurant alongside conference facilities. The Highgate Society expressed guarded support for both schemes, although neither obtained planning approval. Later, between 2002 and 2004, Witanhurst was leased to the BBC for use as the home for the hit TV show *Fame Academy*, during which time it was rumoured that the interior of the house had decayed through carelessness and neglect.

Southwood Hospital

The Society campaigned fiercely against plans put forward in 1997 to demolish the redundant Southwood Hospital in Southwood Lane and to redevelop the site as a contemporary apartment complex. The Environment Committee put forward an alternative involving the removal of the unattractive inter-war extension blocks but retaining the authentic 1799 facade of the building, thus allowing a series of townhouses to be constructed behind.

Despite warnings of the impact such an obtrusive block of flats would have on the Conservation Area, Haringey confirmed their reputation for submitting too easily to developer demands by granting permission. To the relief of the Society, the development was put on hold by a financial recession, as it had done some years previously when Haringey planners had given permission, against the Society's advice, for a substantial apartment block to be built in place of Furnival House in Cholmeley Park.

The site was sold in the early 2000s to a local developer who redeveloped it sensitively. The original 1799 building was restored and the undistinguished 1920s hospital extension was adapted and extended. A detached modern-style house that had been built in the grounds was included in one summer programme of the Walks Group. Visitors were hugely impressed by the host of state-of-the-art energy saving features that they saw there.

Management of the Kenwood Estate

In 1925, the first Earl of Iveagh had arranged for Kenwood House and its grounds to be left to the nation. Initially the house and its grounds were managed by the LCC. In 1986 control had moved to English Heritage. During the 1990s, the Society was one among many local groups and residents to become concerned by way in which English Heritage allowed summer concerts to be staged in its grounds. Conceived as a means of responding to the pressure English Heritage was under to raise more funds, the concert programme was modified so as to appeal to a wider and larger audience. To this end the traditional symphony concert or opera format was replaced by a more popular line-up of contemporary performers, with greater sound volumes and frequently with firework finales. These, it was feared, would heavily pollute the Kenwood Site of Special Scientific Interest. Concern was also expressed over the level of sound pollution which affected not just those living in the immediate vicinity but residents living as far away as Highgate Village.

There was also growing concern that the Kenwood Estate management was acting with little regard for the views of the public and was reluctant to consult the local amenity organisations. The formation of the Kenwood Landscape Forum in 1997 seemed improve relations, although disagreements over issues surrounding the concert administration and format persisted.

No. 10 Fitzroy Park

Determined action was also waged by the Society over the future of No. 10 Fitzroy Park. This spacious house, set in extensive and well-landscaped gardens, had been left to the Borough of St Pancras by its owner, the architect Emmanuel Vincent Harris, who had done much work for the GLC. When London local government was reorganised, the property became the responsibility of Camden. Harris's bequest contained a restrictive covenant requiring the preservation of its grounds and gardens as well as a recommendation that the house itself be designated as a mayoral residence or for some other public use. Local communities were canvassed but even ten years after Harris's death no viable use had been suggested. Rumours then began to circulate that Camden was looking to have the covenant removed to enable a sale to be sold to a purchaser who would then apply for permission to demolish and replace with a luxury development.

A sale was finally agreed in 2000 after vituperative exchanges between Camden and local groups. It was for approximately £4 million, a considerable figure at that time. To the relief of protestors the new owner was a private individual who planned to restore the house for his own occupation. Money from the sale was then allocated to the Borough's Emmanuel Vincent Harris Trust which was set up to provide grants to locally-based social or community projects, thus respecting to a large degree the original charitable stipulations of Harris's bequest. Several years later, when it was proposed that a basement be excavated beneath the garden, the owner was quick to withdraw his application when told of the history of local opposition to a scheme which threatened so much damage and upheaval to the gardens of the property.

Supporting the High Street

The Highgate Society was also keen to protect the Village's High Street, both in terms of its historic, appearance and the range of businesses it supported. But despite strenuous attempts, it proved impossible to stem the encroachment of ever more bistros, cafés, estate agencies, even a Tesco Express, all of which displace the independent traders who contribute to the High Street's character. The Society has had some success in preserving the historic shop fronts of a number of the premises. The corner shop at the junction with Southwood Lane was one retailer who had found it difficult to remain

6.11 Raj Kara-Rajani

in business due to escalating rents and the lack of parking for delivery vehicles. On more than one occasion the Society played a role, behind the scenes, in averting its closure. However in February 2016, Raj closed the shop for the final time. The Society organised a farewell party for him, presenting him with an antique photo of his shop in appreciation of the years of service he had given to the community.

Archway Road

Less successful were repeated attempts to reverse the degeneration of Archway Road where shops and services ceased trading all too frequently. In 2002, after local pressure for the area to be treated as more than a deteriorating motorway suffering from planning blight, Haringey invited the Society, and the recently formed ARRBA, to produce an Archway Road Regeneration Plan, since Haringey did not have the resources to write it themselves.

This plan was focused very specifically on improving waste collection; widening the pavement near the underground station to provide a safer pedestrian environment; creating a small open space at the junction with Southwood Lane and, most urgently, measures to halt the deterioration of the shopping facilities, including grants to provide internal shop window shutters – too many of the shops had forbidding external shutters which did not encourage evening visitors. A plan was duly completed and presented to Haringey, never to be seen again. After five years it was out of date and Haringey, under pressure from the Society and *ARRBA*, asked if they could write an updated version which they did. The report was completed, submitted, and seemingly consigned to oblivion. When the Society asked the then Head of Planning why it had not been implemented, it was calmly told

6.12 Archway Road shops and bridge

that "Archway Road is a declining area and will have to be sacrificed."

Highgate Pubs

A new competition began in 1998, "Aspects of Highgate", in which Highgate's eighteen pubs had their exteriors judged jointly by the Society and the Highgate Horticultural Society. The prize was a congratulatory plaque, on one occasion presented by the film star Juliet Stevenson. The Red Lion and Sun was a particularly successful entrant, winning in 1998, 1999 and 2002; The Gatehouse and The Victoria also earned plaques. One of Highgate's best known establishments, The Flask, to general surprise, was judged one year as "poor".

A number of pubs fell victim to the trend of conversion to restaurants, often accompanied by confusing or seemingly unnecessary changes to their names. *The Bull* was briefly re-branded *Idaho*, but returned to being a traditional pub in 2011, and as a result of the Society's lobbying, also assumed its original

name. The 2003 summer edition of *Buzz* celebrated another similar victory:

The new landlord of the *Rose & Crown* visited us a few weeks ago to explain his plans for promoting it as a gastro pub, for putting in a new, more open shopfront to the pub and changing its name to something more 'modern' and upbeat. Without, we hope, being in any way discouraging we politely explained that the front was an original Victorian façade in an important Conservation Area, and that people in Highgate were immensely proud of the area's history and the significance of such things as historic place names – the *Rose & Crown* having gone by that name since at least 1722, and commemorating events five and a half centuries ago – relating how we prevented the Wrestlers, so named since 1548, becoming the Slug and Lettuce in 1993 some years ago. We gave him a five-minute crash course on Highgate history and character, and hopefully persuaded him to concentrate on giving good service and exceptional food.

The name *Rose & Crown* was retained, but ten years later the pub was replaced by an outlet of *Le Pain Quotidien* bakery chain.

Open Spaces

On the whole, the Society enjoyed a good relationship with the City of London in its capacity as owners and managers of both the Heath and Highgate Wood, this to a large part the result of the constructive efforts made by the Hampstead Heath Consultative Committee. Recognition for the efforts of all involved in these open spaces has come in the form of Green Flag and Green Heritage awards for both parks. In 2005, under the direction of Ray Poole, Highgate Wood won the Green Flag for the ninth consecutive year. This prestigious award identifies and rewards "excellence in the management of … public space". The Heath has received eight awards, a laudable achievement considering this number of benchmark standards which are rigorously applied nationwide before the award is granted.

One unexpected development in Highgate Wood was Michael Hammerson's discovery in 1997 of a previously unknown earthwork. Although English Heritage examined the site to establish whether it was pre-historic or medieval, it failed to come up with an explanation of its origin or function. Another curiously-shaped feature proved easier to identify – a World War II bomb crater.

In 2015, Michael's survey of moths in Highgate Wood celebrated its thirteenth anniversary. The Wildlife Information Hut displays photographs of some of the 360 species recorded in the Wood. The idea for such a centre was proposed by the Society and enthusiastically adopted by the City of London. It is now a popular destination for visitors, local naturalists and visiting schoolchildren.

The group under the name Conservation and Urban Ecology, which had converted the derelict lodge in Queen's Wood, mounted demonstrations of sustainable eco-friendly houses, part of a movement that was shortly to become a major new activity under Catherine Budgett-Meakin, Denzil Budgett-Meakin's daughter (p105).

Litter and graffiti

It proved hard for the Keep Highgate Tidy team to keep up the momentum of litter picking in the streets and badgering of the Councils' frequently-changing refuse collection officers. Sue Hall took over from Christina Nolan in 1999 but in 2002 was somewhat dispiritedly reporting little improvement. She urged members either to bombard Councils, the police, and local politicians with complaints, or to use encouragement where it was judged that that would have more effect. When she handed over the reins in 2004 to Marguerite Clark, Marguerite was able to report progress, particularly in the High Street.

Meanwhile a rash of graffiti was beginning to occur on white Highgate walls. This was first reported in 2002 by "Sean O'Meara" who had discovered that Haringey Council's policy was to clean off only racist and obscene messages. In 2004 a group of homeowners in Southwood Lane, Jacksons Lane, Southwood Avenue, Southwood Lawn Road, Highgate Avenue and Hillside Gardens, instead of waiting for

6.13 Highgate Wood Heritage Day

6.14 Litter pickers

the Council to act, raised £5,000 and formed the company Graffiti Busters to engage a team that worked for Haringey to clean their walls. The Society's Derek Hall monitored and audited the work, pointing out in *Buzz* that this sum was more than offset by the increase in property value that would ensue. Highgate Society Chairman Robin Fairlie reported that Haringey had removed 24,000 square feet of graffiti after the Society had exposed the problem. It was explained that a fairly large number of streets needed to be involved in the scheme for it to be financially viable. Gratifyingly, the graffiti did not reappear and was thought to be the work of a "day-tripper" graffiti artist from South London.

6.15 Graffiti, Broadlands Road

An indication of increased cooperation with Councils and the police was the publication in the autumn 2006 *Buzz* of a list of telephone numbers for reporting environmental nuisances. These included graffiti, dumped rubbish, abandoned cars, noise and environmental concerns, defective street lighting and possible terrorist activity. The last was not entirely unimaginable since in the 1980s an IRA device had been placed beneath the canopy of 84 High Street. Fortunately it caused little damage.

Charitable status

Newly-appointed chairmen of the Society often set themselves specific challenges for their three-year tenure. On his appointment in 2003, one of the challenges taken up by Robin Fairlie was for the Society to achieve charitable status. Such a change would allow the Society to recover up to £3,000 in tax relief on member subscriptions each year, not a small figure in relation to the annual £1,800 surplus of income over expenditure common at that time.

In order to comply with the requirements of the Charity Commission, members were asked to approve what it was assumed would be a series of relatively modest changes to the Society's constitution. A team containing members with legal expertise was charged with drafting a revised constitution. After it reported back and after more heated debate than had been anticipated which led to further revisions, a copy of the proposed new constitution was inserted in the summer 2004 issue of *Buzz*. The Charity Commission required that any draft constitution submitted to it had to be approved by two-thirds of the members voting at a meeting containing at least fifty members. At an Extraordinary General Meeting in January 2005, seventy-three of the eighty-three members present voted in favour of the draft.

Raising revenue

The Society had a good record of devising new ways to raise money and regularly donated to one of a number of local charities. For example, the Highgate Self Portrait calendar, published in 2001 and sold for £5.95, raised £4,500 on behalf of the FOHC, St Michael's Church and the United Reformed Church. Who knows whether any additional income from charitable status would not have been given away to other charities?

View over London from the spire of St Michael's Church, c1880

7.01 Buses struggling to find a berth in Pond Square

CHAPTER 7:
THE FIFTH DECADE (2006 - 2016)

"The kind of Highgate you want"

Any anniversary is an opportunity for taking stock. Now with over 1,000 members, the Society decided a concerted attempt should be made to find out whether members felt its priorities needed to be reviewed.

According to the spring 2006 *Buzz* a survey was answered by over 150 Highgate residents, one in six of whom also worked in Highgate and just under half Highgate Society members. Of issues such as crime, shopping, residents' parking, speed limits, recycling and extension of pub licensing hours that respondents were invited to comment on, the four top priorities were to:

Conserve the historic nature of Highgate
Do more to combat crime, with a more visible police presence
Encourage more varied shops, with fewer estate agents
Take action to deal with graffiti

Other concerns were the reopening of the Pond Square toilets which Camden had closed in 2005 without prior consultation despite their meeting the needs of visitors, shoppers and, more particularly, drivers of the 271 buses that terminated in Highgate Village. It took a year of lobbying by the Society and the HLSI before they were reopened.

The Society opened its fifth decade with a series of three debates. The first of these, in late January, was entitled *What does Highgate say it wants?* The debate was introduced with a presentation of the results of the survey of Highgate residents and employees. The following month the Society invited people to a discussion entitled *The great retail challenge* which explored the ways in which the shops in the High Street were used. This event attracted independent retailers, local branches of national chains and representatives of the growing number of estate agents in the High Street. The

97

third and final event, held in late March, was entitled *What can we do about it?* Here the concerns that had been raised during previous meetings were put to a panel of councillors and officers from Camden and Haringey Councils.

As any Society anniversary approaches there is a call for some form of celebratory party. The fortieth anniversary was no exception. This time the decision was taken to celebrate with a Grand Ball.

7.02 Organising group for the fortieth Anniversary Ball[xxviii].

The weather on the day of the Ball could not have been better. The Headmaster of Highgate School had given permission for the event to be held at the school's dining hall in Bishopswood Road, the playing field beside it providing the perfect setting for the drinks which preceded the dinner. The occasion was supported by a long list of local businesses as well as some national ones. Local estate agents Prickett & Ellis, Underhill sponsored the pre-dinner champagne, Benham & Reeves the orchestra and Day Morris the table magicians. Majestic Wine supplied the wine and Marks and Spencer the canapés.

Among those who donated goods for the auction were Highgate Fine Art, Highgate Travel, Walter Castellazzo Designs, Second Nature and the San Carlo Restaurant. Indeed

so numerous were the sponsors and so generous their sponsorship that the organising committee ended the night with a surplus of over £2,000, enabling £1,000 to be donated to each of the Harington Scheme and the FOHC.

Lynne Featherstone, a long-term resident of Highgate who in 2005 was elected the Liberal Democrat MP for Hornsey & Wood Green, contributed an account of the Ball for the anniversary issue of *Buzz*. Many of its other pages were devoted to recalling the early days of the Society. Among the first generation of members invited to attend the AGM in May were Judy Bernstein, Richard and Audrey Downer, Quentin Edwards, Peter Mostyn, Sir Robin and Wendy Williams, Adrian Mayer, Freda Patton and Jean Pateman.

Unexpected successes

The decade opened with two positive and unanticipated developments. On related to policing where, within a year, Safer Neighbourhood officers were appointed in the Highgate wards of both Camden and Haringey. They spent an evening talking to members at 10A.

There was also promise of real regeneration among the shops fronting Archway Road. The Ministry of Transport's threat in the 1960s to widen the roadway and demolish the shops on one of its sides had condemned the area to decades of planning blight. Now Haringey Council, with help from the Society, boosted morale by publishing an *Archway Road Community Directory*, planted attractive boxes outside the shops and relaxed the parking restrictions both for shoppers and for traders. Sean O'Meara contributed an article to *Buzz*, illustrated by Vanessa Whinney, extolling the pleasures of

7.03 Campaigning to keep the toilets open, 2005

shopping on the Archway Road, with a list of several of its more unusual specialty shops and services.

The Builder Center, a building supplier at the northern end of the Archway Road, won consent despite widespread opposition from the local residents, supported by the Society. This caused concern lest an industrial estate develop at the entrance to the Conservation Area. A local resident on the Archway Road obtained a judicial review challenging Haringey's granting of planning permission, but lost his case. The stark impact of the buildings was subsequently slightly ameliorated by shrubs and climbing plants planted by the Harington Gardeners under a tidying and maintenance contract which the Society persuaded the Builder Center to agree to.

The Society was less successful in improving communications between Camden and Haringey. This was starkly exposed when an application for change of use of No. 4

Highgate High Street to an estate agency was agreed by Haringey on the grounds that there were only six other estate agents in the village. The Society pointed out there were actually twelve – Haringey had failed to count the six on the Camden side of the High Street. Permission was nevertheless granted.

The community's busy life

Meanwhile, those living or working in Highgate continued to be offered a plentiful choice of activities, many of them initiated by the Society. The panel below lists the special events included in the *Buzz Diary* of the winter issue of 2005. These were in addition to the regular weekly events in 10A, namely the Monday Club for retired people on Monday afternoons, the Life-Drawing Group on Tuesday mornings, Bridge Group on Tuesday afternoons, the Watercolour Group on Thursday mornings and again in the early afternoon, and the Coffee Morning on Saturdays.

JANUARY

3 Tues
Christmas tree recycling: leave tree by any gate at Highgate Wood, 7:30am-4:30pm (mulch bags provided)

4 Wed
FRENCH CIRCLE: Fête des Rois. Traditional Epiphany celebration with wine, galettes and music. We choose and crown our King and Queen. 8pm at 10A

11 Wed
HORNSEY HISTORICAL SOCIETY: Union Church Hall, corner of Ferme Park Rd and Weston Park, N8. "Law and Order in 18th Century Middlesex" talk by Paul Carter at 8pm.

12 Thurs
HS COUNCIL MEETING: 7:30 for 8pm at 10A

12 Thurs
HIGHGATE FILM SOCIETY: "Nowhere in Africa" (German with subtitles) at HLSI, 8pm. Refreshments on sale at 7:15. All welcome. Enquiries and subscriptions from HLSI (8340-3343)

14 Sat
NORTH LONDON CHORUS: Bach Mass in B minor (period instruments) 7:30pm at St James' Church, Muswell Hill. Tickets £16, £12, £8 (conc.). Box Office 07787 788 246 or Les Aldrich or on door.

18 Wed
NORTHERN HEIGHTS PROBUS CLUB LUNCH at Sparta Restaurant, 225 Regents Park Road. 12:30pm. Talk by Andrew McIntosh "Doing Time, Life in the House of Lords". Probus details from 8348 4191

18 Wed
PLANNING MEETING: 8pm at 10A

23 Mon
BLOOD DONORS: United Reformed Church, Pond Square 9:15am-12:30pm and 2pm-4pm

25 Wed
TALK: "What Do We Want Highgate To Be?" First of a series of three talks. 7:30 for 8pm at 10A.

26 Thurs
HIGHGATE FILM SOCIETY: "Dmitri Shostakovitch" A film biography. 8pm at HLSI. Refreshments on sale at 7:15. All welcome.

29 Sun
HIGHGATE CHAMBER MUSIC SOCIETY: The Beckmann Quartet with Adrian Turner, viola. HLSI at 7:30pm. Tickets £12, Students £5.

FEBRUARY

1 Wed
FRENCH CIRCLE: "Naissance d'un Premier Roman". Virginie le Chevallier Bennett talks about the writing and publishing of her first novel. 8pm at 10A.

8 Wed
HORNSEY HISTORICAL SOCIETY: Union Church Hall. "Your Victorian Ancestors: facts you may not know" Talk by George Smith at 8pm.

9 Thurs
HIGHGATE FILM SOCIETY: "The Madness of King George" at HLSI, 8pm. Refreshments on sale from 7:15.

15 Wed
NORTHERN HEIGHTS PROBUS CLUB LUNCH: Sparta Restaurant, 225 Regents Park Rd. 12:30pm. Talk by Gill Perrin: "Wednesday's Child" Founder Chairman describes work of this Hampstead Charity.

15 Wed
PLANNING MEETING: 8pm at 10A

22 Wed
TALK: "What Do We Want Highgate To Be?" Meeting with retailers. 7:30 for 8pm at 10A.

23 Thurs
COUNCIL MEETING: 7:30 for 8pm at 10A

The rest of the year was no less busy. Society events were interspersed with regular meetings of the Hornsey Historical Society, Highgate Film Society, Highgate Horticultural Society, Highgate Chamber Music Society, Highgate Choral Society, North London Chorus and, in the summer months, Hampstead and Highgate Festival events. In addition to the regular weekly events in 10A the following Society events were scheduled:

APRIL

4
Council meeting

5
French Circle (French Crossword evening)

25
Annual Quiz against HLSI

26
Talk: Helen Day, author of London Born, plays recordings and talks about her grandfather's life in Highgate

30
Music in Highgate Homes: Harp and cello recital

MAY

3
Walk in Highgate Wood (places of historical interest)

3
French Circle: Competitive wine tasting

13
Harington Open Day and Spring Plant Sale

13
Highgate Society Anniversary Tea at 10A

22
Blood Donors session

24
AGM

25
Council Meeting

JUNE

3
Walk in Highgate Wood Identifying birds and their song

7
French Circle Annual dinner in local French restaurant

17
Highgate Festival in Pond Square

JULY

15
Fortieth Anniversary Ball

20
Council Meeting

AUGUST

3
Watercolour Group outing to Maldon, Essex

16
Highgate Wood Birds of prey display

26
Highgate Wood Summer guided walk

SEPTEMBER

5
Highgate Wood Places of historical interest

6
French Circle La Rentrée

16
Friends of Harington Charity Concert
Schubert's Winterreise

21
Council Meeting

24
Harington Scheme Sponsored Walk

OCTOBER

4
French Circle Vente des livres

9
Highgate Police Team at 10A

11
Highgate Wood Fungi

15
Sponsored walk in aid of North London
Hospice

24-31
Halloween Celebrations at Lauderdale
House

28
Highgate Wood Autumn guided walk

30
Blood donor session

NOVEMBER

4
French Circle La Vie Triste d'Edith Piaf

15
HS Walks and Talks Highgate Cemetery
special tour

21
Council meeting

24
Watercolour Group annual exhibition
Lauderdale House

Wine tasting Premium Australian wines

DECEMBER

9
French Circle Fête Saint Nicolas

9
Harington Christmas Sale

14
Highgate Wood Winter guided walk

Carols in Pond Square

Rejection of charitable status

Contrary to expectations, the charitable status of the Society still hung in the balance at the end of the decade. The chairman, Robin Fairlie, had announced at the AGM in May 2006 that:

> The Charity Commission…has written to say that it will register us as a charity only if we will modify the wording of two of the Objects in our constitution. These changes are, in my opinion, fiddling and trivial, but unfortunately, we cannot finalise the matter at this AGM because the Commission's letter did not reach us in enough time to give the necessary notice to members of the matter to be discussed.

Robin's claim at the 2006 AGM that the Society could look forward with some confidence to its achieving charitable status within the next year proved to be somewhat over-optimistic. Meetings of the Society's Council during 2006 were repeatedly marked by discussion of how to respond to the negative tone of the correspondence from the Charity Commission.

It had been assumed that because amenities societies such as the Heath & Hampstead Society and the umbrella organisation, the London Forum of Amenity and Civic Societies, had similar purposes to the Highgate Society the charitable status that they had been granted would be granted to the Society too. In the account of the negotiations which he gave at the 2007 AGM the new Chairman, Gordon Forbes, referring to Robin Fairlie's opinion that the remaining points raised by the Commissioners were "fiddling and trivial" said:

Unfortunately, on further consultation with the Commission, those points proved to be more significant. Our Constitution, issued in draft in the summer 2004 issue of *Buzz*, and adopted at the Extraordinary General Meeting held on January 19th 2005, sets out at Clause 2 the five Objects of the Society:

(i) To promote a vigorous community life in the area of benefit

(ii) To promote high standards of planning and architecture in or affecting the areas of benefit

(iii) To educate the public in the geography, history, natural history and architecture of the areas of benefit

(iv) To secure the preservation, protection, development and improvement of features of historic or public interest in the area of benefit

(v) To promote improved transport (especially public transport) and traffic management to serve the area of benefit.

The Charity Commission require our Objects (i) and (v) to be:

(i) To promote for the benefit of the inhabitants of the area of benefit the provision of leisure time occupations in the interests of social welfare and with the object of improving the conditions of life of the said inhabitants

(v) To provide transport facilities in the area of benefit for people who have special need of such facilities because they are elderly, poor or disabled, people with young children, or where there are no adequate pubic transport facilities.

This was pursued with the Commission, who insisted that either Objects 1 and 5 of our Society be amended to conform with the Recreational Charities Act (1958), or that they be deleted altogether.

The matter was discussed with your Council, and their opinion was sought on the course of action to be pursued. After fairly extensive discussion with the Civic Trust, the matter was again brought before Council, who by a substantial majority expressed the wish neither to alter the existing wording of the two Objects in question, nor to delete them:

[Clearly,] the Highgate Society is not willing to restrict itself to … concerning itself solely with the welfare of the elderly, poor or disabled, people with young children, or where there are no adequate public transport facilities. Admirable as these latter objects may be, and indeed although they form part of our work, they would constrict the basis upon which the Society was founded, and upon which our activities are centred today.

The application for charitable status has therefore been abandoned for the present.

It had become evident that there were subtle respects in which the Highgate Society differed from other amenity societies, for which knitting their communities together and fighting for better transport facilities might not be critical objectives. The particular strength of the Highgate Society, it could be argued, comes from the fact that members enjoy a host of cultural and social events together. The lasting friendships forged in this process do contribute to the energy, power and authority to contest poorly thought-through planning regulations and to scrutinise a seemingly endless series of planning applications in a spirit of mutually supportive camaraderie.

The quest for charitable status was laid to rest. The Highgate Society pressed on as before, raising the funds it needed from subscriptions and donations without the financial benefits that result from charitable status. Some considered that a society made up mostly of members on comfortable incomes should not be seeking to avoid tax at a level of barely £1 per member per year, and that the Society had little reason for trying to raise income in this manner.

Planning de-regulation

The Highgate Society had long been pressing Camden and Haringey Councils to commission Conservation Area Appraisals – a description of the Conservation Area, setting out its character, value, positive and negative contributors, and how future development should reflect its special character. Eventually, in 2009, Camden published a draft for the Society's comment, and *Buzz* urged members to respond to it not just by enumerating the historic buildings of the area but, just as importantly, their favourite views. Haringey was less forthcoming, and in an effort to chivvy them along *Buzz* repeated the message in 2012: "Take a camera and ask 'What do I like about this place? What do I dislike about it? What do we need to work on?' And look behind shops, up at façades, down at the pavement."

Eventually, as a result of staff shortages, Haringey invited the Society to draft a Conservation Area Appraisal for the Haringey section of the Highgate Conservation Area – an offer which it took up enthusiastically, working with the Conservation Area Advisory Committee (CAAC) to compile the majority of the material that was eventually included in Haringey's Highgate Conservation Area Appraisal. However, the Society failed to persuade Camden and Haringey that there should be a single, consistent appraisal for the whole Highgate Conservation Area; but at least it remedied the unsatisfactory situation where

one half of the historic village of Highgate and its environs had an appraisal and the other half did not.

This increased workload resulted in the reorganisation of the Environment Committee, with architect Elspeth Clements taking over the chairmanship the Planning Group from Michael Hammerson who was able to step down after more than twenty years in this position. The Environment Committee continued to meet on a regular basis to look at larger, wider or more specialist topics, forming ad hoc project groups to address issues such as preparing the Conservation Area Appraisal in conjunction with the CAAC.

Government initiatives to encourage development to ease the economic difficulties of 2008 also increased the Committee's workload, insofar as local authorities were urged to rubber stamp new building applications in all but the most exceptional cases. Camden and Islington were two of the London Boroughs that applied for exemption from this policy on account of their heritage assets but neither was successful. In addition, in what was felt to be an alarming new development, the national planning system appeared to have been reduced to the status of a lottery, as the presumption in favour of development encouraged the promoters of rejected applications to use the appeal system as a "second throw of the dice".

Although the Highgate Society generally stood firmly behind the boroughs when they decided to contest appeals, not only did the exercise drain Councils of time and money, but also carried with it the potential for ever greater expense should the Planning Inspectorate rule in favour of the appellant.

Among the prominent figures vehemently opposed to this policy was Nicky Gavron, who was the Deputy Mayor of London until 2010 and who has since chaired the Greater London Authority Planning Committee. As concern grew over the policy's implications, there was a growing acceptance of the need to consult with local communities on large development schemes. This led in 2011 to the introduction of the Localism Act. This legislation aimed to encourage and support the creation of Neighbourhood Plans, which communities could formally rely upon as an additional level of planning policy focused exclusively on a community's goals and wishes.

The new Neighbourhood Forum, established under the aegis of the Highgate Society in 2012 and empowered by the Localism Act was tasked with producing a plan for Highgate. The Society was proud of its success in having this act amended so that the area covered by a Neighbourhood Forum could cross borough boundaries, reflecting the fact that there were many cases similar to Highgate where the boundaries of local authorities cut across the natural boundaries of local communities.

Environment reports in *Buzz* nevertheless argued that government statements in favour of "localism", whereby local communities were empowered to have more of a say in how they wanted their areas to develop, conflicted with its growing assault on the planning system and on the historic environment, both of which it believed were responsible for holding back the economy. Allowing offices to be converted to housing without the need for planning permission, it was argued, would result in an explosion in the supply of luxury housing for the overseas investment market delivering little benefit to people no longer able to find accommodation at a price they could afford.

At the beginning of 2012, preliminary meetings were held to establish the Forum. It was officially ratified by both Haringey and Camden Councils by the end of the year.

The Forum's first and extremely demanding task was the production of The Highgate Neighbourhood Plan, which had to be written using the terminology of planners but in language which could be understood by the general public, no mean challenge. The requirement that the plan should not conflict with national or borough-wide planning policies ruled out many of the policies that members would have liked it to include. Two years later, the winter edition of *Buzz* was able to report that Council officials from Haringey and Camden were at last now meeting and talking to each other; that a consultation draft of The Plan would shortly be published on the Forum and Highgate Society websites; and that once this consultation process was complete, the Highgate Neighbourhood Plan would be put to a referendum some time in 2016.

Sustainability

Catherine Budgett-Meakin and her husband John Mead had for some years organised a campaign group to raise awareness of the threat to the world's population caused by climate change. Some members of the group contributed articles to a 'Green' issue of *Buzz* which was published in summer 2007. For its cover, Vanessa Whinney was asked to create an imaginary view of a "Highgate-on-Sea" that would result from a dramatic rise in sea level. Catherine and John then formed the *Highgate Climate Action Network (HiCAN)*, its remit being to raise awareness locally of the threat of climate change and to champion a community less dependent on fossil fuel and with lower emissions of carbon dioxide. The Network focused on lobbying politicians and on informing neighbours. It arranged a series of lectures from authorities on climate change, many of which were held at 10A. HiCAN members also undertook a survey of local shops' and restaurants' use of foodstuffs produced fewer than a hundred miles away. The results were published in *Buzz* and tips on recycling were posted on the Society's website.

In 2012 HiCAN decided to affiliate to the worldwide Transition movement and rebrand itself Transition Highgate. This did not diminish its political activities, which included lobbying local and national politicians and, before elections, collaborating with other local groups to organise hustings where the position of candidates on green issues could be questioned.

Members also encouraged the growing of food locally and the retrofitting of homes so as to be more carbon-efficient, publishing a regular newsletter to over 230 supporters and organising a 'green' book club. The group was also responsible for John Doggart, Chairman of the Sustainable Energy Academy, being invited to deliver a talk on retrofitting Victorian houses at the Society's 2010 AGM.

7.04 Highgate-on-Sea

Key members of the group, Catherine Budgett-Meakin and Jackie Jones, were instrumental in the formation of a Sustainable Homes Group in 2011. Its aim was very practical: to inspire Highgate householders to improve their lives by making their homes more comfortable

7.05 Sustainable Homes event, 10A

while reducing their energy bills and without compromising Highgate's architectural heritage. The Group sought the agreement of owners of a number of homes that had installed energy-saving technologies to open them to the public so that others could see these improvements for themselves. They also organised a number of events, with expert speakers and exhibits by local companies, at local schools and at 10A. One of its most ambitious projects was to publish Homeowner Packs for estate agents to give to people who had just bought a property. The purpose was to help new owners save time and money by installing energy-saving features before they moved into the house they had bought.

A more broadly based-group that emerged within the Society also contributed to the content of the Highgate Neighbourhood Plan, its members participating in groups working on economic activity, open spaces and the public realm, development and heritage, traffic and transport and social and community.

Green initiatives at this time were not restricted to the Highgate Society. The Harington Scheme introduced a scheme for recycling old mobile phones, both to raise funds and to highlight the environmental benefits of recycling.

Social activities

The annual New Members Party continued to play an important role, enabling new members to identify activities which fitted their interests or skills. Equally evergreen were parties to celebrate Burns Night, often with Scottish dancing, and nationally themed evenings, as for instance the two Hungarian evenings held in 2007 and 2013, an Italian evening and an Indian supper.

Responsibility of these get-togethers lay with the long-established Wine Committee, which organised wine-tastings sessions, Greece in 2007, Hungary in 2008 and Spain and Portugal in 2010. For those too busy to get to these events much could be learned from the reports regularly contributed to *Buzz* by Cornelis van Vessem which focused sometimes on the wines of different countries, at others on one of the wine-producing regions of France. They provided advice on what to buys at the supermarket or at one of the two specialist wine merchants which the High Street was fortunate in having for most of this period.

A Society that had berated itself for many years for its meagre offering for children was lucky to engage the energy of Liz Morris, later to be elected a councillor for Highgate's Haringey ward, who in 2006 initiated what was to become a very successful annual Trick-or-Treat trail at Halloween and that of Amy Brown who in 2010 hid Easter eggs for children to search for in locations in Pond Square. The Trick-or-Treat event was soon attracting as many as a hundred children and their parents. Assembling in South Grove outside Café Rouge the children were given maps of the local area marking where doors were likely to open in the event that their bells were rung by a young visitor wearing a scary outfit.

Only one instance of a mishap was reported in *Buzz*. Adults in one of the houses marked on the map had not been made aware of the event. The organising team sent an apology along with a bottle of wine, perhaps chosen on the advice of Cornelis van Vessem, small change in comparison with the £200 cheque that they sent to Great Ormond Street Hospital. Were it not for the success of these ventures it is unlikely that Anne Isaksson would have decided in 2012 to organise a children's baking class. Held initially during the half-term holiday, the event was so well-attended that it was repeated during the Christmas school holiday.

7.06 Halloween, 2009

For families with children, one of the Society's most popular get-togethers has always been the annual carol singing in Pond Square. For much of this and the previous decade this event was compèred by Gavin Doyle. His shoes were filled between 2007 and 2010 by Derek Hall. During this time the standard of music was much improved by the accompaniment of musicians from Highgate School under the leadership of its then music director John Marsh. Many children and indeed some of their parents were no longer familiar with carols and their tunes so this may have been a rare opportunity for them to participate in this form of communal activity.

Carol sheets distributed, carols sung and tins rattled by Society volunteers, families then repaired to 10A to escape the chill, to revive themselves with mulled wine and mince pies and in doing so be exposed to information on the various other activities of the Society.

Walking in London cemeteries is not among the most favourite of summer activities today but such a summer stroll was particularly popular in Victorian times. So at this time local resident John Caird, best known in Highgate as a host to Music in Highgate Homes and a Highgate Cemetery trustee and more widely as a distinguished theatre director, recognised the potential role of Highgate Cemetery as a venue for cultural events. In summer 2010 he organised an hour's walk which took guests along a route where, on reaching particularly apposite gravestones, they were briefly serenaded by music played by talented performers.

The role of the cemetery as a venue for the arts was further enhanced when the Anglican chapel next to the entrance arch to the West Cemetery was refurbished. Redecorated and serviced by an effective heating system, the chapel became the venue for an annual lecture, organised by the Cemetery, on a topic with some local connection.

The French Circle went from strength to strength, celebrating its 25th anniversary in 2008 under the leadership of Elizabeth Woodman. She regularly devised new forms of entertainment, such as Guess the Cheese, as a change from Guess the Wine; identifying a public figure from his/her silhouette; a talk on Yves Montand or Edith Piaf; and a bring-and-buy sale in aid of Médecins sans Frontières. Such evenings were complemented each year by the three parties, Fête St Nicolas in December, Fête des Rois in January and dinner at a local French restaurant in June.

7.07 Ruth Hazeldine and Elizabeth Woodman baking for the French Circle

Elizabeth had taken over the Presidency from Mat Schwitzer in 1999 and in 2014 she was succeeded by Ruth Hazeldine, one of the Circle's founders.

Walks and guides

The idea of organising private visits to architecturally interesting homes was brought to Highgate by Christina Nolan who had enjoyed such visits when a residents of Washington, DC. Given the diversity of Highgate's domestic architecture and the cultural interests of the Society's members, such activity seemed a natural extension to its social and cultural programme.

Accordingly, each summer Christina and Richard Webber organised a couple of House Visit afternoons, each visit typically involving two mystery buildings of contrasting style. Some of the buildings were ones members could have visited on a London Open House Weekend, but only after a long wait. Others were landmark houses which, if members were familiar with them, it would be only from the outside. Which home members of the party could see themselves living in was a common source of discussion during the tea which concluded the afternoon.

Particularly memorable were visits to Highpoint I, to the recently-built, energy-efficient house in Southwood Lane and to the Tamil Murugan Temple on the Archway Road which the Queen had visited in 2002. One year, following an interesting talk by Simon Lee, Superintendent of Hampstead Heath, one of his Heath ecologists was made available to lead a tour of some of the interesting but less well-known natural features of the Heath.

7.08 House visit to the Murugan Temple, Archway Road

These activities did not focus exclusively on Highgate: the 2012 Walks and Talks programme included a visit by members of the Blackheath Society, followed the next month by a guided walk which they led through the historic parts Blackheath. The two Societies concluded that the two villages had a lot in common, fine open spaces, historic houses, great views, problems of being divided between two London Boroughs, a history of fighting against the MoT's motorway proposals,

in the case of Highgate the A1, in the case of Blackheath the A2.

Unlike the Heath & Hampstead Society, which operates a programme of guided walks covering the historic architecture of Hampstead and the natural history of the Heath, the Highgate Society had no tradition of organising guided walks. However, as a result of the walk led by the Heath ecologist, a proposal was developed for the publication of a series of self-guided walks covering both the historic sites of Highgate Village and the less frequently visited sections of Hampstead Heath.

In 2012 Council approved the publication of the first two of what was to become a series of five booklets which, in combination, took readers on an eight-mile circular walk around Highgate and the Heath. Sold by bookshops as well as directly to members, the first two booklets proved sufficiently popular that the Society decided to invest in the publication of the booklets covering the three remaining sections. The success of the first two booklets also resulted in Richard Webber, on behalf of the Society, being invited by the Heath & Hampstead Society, the Hampstead Garden Suburb Trust and the Hornsey Historical Society to design, publish and organise the distribution of a second series of five connecting walks in a similar format, linking Camden Town to Alexandra Palace via the Hampstead Garden Suburb. This led to the formation of Northern Heights Publications, the publisher and distributer of this book.

7.09 Section two of the Circular Walk

The booklets, costing between £3.00 and £4.50, continue to be stocked in local bookshops and visitor attractions and the Society was awarded a prize by the London Forum of Amenity and Civic Societies in 2014. Encouraged by these successes, the Publications Group applied for and was awarded a grant by Haringey to design and erect an information board outside *The Bull* on North Hill. This highlighted the variety of architectural styles and periods represented by the homes along the road. Attempts to develop a series of sign posts and information panels along the route between Highgate Underground Station and Highgate Cemetery have so far proved less successful.

Meanwhile Michael Hammerson wrote and had published a booklet of historical and archaeological walks in Highgate Wood which the City of London gives to visitors to the Wood.

Intellectual and cultural affairs

Quizzes grew in popularity during this decade and the annual contest for the *Merry Mug* with the HLSI was no exception. The margins of victory were invariably narrow but, unlike the boat race, no reliable tally has been kept of which side has won most times. The quizmasters are instructed to avoid asking questions relating to television programmes or popular sport. Players cluster together on separate tables, typically six tables of six on each side, and those on each table are allowed to confer. Each table then submits its own answers. This has proved a popular format and an effective way not just of conducting the competition but of enabling members to get to know each other better, informed by a clearer understanding of their different fields of knowledge.

7.10 *Scoring at the HLSI / Highgate Society Quiz, 2004*

Indefatigable is a term used frequently, but not excessively, to describe organisers of the Society's most valued activities. It is a term aptly used to describe Sara Kaye who throughout this decade maintained the programme of concerts by up-and-coming young musicians that were held in a number of Highgate homes. An addition to the Society's cultural programme was the introduction of a Theatre Dinner at Upstairs at the Gatehouse. The format of this event began with a drink in the theatre's warehouse after which guests were entertained by the performance of a musical. The audience were then given an opportunity to quiz a panel containing the director, a lead actor and/ or librettist. Discussion of the performance continued over a meal at nearby Highgate restaurants.

Upstairs at the Gatehouse was by now a vital part of Highgate's cultural life. Though musicals are the passion of its owners and directors, the theatre also puts on plays and, until 2015 when it moved back to the Suburb, it had an arrangement with the Hampstead Garden Opera – whose productions have included The Marriage of Figaro and, in 2009, an ambitious combination of Purcell's Dido and Aeneas with Blow's Venus and Adonis.

Given the attention that Geoffrey Salmon had paid, when redesigning 10A, to making it possible for the hall to host exhibitions, it was disappointing how seldom in recent years it had been used for this purpose. This omission was in part rectified on the initiative of Marius Reynolds and friends who decided to celebrate the centenary of graphic designer Hans Unger with an exhibition of his work. Hans lived and worked in Highgate for many years: first on Shepherds Hill, then on Muswell Hill Road where he had a studio for graphic art work and for mosaics. A refugee from Germany who had reached Britain via South Africa, he was noted in particular for his memorable poster designs, many of them for London Transport. Some twenty of these were collected for display, together with memorabilia.

Kenwood concerts

In 1927 Lord Iveagh, who had purchased Kenwood House and part of the former Kenwood Estate from the Earl of Mansfield in 1925 in order to protect it from development, bequeathed the grounds of Kenwood House to the nation. Since 1986 responsibility for the management of the estate had lain with English Heritage. To raise money for its upkeep, an agreement had been made with IMG permitting it to hold a series of outdoor concerts in a spectacular parkland setting.

For them to be financially viable, IMG insisted that there would need to be a minimum of ten

concerts, each with a paying audience in the region of ten thousand. In 2006 complaints from local residents about excessive noise resulted in Camden Council, the licencing authority, restricting the number of concerts to eight. IMG argued that such a reduction would result in the loss of a quarter of a million pounds for the 2006 season and, when its appeal against the restrictions was refused, decided not to proceed with its plans for a 2007 season.

In conjunction with other local groups the Society argued in Camden's defence that local residents were not necessarily hostile to the practice of holding concerts. But they did want fewer tickets sold and the power of the amplification system to be reduced so as not to unduly disturb their summer evenings. After taking steps to curb excessive noise IMG resumed its concert programme in 2008 and the focus of the Society's attention shifted to the tardiness of English Heritage in repairing damage to the turf caused during previous concert seasons.

Underlying these disputes over the Kenwood concerts was wider problem: how to raise money for the maintenance of historic buildings without damaging either the grounds or their enjoyment by the public. This problem became even more critical in 2015 when the two distinct functions of English Heritage were placed in separate organisations. A new English Heritage was formed, with a one-off grant of £80 million to carry out necessary repairs to its 400 properties, thereafter to become a charitable trust obliged be self-financing by 2020. A separate organisation, Historic England, was tasked with giving advice on preserving and conserving heritage.

In 2015 proposals which would make it easier to generate commercial income to defray the operating costs of Hampstead Heath were also considered. The City of London claimed that legislation governing the use of its open spaces such as the Heath were too inconsistent to make holistic management possible. Fears were expressed by voluntary organisations that this claim was merely a ploy to facilitate more commercial use of the Heath to raise revenue. After all, even the City had been hit by the recession. Lobbying by the Heath & Hampstead Society in particular resulted in concessions which brought reassurance to members of the Consultative Committee.

The dams project

In 2010 modifications were made to the Reservoirs Act of 1975. These were intended to identify and register reservoirs where, in the view of the Environment Agency, 'in the event of an uncontrolled release of water from the reservoir, human life could be endangered'. This resulted in advice to the Corporation of London that, in its capacity as the owner of Hampstead Heath, it should reinforce the Heath Ponds in order to preclude any risk of and liability resulting from an overflow.

Statistical models gave a one in 400,000 year probability that a sudden deluge could cause the dams to break and water overwhelm areas of Gospel Oak and South End Green downstream from the Heath. Concerned by the potential repercussions of this assessment, The Heath & Hampstead Society sought guidance from its own legal advisors. They concluded not only that the estimate of potential damage was miscalculated, but that the legislation in question did not apply to the Heath's chain of ponds since their use as reservoirs had ceased long ago.

Spurred on by these conclusions and a vociferous campaign waged in the local press

for and against the proposed engineering works, both sides put pressure on Camden Council to approve or reject the proposals. Quite apart from their disruptive impact on Heath users, the cost of the work became a source of contention. Initially set at £15 million, it soon escalated to £23 million. In the summer of 2014, the Highgate Society reported on the issue in the following terms:

The critical issue is not 'Is the work necessary?' but 'Is the legislation being properly interpreted?' The City of London has a top counsel's opinion that it is. The Heath & Hampstead Society have one from an equally top counsel that it is not, and that the work proposed is excessive. The Heath & Hampstead Society has shared its advice with the City, but the City will not share its advice with the Society, saying only that they are satisfied that their advice is correct and that they must proceed with the work. It would be logical for the City to adopt the Heath & Hampstead Society's proposal to seek a joint legal determination of which interpretation is correct, not least because it could save a significant part of the £15 million the City has set aside for the works. The City's lead officer for the project admitted, at the public meeting on 4th June, that they would welcome a Court decision that they did not need to do the work.

After Camden approved the proposals the Heath & Hampstead Society used a High Court to challenge the Corporation of London's analysis of the evidence as well as its conclusions. When the case was lost, works on the Heath started in May 2015. For its part, although genuinely concerned over the impending disturbance and damage to the landscape of the Heath, the Highgate Society was more measured in its criticism of the plans, possibly due to the general belief conveyed by the Heath Consultative Committee members that the Corporation of London had always administered the Heath in a sensible and conscientious manner. In the end, while most people regretted the upheaval and, particularly, the loss of a large number of mature trees, it was hoped that the contractors would honour their pledge to keep disruption to a minimum. Notwithstanding the efforts of the contractors it was evident to most that the landscape of Heath would be radically and irreversibly changed.

The flower stall

Situated at the prominent Village gateway junction between the High Street and Highgate West Hill is a diminutive brick building, probably constructed in the nineteenth century as a cattle byre. Once home to a clockmaker's workshop, it now serves primarily as a backdrop to the adjacent flower stall. It also encloses the northerly flank of a narrow passageway which leads directly to Pond Square.

In 2010 a planning application was submitted for the redevelopment of this corner site with the construction of a contemporary commercial building four storeys high. The Society's objections were supported by English Heritage on the grounds of heritage, Conservation Area status and proposed design. The debate continued for three years as the applicants tried to convince the planners and public that their new building would provide an 'iconic gateway to the Village'. However Camden took the side of the Society and other campaigners. It would cause immense damage to the historic Village and planning permission was refused.

When the developers appealed against this decision, their appeal was upheld by the Planning Inspector Terry Phillimore. Castigated in the press for having permitted the construction of the 2013 "Carbuncle of the Year" in Islington, his decision in the Highgate case was highlighted by the *Guardian* as another flagrant example of how local feeling could be over-ridden:

7.11 The flower stall, 2015

"Localism is dead" is the cry nationwide in the face of a similar local Appeal decision. Richmond MP Zac Goldsmith said of the Planning Inspectorate: "If I were asked to design a body with the specific goal of alienating and enraging communities, I do not think I could do better. Even where local people are absolutely united and backed up by their councillors, they are still routinely overruled."

Both English Heritage and Camden Council considered applying for a Judicial Review. However, as any appeal would have to be justified on the basis of the manner in which the decision was arrived at and not the reasonableness of the decision, the costs incurred in the event of a loss did not justify the low chance of success. *Buzz* drew attention to a recent decision of the Planning Inspectorate which had been overturned in the High Court when appealed by North Norfolk District Council, the Judge finding that the Inspector had not complied with the statutory requirement to give "special regard" to the preservation of listed buildings and their settings. "If only Camden and English Heritage had shown similar resolve."

Archway Road

Despite Haringey's failure to act on its 2002 Archway Road Regeneration Plan the Society continued to support the plan, encouraging members to make more use of the various shops and services along the road. "Signwriter" noted that within the short distance between St Augustine's Church and the junction with Cholmeley Park there were a dozen restaurants or cafés, and long-standing Society member Shirley Shelton enthused about the surprising collection of unique stores and boutiques along this section of the road.

7.12 *The Red Hedgehog, Archway Road, 2016*

Successfully repaired after storm damage in 2008, Jacksons Lane Community Centre, on the corner of Archway Road and Southwood Lane, was once again providing a host of workshops and courses, many popular with retired people. By 2010 a circus had taken up residence there. The curiously named venue at No. 255 Archway Road, *The Red Hedgehog*, also featured in *Buzz* that year. Established as a friendly setting for live performances, the name comes from Zum Roten Igel, a coffee house in Vienna which was once the favourite haunt of Johannes Brahms. Peter Katin, Emma Kirkby and Steven Isserlis are just some of the artists who have performed there, attracted by its relaxed and very personal atmosphere.

In spite of these encouraging signs – and in spite of its importance as the Victorian element of Highgate's Conservation Area, with a substantial residential population – Archway Road in 2016 continues to suffer the environmental problems associated with any major traffic route. For several years conditions were not helped by TfL's erection of an acoustic barrier along the north eastern side of the road by Highgate Underground Station, part of a project to stabilise the embankment, which had the effect of reflecting traffic noise onto the parade of shops and restaurants opposite. Only after several years' constant campaigning were they persuaded to remove it, by which time the trees

TfL had planted to replace the ones cut down during the works had grown sufficiently to prove a barrier for both the noise and the pollution. A further improvement was the widening of the narrow pavement which obliged pedestrians to walk dangerously close to passing lorries.

The road continues to be blighted by the permission granted to developers to replace the former Archway Road magistrates' court by an apartment block towering up to seven storeys instead of the five formerly applied for. Permission was granted in the face of vehement objections by the Highgate Society, the Conservation Area Advisory Committee, a hundred-strong residents' group, local councillors and the City of London in its capacity as owner of Highgate Wood which the development will overlook.

Basements, extensions and railings

This decade saw the rise of a new threat which was to affect the more affluent parts of London, a seemingly endless series of applications for the construction of enormous basements. In some instances multi-storey "icebergs" reached well beyond the house footprint and into previously undeveloped garden land. This practice was particularly prevalent in the Bishops area to the west of the Village, where many spacious detached houses were being bought by non-resident, overseas investors, often seemingly interested only in maximising financial returns available from a given square footage regardless of the setting of their homes within a Conservation Area. Outstanding among these development is Witanhurst, now sporting a basement of 12,000 cubic metres.

Whilst applications in central London typically involved the construction of basements under existing houses, in Highgate an application

has been more likely to involve the demolition of existing houses altogether and their replacement by larger houses in a different style. The character of streets is not enhanced when owners seek the protection of metal security fencing, often topped with decorative barbs.

The purpose of these basements was often to provide leisure facilities such as a swimming pool, sauna or media room or to provide secure underground car parking. The rationale was that, if over-ground extension was not permitted upwards or sideways, underground rooms should be unobjectionable because they were invisible once built. Such arguments disregarded the nuisance for the neighbours during months of construction work and the dangers of subsidence, diversion of underground watercourses, damage to veteran trees or undermining of the roadway. However often these nuisances were raised by conservation and amenity groups, permission was rarely refused in the face of government guidance favouring development over conservation. Haringey in particular appeared inconsistent in its response to planning applications of this kind, not that Camden's controls were much better despite having a stronger policy.

In spite of the Society's determined objections, it was unable to prevent the demolition of a

7.13 Gilded spikes, View Road

7.14 21 Broadlands Road

number of attractive Arts and Crafts houses and their replacement by larger buildings contrasting in style and out of scale with their neighbours but it did score a few successes – notably at 21 Broadlands Road. This was one of a still-intact sequence of attractive Edwardian houses. It had been threatened with demolition and replacement by a huge dwelling in Jacobean pastiche style with an oversized basement.

That the application was refused and a subsequent appeal decisively rejected was largely on account of the Society's arguments, but much damage had already been done to neighbouring streets such as View Road, Grange Road, Denewood Road and Sheldon Avenue, and by 2016 further applications of this sort were being made in Stormont Road as well as elsewhere on Broadlands Road. The battle to conserve Highgate's heritage from this form of development was seemingly never-

7.15 Neo-classical pastiche, Courtenay Avenue, 2012

ending, and Highgate residents will no doubt be contesting basement redevelopments for decades to come.

Objecting to the erection of tall, pretentious railings around a property may seem trivial by comparison, but whatever sense of community a street may have can be quickly eroded by such barriers. In one case, where it was necessary to erect some form of security fencing in order to guard against repeated criminal activity, members of the Society's Environment Committee were successful in negotiating a compromise in which the homeowner agreed to conceal the fence within a hedge at the pavement edge.

Increasingly Highgate was becoming the preferred residential location of an international elite of very wealthy people whose sense of what constitutes a desirable house to live in is very different to that to which Highgate has been accustomed in the past. As is explained in more detail in chapter 9, the streets to the west of Highgate in particular form the front line of a deep-seated conflict between two cultures, one favouring the conservation of historic buildings, the other a rejection of historicism in favour of pastiche.

The story ends

By 2016 Highgate's public toilets were under renewed threat due to pressures on Camden's budget. A campaign team led by Andrew Sulston found itself working with Camden Council on possible solutions which might be applied more widely across the Borough. This became yet another of the Society's campaigns to attract national media coverage when *Sky News* featured the story and on March 12th local journalist Jenny McCartney wrote in *The Spectator* that the Highgate Society is putting up "a spirited protest" and has made "many powerful points".

The contents of this and preceding chapters have been based on information recorded in print. During the last few of its fifty years existence Ian Henghes has masterminded the Society's effort to take advantage of the arrival of new digital technologies. As of the start of the fiftieth anniversary year the Society now has a website at www.highgatesociety.com which enables visitors to access a calendar of local community events and to sign up for the email newsletter that it now uses to supplement *Buzz*. The public are encouraged to submit events via www.highgatecalendar. org and items of interest are regularly provided by members of the Society for the newsletter and website. News is also circulated using social media via Facebook, Twitter and Streetlife. Website visitors can also check room bookings – useful for avoiding inadvertently interrupting a booked event – and they can request a room booking. The Society now also offers free Wi-Fi internet access to users of 10A.

This, and the establishment of a system for sharing documents using Google Drive, may one day assist whoever compiles the story of the next fifty years of the Society's activities. Certainly this will be an easier task than searching the seventy boxes containing a complete set of the minutes of the meetings of the Society's Council during its first fifty years.

This story ends in April 2016, the fiftieth anniversary of the month in which the Society was founded. Not for the first time shops in the High Street carry the posters campaigning about the proposed closure of the Pond Square toilets. Some also carry posters opposing TfL's

7.16 Sky News covers opposition to toilet closure

plans to relocate the terminus of the 271 to a so-called bus "depot" in North Road. There is a flurry of emails between members of the Environment Committee lobbying against proposed alterations to the Archway gyratory while another flurry canvasses views on how Highgate should respond to the decision of Islington Council to extend the hours of the CPZ system in streets surrounding the Whittington Hospital.

Unlike previous anniversaries, the fiftieth will be celebrated by events spread across an entire calendar year. The Editor of the Anniversary issue of *Buzz*, Tamar Karet, announced to members that the programme would start with a repeat at Upstairs at the Gatehouse of *The People on the Hill*, the production Brendan Nolan wrote to celebrate its tenth anniversary. This would be followed by a series of cultural events: a sing-along with Highgate Choral Society at St Michael's church in April, a literary walk and Music in Highgate Homes in May and an exhibition on the grand houses of Highgate and the visionaries who lived in them in June. A second exhibition, of the contribution of modern architecture to Highgate, is scheduled for October, highlighting the successes and failures in the design of new residential buildings during the last fifty years. In July the Watercolour Group plan to set up their easels throughout Highgate Village so that passing residents can watch them working.

Since no anniversary would be complete without wining and dining, the celebratory year culminates in an Anniversary Dinner in November. Before then, in September, the Society will have celebrated the publication of the book you are currently reading, *The Story of the Highgate Society: 1966-2016*.

The Old Forge, 45 North Road, in 1905

Ongoing issues

CHAPTER 8:
TRAFFIC AND TRANSPORT

The foregoing chapters 3 to 7 have provided a chronological account of how the Highgate Society has evolved and adapted over the fifty years since its formation.

In contrast with most of those activities described in earlier chapters, many of which reflect the interests and initiatives of individual members, there have been a number of more persistent issues which have involved the Society in every period of its existence. One of these is how to balance the growth in the use of private transport with the need for an efficient public transport system, an issue which affects the whole of London, not just Highgate.

The Archway Road

From its earliest days Highgate has enjoyed – or suffered – from its position on the principal

route from London to the North, astride what since 1923 has been designated the A1.

Traffic congestion was a problem as early as 1813 when the Archway Road was constructed to bypass the bottleneck of Highgate Village and to avoid its steep and muddy hills. But, a century later, it was not wide enough and by the 1960s the problem of getting traffic from the north into central London – and out again – was becoming critical once more. As was explained in chapter 2, a proposal surfaced in 1962 which involved making the Archway Road one-way south-bound, and Highgate High Street north-bound, having been widened by the demolition of the buildings on its east side. Outrage in Highgate was universal; a Save Highgate Committee was formed, and the resistance caused by this threat led to the creation of the Highgate Society.

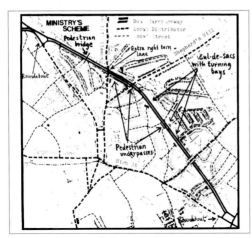

8.01 Draft proposals for a dual carriageway, Archway Road, 1962

When protests caused this particular solution to be abandoned, various schemes were then advanced for the widening of Archway Road, part of which was implemented in the 1970s when a dual carriageway was built along the stretch from the Archway gyratory to the Archway Bridge. The MoT's intention was to extend the dual carriageway north to the Wellington at the foot of North Hill. Opinion in the Society was divided: some were wholly opposed; some accepted the need for widening but sought, through an expert critique of the Ministry's plans which had formed the basis of a representation the Society had made to Parliament, to mitigate their worst effects.

There were uncomfortable suspicions that some of those living higher up the hill than the Archway Road were prepared to sacrifice the interests of their neighbours down the hill, in exchange for a relief from traffic in the historic section of the Village. And then there were some, on the fringe, who sought not to argue the opposition case but to disrupt successive planning enquiries, misleadingly characterising the scheme as a 'motorway', and refusing to debate the issues, or to allow others to do so.

The row culminated in a Special General Meeting of the Society in December 1985 at which it debated whether Society members as a whole should always be consulted via an AGM or Special General Meeting about public statements on the Archway Road, or whether the elected members of the Environment Committee could be empowered to speak on behalf of the membership. Neither of these propositions was accepted, but a compromise resolution was eventually passed which required the Council of the Society to decide *how* the membership should be consulted on any important issue, for example by circulating a written survey or other means.

The debate became so acrimonious that the Chairman and Council felt obliged to expel from the Society one of its members, veteran campaigner George Stern, on the grounds that he repeatedly disrupted meetings and refused to abide by the chairman's rulings. The fuss generated by this decision led to the convening of yet another meeting of Council, this time a Special Meeting to debate whether the actions of the previous Council meeting were consistent with the Society's constitution. The outcome was to uphold the original decision. Such disputes were in danger of damaging the reputation of the Society, so the editor of subsequent issues of *Buzz* decided to publish the letters they had been sent by Mr Stern and his supporters, but took care themselves to avoid any direct mention of the controversy to which these letters were referring.

Separatist propaganda on a wall near the Archway. Any takers for an Isle of Dogs on Highgate Hill?

8.02 Anger beside the Archway Road

After four successive public enquiries had ended in mayhem, it increasingly became evident that the problem was solving itself: as container ships began to dock at Tilbury and Felixstowe and the section of the M25 between St Albans and the Dartford Tunnel, completed in 1982, carried international freight traffic eastwards, the traffic on the Archway Road was falling far short of earlier predictions. Nonetheless it took until 1991 for the MoT to abandon further proposals for Archway Road widening.

Meanwhile, the Ministry, convinced of the force of their arguments, had compulsorily purchased properties on the west side of the road and when plans for widening were abandoned, had sold the properties on to developers without consulting the tenants. The consequent planning blight along the whole road continued to affect Highgate twenty-five years later.

That left the gyratory system at Archway. It was introduced in 1969; the resulting orientation of the roads attracted through traffic up Highgate Hill rather than Archway Road, and representations by the Society resulted in notices at the foot of the hill seeking, ineffectively as it turned out, to direct heavy traffic onto Archway Road. By the 1980s it had become evident that growth in traffic volumes had made it difficult for pedestrians to reach shops and offices inside the gyratory. As a result in 2005 Islington started consultations on three options for development of the area around Archway Tube station: tall buildings such as at Canary Wharf; high density, low rise development such as at Queensway; or a mixture such as Putney Wharf.

Thirty years of discussion and a generation of lobbying by the Better Archway Forum has resulted in a decision by Islington Council to terminate the use of Archway as a traffic gyratory and to reconfigure traffic so as to make the part of the shopping centre isolated by the gyratory more accessible to pedestrians and shoppers. Attractive though this may be to people living in the immediate vicinity of Archway, there is increasing concern about the capacity of the revised road lay-out and that much of the Archway Road and Holloway Road will suffer once again from the tail-backs that so blighted the area in the 1960s.

Public Transport

The government's attitudes towards transport has changed enormously during the half-century since the formation of the Society. When the Society was founded, private cars and public transport competed for limited road space without intervention by transport planners. By the 1990s Councils had become committed to giving much higher priority to public transport, both to counter the deterioration in journey times caused by increased congestion and to persuade car owners to abandon their cars in favour of public transport.

The Traffic and Transport Committee which was set up with John Oakes as Chairman in 1999, succeeded by Robin Fairlie and subsequently David Shelbourn, set about designing a bus lane on Highgate Hill which would be one-way downhill in the morning and uphill during the afternoon rush-hour. This proposal was defeated after careful cost-benefit analysis by former Society Chairman Derek Hall and numerous other objections. The committee also addressed the appropriateness of the location of bus stops and the urgent re-opening of the faulty escalators at Highgate Tube station, the latter rectified after the attendance of Northern Line management at a public meeting demanded by the Society.

Highgate is well-served by buses to and from the City of London, but the Society has for long complained to Transport for London (TfL) of

121

the absence of a direct route to the West End, and the near-total absence of orbital routes – connecting, for example, Haringey Council offices at Wood Green by way of Muswell Hill to Highgate and on to Hampstead, Swiss Cottage, and Paddington.

In 1998 the Society had conducted an extensive survey of how pupils travelled to the eight schools in Highgate, and used the results to campaign for a service between Wood Green and Paddington via Highgate, emphasising the needs of the schools in particular. These were repeatedly rejected. Nevertheless, years of pressure by the Society and foot-dragging by TfL led in 2005 to Mayor Livingstone intervening in a meeting attended by the Chairman of the GLA's Transport Committee, the head of London Buses, and representatives of the Society, which had the effect of initiating a new 603 service from Muswell Hill to Swiss Cottage via Highgate and Hampstead and back again. Specifically designed for schoolchildren, this service offers just two buses in each direction each morning Monday to Friday, and two buses in each direction each afternoon. TfL, having hotly disputed the need for this 'concession', continues to deny the existence of sufficient demand to justify a regular day-long and/or extended service on this route. The fight continues.

The other long-running debate with TfL concerns the turn-around of the 271 bus in the entry to South Grove and Pond Square. The Society has consistently argued that this turn-around is dangerous, unhealthy, productive of traffic snarl-ups, and a blot on the Village; as a result of an extensive survey of bus usage in Highgate Village, it produced a series of cost-analyses of alternative configurations which would be cost-neutral to TfL. In February 2012 TfL's head of surface transport, Leon Daniels took part in a public meeting at Highgate School attended by over a hundred residents.

He left with the clear understanding that the issue was one which concerned the entire community, not just a few public transport enthusiasts.

8.03 Campaign to relocate 271 bus turnaround

For year after year the response from TfL was a flat negative, and there was no apparent attempt to engage with the Society's arguments, or to respond to constructive proposals even after the Society formed an alliance with the Neighbourhood Forum, councillors from Camden and Haringey and elected representatives on the GLA to press TfL for action. However in February 2016 TfL unexpectedly announced a consultation on its proposals to build a new mini-roundabout outside the main entrance to Highgate School in North Road and to relocate the 271 terminus so that it shared the same terminus as the 214 in North Road.

This change would offer real opportunities for using the space at the end of South Grove to revitalise the village core, but residents of North Road were among many who considered the scheme over-engineered and TfL agreed to return with revised proposals, maintaining the bus turnaround in North Road but having both the 214 and the 271 turning at the mini-roundabout at its junction with Castle Yard.

In 1993, after many requests from the Society, TfL introduced a bus service up West Hill by extending the 214 bus service from Moorgate to Parliament Hill into the Village. This was chosen in preference to the extension of the C2 service from Victoria, which the Society had advocated because it would have linked Highgate with the West End, complementing Highgate's existing transport connections to the City of London. And in 2000 the Transport and Traffic Committee secured a night bus extension of the 214 service. It is astonishing how many years it took and what persistence was needed to achieve these successes.

In 2001 after years of agitating, a left turn out of Archway Road into Muswell Hill Road, prohibited by Haringey, was restored, and the bus shelter on the west side of North Hill was relocated to make it more convenient for visitors to the Highgate Group Practice, though it took another nine years to get a bus stop on the opposite side for patients visiting the surgery from the other direction.

Parking

The growth of car ownership since the formation of the Society in 1966 has resulted in increased competition for a limited number of spaces where motorists may park. This has resulted in parking controls being subject to constant discussion and review. The success of these schemes has required careful balancing of the interests of five different groups: residents, shoppers, visitors, traders, and commuters.

8.04 Parking in Pond Square

For years the Society watched the gradual spread of Controlled Parking Zones (CPZs) outward from central London until, shortly after the millennium, it became evident that CPZs must arrive in Highgate too. Opinions over when, where, and how, were varied. The Society declined to oppose outright the creation of CPZs; rather it took the line that local authorities must follow their statutory duty to consult with their constituents on whether, and if so how, CPZs should cover Highgate. The Society's role would be to ensure that consultation was full, transparent, and fair. In particular it took the lead in chairing an initial meeting between the responsible officers in Camden and Haringey, to ensure that the proposals of the two boroughs were consistent, and played a part in designing the questionnaires that their residents were invited to answer.

Such a level of coordination between the two councils was, at least in Highgate, unprecedented, and helped to make the installation of CPZs across Highgate in 2005/6 a relatively uncontentious affair. In the event large majorities in both boroughs were content with restricted parking Monday to Friday from 10-12 noon; this has had the desired effect of preventing all-day street parking, except in residents' spaces. It seemed that the Society had learned some lessons from the Archway Road debacle on how to handle internally difficult and potentially disputatious issues.

Traffic circulation

There have been very few periods when the Society has not been in discussion with Haringey, Camden or TfL over issues of road design and traffic circulation, often involving the detail of proposals for the siting and design of bus stops, pedestrian crossings or cycle racks. The Society, in these as in many other

8.05 Controlled Parking Zone, Church Road, 2016

matters, has been extremely well-served by local councillors who have communicated the Society's views to the hard-pressed officers responsible for these decisions.

1993 saw the abandonment of the notorious Village one-way system of traffic, introduced in 1969 (see chapter 2), which used the block between North Road and Southwood Lane as a gyratory system. However, despite the Society having persistently lobbied for its removal and welcomed the proposals, it was concerned that the three proposed mini-roundabouts would confuse drivers. On this issue the Society's fears turned out to be unjustified: the roundabouts were installed and have proved capable of handling traffic volumes.

The 1990s was a period when "traffic calming" first became an accepted policy. In 1993 there was widespread criticism of Camden's traffic calming measures as piecemeal and not integrated across the borough. One of the criticisms, of the size and positioning of the mini-roundabout at the foot of West Hill,

proved to have been justified as it had to be re-designed following a series of accidents. Camden also proposed a series of traffic calming measures for West Hill which the Society considered inappropriate, and the engineering consultants brought in by Camden "seemed to be unaware of PPG15 [official guidance] on Planning in a Historic Environment."

A good deal of angst was also expressed about the proposal that the part of Swain's Lane above Highgate Cemetery should be restricted to one-way traffic; although Camden's 'consultation' produced ninety-seven votes against and only nineteen in favour, the scheme was implemented.

Richard Webber, for the Traffic and Transport Committee, was successful in persuading the Council to change traffic priorities at the junction of South Grove, The Grove and West Hill, resulting in a significant reduction in road rage. More recently, Section 106[xxix] money from Witanhurst has been used to upgrade the kerbs and pavements at this junction.

In 2015 irritation was expressed at Haringey's decision to create a 20-mph speed limit on the borough's roads, not least because of the rejection of a blanket 20-mph zone by residents. The erection of the rash of "repeater" signs required to comply with the provisions of Department of Transport standards has been severely criticised both in terms of cost and visual impact. However 2015 did see the success of a long-standing campaign when the Society assisted residents in North Hill in persuading Haringey to introduce a light controlled pedestrian crossing at the junction of North Hill with View Road and Church Road.

Map Three: Key planning issues

CHAPTER 9:
MANSIONS FOR THE MONEYED CLASSES

Traffic and public transport are by no means the only issues to have engaged the Society throughout its fifty year existence. Another is the increasing pressure to satisfy the demand among the super-rich for luxury homes of the highest specification. The impact of this demand for what the press commonly describe as "mansions" is exacerbated by the extraordinary increase in the price of London homes, with the result that the value of the land that a property sits on is now often greater than the cost of its construction.

The pressures for the construction of luxury homes for the super-rich have been particularly strong in two parts of Highgate, in the Highgate Bowl and along the Highgate – Hampstead ridge.

The Highgate Bowl

The Highgate Bowl is the large open area sloping down from the east of the High Street. It is accessed through the narrow neck of Townsend Yard. Prized as one of the green areas by which Highgate is surrounded, the Bowl has historic significance as a rare if not unique survival of grazing land for the cattle droves. It contributes significantly to Highgate's appearance as a hill-top village. For the first half of the twentieth century it was owned by Highgate Cemetery and used for growing its flowers. Later it was cultivated as Bates' Nursery.

In 1967 there were two applications for large housing developments, one of 100 units, and the threat of redevelopment has hung over it ever since. The Society was amongst those objecting in 1967; in 1969 the Borough of Haringey refused both. Both were dismissed at appeal and the decisions confirmed by the Minister of State for the Environment.

However when the nursery closed in the early seventies a renewed threat was averted only after

9.01 The Highgate Bowl

agitation by the Society: the summer 1971 issue of *Buzz* recounts how the land was now being again laid out as a nursery by Chris Southwood.

However, after a further application for twenty-five houses was rejected in 1975, the Society responded imaginatively. A group of local residents realised that they could not succeed in fighting off development proposals for parts of the Bowl indefinitely without a positive approach to its future use. The driving force was Dame Geraldine Aves, a retired civil servant whose unassuming manner concealed great determination and force of character.

Their concept became the Harington Scheme, its name reflecting the interests of the Borough of Haringey and that of the Camden and Islington Area Health Authority. It still provides training for young people with learning difficulties. In 1980 it recruited its first fifteen trainees, who would learn gardening skills on land that formed part of the grounds of Furnival House nurses' home in Cholmeley Park. The land belonged to the Health Authority, which had granted the Scheme an initial four-year lease.

Other parts of the Bowl have remained under threat. During the nineties several onslaughts were successfully fought off. Perhaps the most divisive came in 1995 when Highgate School proposed to build a science block on the parade ground below Dyne House. Many of the society's members had close connections with the school but the majority view which emerged could be summarised as: "Of course the School must have a new science block, but do they really need to build it in the Bowl?" When the scheme was eventually withdrawn after opposition from Kingsley Place residents, the then Headmaster blamed the Society. It took many years for good relations between the two parties to be restored.

In the centre of the Bowl more than one developer proved keen to build residential property on the old nursery lands, while at the southern end the Health Authority wanted to build a further tall block of flats on the tennis court next to Furnival House. The latter was actually given planning permission, but the developers overstepped the mark by making deep excavations far too close to the roots of ancient trees. They were forced to fill them in and pay swingeing fines to fund replacing the trees and the monitoring of tree growth over the following five years.

During this period no fewer than six appeals against refusal of permission for development on various sites were rejected, including one proposing the construction of twenty-eight terraced houses. Each was fought tenaciously by the Society and each was dismissed, the inspectors unanimously agreeing on the contribution that the open land made to the character of Highgate. One even describe the land as of "national importance" for its contribution to the character of the Village.

The beginning of the new century saw a period of comparative calm, but continued vigilance, with the Society concentrating on resisting small-scale buildings on what was now the Capital Gardens Garden Centre. But in 2010 an application to build three luxury houses on the site was lodged by developers, justified on the grounds that the garden centre was uneconomic. This application too was refused by Haringey and yet again dismissed on Appeal. Only a few months later a new application for three more houses, apparently designed to mimic the greenhouses on the site, was submitted. When this went to Appeal in 2013, the Society raised over £10,000 to brief a barrister whose arguments against the development were successful.

In her judgment, the inspector, Joanna Reid, said significantly that 'the proposal would seriously erode the significance of this part of the Bowl as a historically important back-land and its important heritage value as a setting for the village'. Her comments were considered sufficiently strong to rule out any possibility of further attempts to develop the land.

Following the rejection, members of the Society, with support from the newly-formed Highgate Neighbourhood Forum, the CAAC and the Harington Scheme, have established a charity, the Friends of the Highgate Bowl, with the objective of purchasing the garden centre land to protect it from yet more attempts at development and retain it as open land for community use.

The campaign continues.

Witanhurst

Witanhurst is Highgate's most prominent mansion, situated at the summit of West Hill. Known as Parkfield when it was bought by soap magnate Sir Arthur Crosfield MP in 1912, the house was surrounded by extensive grounds, sufficient to host what became an annual tennis tournament in the weeks following Wimbledon which became a major

9.02 Celebrating the inspector's judgment on the Bowl case, November 2014

9.03 Witanhurst, seen from Hampstead Heath, c 1980

In 1965 Witanhurst was sold by Crosfield's widow to his son Paul Crosfield. He in turn sold it to developers who applied for planning permission to build over 100 houses in its grounds. The Society, in partnership with the Heath & Hampstead Society, mounted vigorous opposition and the case was eventually referred to the Secretary of State. His ruling in October 1972 disappointed those who had hoped for complete rejection; though it was a bitter defeat, their disappointment was softened by the permitted number of houses being reduced from 121 to 63, resulting in what is still Highgate's largest gated development.

event in the London social calendar. When Crosfield decided to demolish the original house and replace it with a new one in the style of a French château, completed in 1920, it assumed the name Witanhurst.

The 31 January 1980 edition of the *Country Life* featured a piece by Michael Wright, chairman of the Society, entitled *Witanhurst under Attack*. It was illustrated by a number of photographs by John Gay.

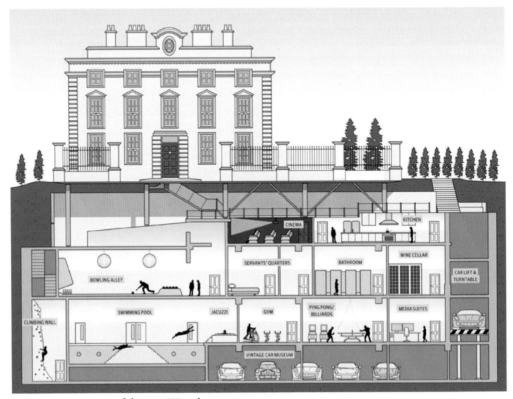

9.04 Service quarters of the new Witanhurst

In 2007 the house was re-sold, allegedly to a "European family which wants to adapt it as a simple family home". By 2009 a planning application had been made proposing no external modifications to the house itself but seeking to replace the original service wing, an integral part of the building, with an orangery, designed by Robert Adam in neo-Classical style, a new entrance off West Hill, and, to the disbelief of the community, a 12,000 cubic metre double basement. Camden Planning Committee refused the application. An appeal was launched, and, to widespread dismay, it was upheld. Following construction of the basement the Society received complaints of rising damp and even flooding from adjacent properties. A further application for an additional basement was lodged, the justification being that it would protect the owners from the sight of staff walking round the site.

In June 2015 the identity of the owner, formerly hidden behind the screen of an offshore company, was revealed by Ed Caesar in an article in the *New Yorker* to be Andrey Guryev, former Russian senator and owner of a fertiliser factory and a number of other businesses. The orangery was built, justified as a necessary separate home for Guryev's children and their families, and the extra basement was permitted despite many objections. Though the house was supposed to be finished in time for the London Olympics, the main house was still shrouded in tarpaulin three years later. The large number of contractors who used the limited number of parking spaces in South Grove caused difficulties for Highgate shoppers but their trade did contribute hugely to the viability of the shops selling lunchtime snacks. The fine avenue of mature lime trees, felled to enable the wall along West Hill to be repaired, is yet to be replanted as required under the original consent.

Athlone House: Act One

Unlike the Highgate Bowl and Witanhurst, it was only comparatively recently that the future of Athlone House became a major issue. Yet in the twenty years since it came on the market it has been the centre of the Society's most high-profile campaigns.

The mansion, built as Caen Wood Towers in 1872 by wealthy industrialist Edward Brooke, is situated on the Highgate-Hampstead ridge on a brow overlooking Hampstead Heath. It is accessed from Hampstead Lane. During World War II it was requisitioned for use as the headquarters for RAF intelligence. After the war its owner, Sir Edward Waley-Cohen, donated the house to the newly founded National Health Service for use as a convalescent home, and donated an extensive area of grassland which formed part of its grounds, subsequently called Cohen's Field, to form part of Hampstead Heath.

The projected sale of Athlone House by the Camden & Islington Health Authority got off to a bad start: it became public knowledge that, contrary to established practice, Camden had invited the applicants to write the planning brief on which the authority's application for planning consent was to be judged. As the house was visible from many parts of the Heath

9.05 Athlone House from Hampstead Heath

and any building on its grounds of similar or greater height would seriously affect such views, there was an immediate outcry from the Heath & Hampstead Society and the Highgate CAAC as well as from the Highgate Society. They were assured by Camden that there would be a public consultation once the design brief had been approved. Objectors were not allowed to speak at the Council meeting which considered the brief.

However, Councillors Gerry Harrison and Margaret Little brought about a meeting with the developers acting on behalf of the Health Authority. Initial negotiations between the Athlone House Working Group (AHWG) from 1998 to 2005 and the original developers, Dwyer Ltd and their architect, Sir David Chipperfield, were friendly and productive. Dwyer wanted to build three blocks of flats in the grounds of the House and AHWG were determined that these should not be visible from Hampstead Heath and that the splendid, albeit somewhat neglected Victorian house should be saved and restored.

After lengthy but constructive negotiations, the developers accepted the validity of many of the AHWG's comments, particularly those regarding the visual appearance of the apartment blocks proposed for the ground to the east of the main house. In 2005 AHWG was delighted to receive a letter from the developers thanking it for its involvement and acknowledging that the discussions has resulted in a more appropriate scheme. Camden Council approved the application subject to a section 106 agreement which required restoration of the original house. Construction work on the new apartment blocks commenced in 2006, and in the following year AHWG obtained a positive response to its request to Dwyer to donate a hectare of the gardens to Hampstead Heath. Thus was achieved the largest addition to the extent of the Heath for eighty years.

These positive outcomes appeared to confirm the Society's belief that discussion of developers plans with local amenity groups before making an application was likely to improve the likelihood of a proposal's approval. The flats were built, but, to AHWG's consternation there was no evidence of restoration work having been started on the principal house within the forty-two months stipulated in the Section 106 Agreement.

Athlone House: Act two

It became apparent in due course that a new owner had acquired that section of the Athlone House site that contained the original house. They were adamant that its condition had deteriorated to such an extent that it was no longer financially viable to restore it as required under the section 106 agreement. They further declared that they were not obliged to observe an agreement which they themselves had not signed. The only viable alternative to a continual decline in the condition of the house was to demolish it and build in its place an edifice whose opulent design did justice to its exceptional location, a task for which the services of the seemingly ubiquitous Robert Adam had been secured.

David Chipperfield, it transpired, would no longer be retained by the new owners, whose identity, it was asserted, was too sensitive for it to be made public or indeed even be revealed to the new architect who would report to the offshore vehicle through which the new owner conducted the transaction. Moreover, in response to AHWG's constant demands that the Section 106 Agreement must be enforced, Camden Council's legal department advised that such an Agreement could not be enforced while a subsequent planning application had not been decided upon. This advice was contested by AHWG

9.06 Athlone House during the 2000s

whose arguments to the contrary were in due course upheld by a planning inspector. Nevertheless, to the relief of the community, Camden refused the application as damaging to the Metropolitan Open Land of Hampstead Heath.

At the public inquiry held in 2011 the *AHWG* urged dismissal of new proposal on a number of grounds. These included the size of the building which was two and a half times the area of the existing building, the choice of a neoclassical design with copper domes and other decorative features alien to the building's countrified setting, and the use of a light white Bath stone. All, it was argued, would detract from the views from the Heath. Other objectors included the City of London, English Heritage, the Victorian Society, Save Britain's Heritage and 1,100 local people.

Though the appeal was dismissed, the inspector's judgement was such as not to discourage a fresh application subject to modifications which might not be too onerous for the developers. By this stage it was rumoured that the beneficial owner was a Kuwaiti family. Whether true or not, in 2014 a fresh application was submitted which repeated the claim that the deterioration of the

fabric of the existing house had now made restoration impossible, accompanied by plans claiming that the footprint of the current house would be exceeded only by a few per cent.

The revised application was no more successful than the previous one. Though the Society was not pleased to learn of the developers' request that the appeal inquiry, scheduled for February 2015, should last a full twelve days, the choice of Colin Ball to act as inspector was considered auspicious. This was because the previous year he had presided over the landmark appeal that saved Smithfield Market from demolition. Equally positive, in the view of the *AHWG*, was the decision of Mr Ball to make a series of site visits to inspect the impact of the new proposals on views from the Heath.

9.07 Save Athlone House campaign

9.08 *The campaign to save Athlone House was the Society's first to use social media*

The twenty-page judgment which was published in June contained a thorough consideration of the planning issues that the *AHWG* had argued were relevant and concluded, without equivocation, that the appeal should be rejected. The inspector rejected the argument that the new building would not be materially larger than the existing one, and asserted that with an increased footprint of 26.7%, increased built volume of 50-51% and above-ground volume of 38%, the proposals were inconsistent with the planning regulations governing development on Metropolitan Open Land.

Ball considered that its appearance was intended to be grandiose and palatial in scale in a setting where a domestic appearance was more appropriate. It was his opinion that these aspects of the design were harmful and outweighed any benefits that the new building might bring, such as for example bringing to an end the years of uncertainty regarding the future of Athlone House and the decades of deterioration.

He accepted that the original restoration programme might no longer be appropriate. But he rejected the developers' claim that it had to be designed in such a way as to satisfy the requirements of the most demanding purchaser. A revised restoration programme

was perfectly feasible and the *AHWG*, he said, had shown that the house was an important heritage asset and, moreover, that it could be repaired without exorbitant expenditure and could find a buyer prepared to accept a lower specification. The *AHWG* made clear its willingness to engage in discussions which might result in such an accommodation.

Finally, the Inspector declared unambiguously that the Section 106 Agreement was legally binding, that it was still valid, and that Camden was in error in maintaining that it could not enforce it while a new application or appeal was current. It should and must be enforced. Nothing could be clearer, more decisive or more confirmative of the arguments made by the Society and its fellow objectors.

Michael Hammerson commented: "Perhaps the planning system, at least when in the hands of a thoughtful and experienced inspector, is not always so weighted against the community as we have been concluding in recent years. This triumph will hopefully give comfort to other amenity groups struggling year after year to conserve their heritage."

The Society took pride in the professionalism of the defence it mounted at the Appeal, against an expensively arrayed battery of expert witnesses called by the appellants. Gail Waldman, an architect member of the Environment Committee, proved a particularly robust and well-informed expert witness demonstrating how exaggerated were the claims of the appellants as regards restoration. She worked closely with Susan Rose, Chairman of the Conservation Area Advisory Committee, to present a comprehensive dossier on the historic importance of the house; another local Heath expert, Deborah Wolton, spoke eloquently on the importance of Athlone House in views from the Heath and the damage the new development would cause.

Impressive too was the number of professional people who acted *pro bono* on behalf of *AHWG*. These included the barrister David Altaras and the distinguished architectural historian Professor Joseph Rykwert CBE. An unexpected reinforcement to the team was John Avent, director of a firm of engineers in Bath specialising in restoration of historic buildings. When he read about the Athlone House saga he was so outraged by the developers' claims that he immediately offered his services to *AHWG* as an expert witness on restoration. He visited the house twice and prepared a submission delivered with telling effect at the inquiry.

The Athlone House affair roused feelings far beyond Highgate and Hampstead. Apart from the major national bodies listed above, another 1,100 people sent objections to Camden or the Planning Inspectorate, while an on-line petition organised by Highgate Society member Jack Boswell, urging Camden to refuse the second application, gathered 5,200 signatures from people as far afield as Australia and America who had experienced the pleasures of Hampstead Heath. In February 2015, *Private Eye* published a scathing attack on the developers, calling the affair "a real scandal".

And yet, to widespread astonishment, the developers proceeded to notify the Planning Inspectorate in July 2015 that they would seek a judicial review of the Planning Inspector's decision. Many were aghast at what they felt was a cynical manoeuvre. If this latest action were successful, it would have serious implications for the national planning system, for local democracy, and for the integrity of legally binding agreements. However the High Court found in support of Camden, with the inspector deciding that the developers had no case. He refused leave to appeal further. In January 2016 the house was sold again, conditional on the new owners obtaining planning permission, their intention being to restore Athlone House. The *AHWG* are currently in discussion with them.

Highgate High Street in 1911 in the days of cable cars

THE VOLUNTARY SECTOR

10.01 Highgate Cemetery

CHAPTER 10:
THE WIDENING OF VOLUNTARY ACTIVITIES

Limits to the role of the Highgate Society

When the Society was founded in 1966 few people would have predicted how greatly the role of the voluntary sector would change over the next fifty years. Whereas in 1966 a small number of national charities collected donations from private individuals to fund particular good causes, by 2016 there were many more voluntary organisations who relied on central and local government for their funds. This is because voluntary organisations were increasingly considered to offer a more cost effective means of delivering many public services than government itself. This transformation of the voluntary sector is particularly evident in Highgate.

In 1966 the voluntary sector relied exclusively on volunteers and raised their own funds. The intervening years have seen the emergence

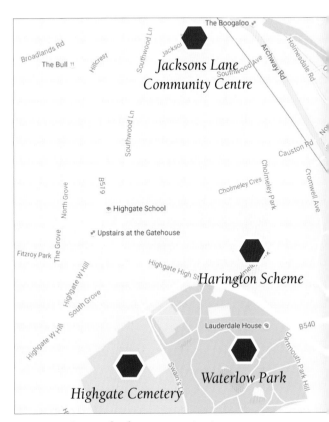

Map Four: Principal voluntary organisations

in Highgate of three voluntary organisations, Highgate Cemetery, Jacksons Lane Community Centre and the Harington Scheme, each funded by government to provide vital services to the local community. Another, the Highgate Neighbourhood Forum, has a defined statutory role in advising Haringey Council although it receives minimal public funding. The Friends of Waterlow Park provides advisory services and expert advice to Camden Council on the management of Waterlow Park but on an entirely voluntary basis.

Many members of the community, and even quite a few in the Society itself, can be confused by the relationship between the Society and these other organisations. A founding member is very clear about the relationship:

> It was the HS who, in the early days of the Highgate Cemetery Trust, gave its dynamic founder Jean Pateman the contacts she needed to network; this is a real legacy of the Society. The Society also initiated action which led to the founding of the Jacksons Lane Centre, The Harington Scheme, and Lauderdale House. However, while it acted as a facilitator for all these, it did not want to take them over, and ensured that they secured their independence while never being in competition with each other. The people involved with them came through the HS.

Earlier pages have noted the involvement in the Society of Nicky Gavron, the driving force behind Jacksons Lane Community Centre, and of Geraldine Aves, the driving force behind the Harington Scheme. Both of these organisations have a much more specific focus than the Highgate Society. This chapter focuses on these and other voluntary organisations to which members of the Highgate Society have given visionary leadership over the last fifty years.

Highgate Cemetery

Highgate cemetery consists of two parts, the original West Cemetery, opened 1839 on one side of Swain's Lane, and the east ground opened in 1855 on the other. By 1975 the West Cemetery, which contained many exceptional Victorian monuments, had become severely overgrown whilst the East Cemetery, which attracted large numbers of visitors since it is where Karl Marx is buried, remained in better condition.

Over the Easter weekend of 1975, fearing an imminent threat of closure to the cemetery, members of the Highgate Society carried out a survey of visitors. A few weeks later its owner, United Cemeteries, decided to close and to give notice to its staff. Camden Council thereupon awarded a limited grant to United Cemeteries which would provide for the eastern part to remain open whilst the western part would open only by arrangement to allow for burials[xxx].

In the May 1975 issue of *Buzz* the Environment Committee reported.

Most members will know that the Company owning the Cemetery has announced its intention of closing the two sections of the Cemetery to both grave-owners and the general public, and has dismissed the staff. Camden Borough Council has decided in principle to try to acquire the Cemetery but needs legislative powers to do so. This would take two years, and in the meantime there is a real danger that vandalism and neglect could do irreparable damage to the buildings, tombs and walls. The [Environment] Committee believes that the Cemetery must be kept open.

"A working group of the Environment Committee has also had a meeting with Camden councillors and officers to urge the setting up of a Trust to act as custodian for the national interest in the Cemetery and to foster the conservation of the monuments and buildings and their setting. In view of recent developments, the Committee feels that the establishment of a Trust is all the more urgent, and is seeking to co-ordinate the efforts of grave owners and organisations with special interest in the Cemetery to keep it open.

The Society, in the person of Michael Wright, Chairman of the Environment Committee, decided that something more formal than an ad hoc working group was needed. He persuaded Jean Pateman and Judith Yuille to recruit a band of volunteers who would become the Friends of Highgate Cemetery. In June John Winter, an architect, was elected its Chairman and Jean Pateman its Secretary.

The November 1975 *Buzz* reported that "The Friends of Highgate Cemetery, inspired by Judith Yuille and launched with the blessing and backing of the Highgate Society, [and which was] now an officially constituted society, held their Inaugural Meeting at the Institution on October 9th. Camden Council under the GLC General Powers Bill is proposing to acquire the Cemetery and legislation is due to be introduced to the House on November 27. Mrs Jean Pateman, the acting Secretary, at 5 View Road N6 would be pleased to answer questions on recent developments and anyone wishing to join the Friends of Highgate Cemetery should contact her." Articles under the heading FOHC soon became regular features in the Society's newsletters.

The formation of the FOHC was crucial to the success and subsequent history of the cemetery. Although the GLC General Powers Act 1976 would have allowed Camden to acquire it, the Borough decided instead to work with the Highgate Society, the FOHC and others to draw up a Trust Deed for the Advisory Trust long advocated by the Society.

Shortly after the FOHC's first AGM, held in the HLSI, work began on clearing the worst of the

10.02 Jean Pateman

undergrowth and the landscape architect Jenny Cox, who was called in as adviser, recommended replacing the overwhelming self-seeded sycamores with mixed oak woodland. From the beginning the FOHC has recognised the need both to preserve the cemetery as a nature reserve and to develop it as a visitor destination, producing an income sufficient to fund essential repairs while respecting its role as a working graveyard.

As part of the Highgate Society's tenth anniversary celebration in 1976, the cemetery held its first open day. By November 1978 the FOHC's membership had grown to 800 and it had produced a booklet on the history of the cemetery, with a preface by Sir John Betjeman who lived nearby in West Hill. In 1980, in the pages of *Buzz*, the Friends recalled with gratitude the strong-willed support of the Society in general and "those of its members whose early zeal helped the Society to launch the Friends of the Highgate Cemetery".

By 1981 the cemetery had been bought for £50 from United Cemeteries by Bryan Morris

10.03 "Mums Army Fights Back"

Fielding, vicar of St Michael's and Vice President of FOHC, appealed for funds for a conservation centre in the north lodge as a memorial to John Gay who, besides taking many celebrated photographs of tomb monuments, had devoted many hours to conservation work at the cemetery.

In 2006, in response to allegations of authoritarian behaviour, Judith Yuille, Jean Pateman and Hilary Deeble-Rogers were photographed in the *Ham and High* under the caption "Mums Army Fights Back". According to the paper:

and June Marriott on behalf of the Friends. In February 1985 FOHC started a campaign to raise funds from conservation bodies. English Heritage contributed £32,250 towards work on the memorial chapels and the Circle of Lebanon, and the Friends began to tackle the East Cemetery.

After 1986 no further articles on the FOHC appeared in *Buzz* for a dozen years, it is thought because of disagreements with the Society implied but not explained in a 1997 issue. However, in 1999 the Friends proudly reported that they had received a Europa Nostra award for the restoration of the Circle of Lebanon, the citation referring to "the inspiring conservation by a volunteer organisation of an important part of a famous historic cemetery, using the best principles of minimum intervention". Clearly, the organisation was now operating strongly as an independent body.

Information on opening times did appear in the Highgate Diary on the inside cover of *Buzz*, and from 2001 Rachel Hawes contributed a series of biographies of distinguished female grave occupants: George Eliot, Christina Rossetti, Stella Gibbons, Claudia Jones, the black activist and inspiration for the Notting Hill Carnival, Elizabeth Lilly, midwife to Queen Victoria – later corrected by John Pateman, the cemetery archivist, to *Mary Lilly*, Victoria's nurse – and Catherine Booth of the Salvation Army. In 1999 the Rev. John

Highgate Cemetery volunteers have hit back at claims they are a brigade of stroppy silver haired ladies. The army of volunteers donned helmets and brandished brooms to prove their point after they were mocked in the 2006 edition of a *Lonely Planet* guide.

By 2015 the Cemetery employed twelve staff and more than a hundred volunteers. More than 75,000 visitors were passing through its gates in a single year.

"The Friends of Highgate Cemetery Trust is an example of the most remarkable success of the voluntary sector. Despite the internal rows, the cemetery is in much better state than it might have been otherwise, and the volunteers add hugely to its quality as a heritage attraction. In these times of austerity it is doubtful that the Council would have had the resources available which the cemetery needs, and it seems only right that the bill to run it should not fall exclusively on Camden council tax payers as it would have done."

Ian Dungavell, Chief Executive
Highgate Cemetery (2016)

Jacksons Lane Community Centre

In 1968 the Highgate Society had set up a playgroup for pre-school children in the crypt of the United Reformed Church. This became a catalyst for a group of young mothers to address the absence of facilities for children across the whole Highgate area.

In 1973 a programme of holiday activities for under-elevens was organised at Highgate Primary School, run by parents. This was so popular that even teenagers in the neighbourhood – many of whom were perceived to be children at risk with nowhere suitable to "hang out", were desperate to be allowed in. Questions then arose about how to provide constructive leisure opportunities for them as well.

10.04 Nicky Gavron

Nicky Gavron, one of the group's members volunteered to run a project for them. She found that some teenagers had been breaking in to the abandoned church at the junction of Archway Road and Jacksons Lane and so, seeing that they were already using it illicitly, she applied to Haringey Council for them to be able to make legal use of it. She then went on to lead a campaign to obtain the Council's agreement for the church to be used as a Community Centre run by local people.

The church had become vacant when the Methodist church decided to consolidate its congregation with that of its church in Archway. The council had intended that the church be demolished and that the site be used for housing and to provide a new home for the Highgate Group Practice, at that time located opposite. These plans were placed in jeopardy both by the delays surrounding the disputed widening of the Archway Road and by a decision by the Department of the Environment to list the building. Meanwhile a council plan to use it as a furniture store was successfully fought off by Sally Whitby, a Society member and one-time Haringey councillor who lived in nearby Highgate Avenue.

Finding that several other groups had applied to the Council to use the church, Nicky formed a team that succeeded in persuading Haringey's Community Development Committee, at that time chaired by councillor Jeremy Corbyn, to recommend that the Council grant the team a temporary but renewable annual licence to use the building as a youth and community centre for a range of activities including the performing arts.

Once an initial and very limited programme of structural improvement had been completed, the centre started setting up self-organising community groups in early 1975. In July of that year Arnold Wesker generously facilitated the first of many local celebrity fundraising events with an electrifying rehearsed reading of his play *The Journalists*. The thirty-two strong cast from the Royal Shakespeare Company was led by Ian McKellen and Sheila Allen. In November 1975 the Centre held its first AGM.

Buzz reported that the Centre provided a daily local information and advice service, and that the space could be hired for rehearsals, meetings and, later on, for weddings, and that by 1978 a Christmas Day Dinner and Entertainment for pensioners had become an annual event.

10.05 Jacksons Lane Community Centre

In 1978 the Centre was still run entirely by volunteers and *Buzz* reported that there was an urgent need of funds for permanent staffing. Besides running the activities and looking after the building, the volunteers were busy raising funds for further improvements to the fabric of the building. Though the Highgate Society had no formal involvement in the Centre, its members did play a prominent role in the fund-raising. In 1981 *Buzz* reported that the Centre had raised £90,000 towards the £100,000 needed as a local contribution towards the first phase of its refurbishment,

and was asking the Society to help raise the remaining £10,000.

In 1985 Haringey Council had awarded the centre a long lease so that it could at last embark on the long road of phased conversion of the building, including the creation of a theatre which, with the rest of the ground floor, would be made wheelchair accessible. By March 1986 a significant proportion of the funding for the Centre was being provided by the GLC, so there was considerable anxiety over its future when the GLC was abolished later that year.

An article by Melian Mansfield in the winter 1998 *Buzz* provides information on how the local community used the Centre:

During 1998 there were 280 performances of theatre, dance and music, regular art exhibitions, numerous workshops and classes for people of all ages and a pensioners' lunch club. In addition there was an after school club, a parent and toddler club and ten educational outreach projects for young people with disabilities." Over 200,000 visits had been made to the Centre and in March the Centre achieved certification from Investors in People. There were plans to develop further as a centre for disability arts, to increase the use of our workshop and rehearsal space, to set up a multimedia production base and to hold a festival for children and young people.

At present the Centre is funded by Haringey Council, Arts Council England, Big Lottery and Children in Need. After forty years it is developing its fund-raising strategy to bring the building into the twenty-first century and extend disability access to the upper floor. It remains unusual among community centres in the extent of its local and wider community

10.06 Society members after class at Jacksons Lane

involvement.

Friends of Waterlow Park

In the early 1990s there were numerous complaints about Camden's management of Waterlow Park. When the Council explained that government policy obliged it to put its maintenance out to tender, users retorted that the firm which had been selected employed people with low gardening skills and insufficient training. In 1992 a new charity was formed, the Friends of Waterlow Park. The Society was entitled to nominate a member of the board.

The first meetings between the Friends and Camden were reported as 'encouraging'. One of the Friends' successes was to have the unsightly recycling bins situated at the Lauderdale House entrance to the Park replaced with black ones with gold lettering.

In 1997 the Heritage Lottery Fund awarded £1.1 million for the restoration of Waterlow Park subject to Camden adding a further £400,000 in match-funding. The next few years proved fractious. The Friends complained

10.08 Statue of Sir Sydney Waterlow, Waterlow Park

to Camden about the nature and scale of restoration work. Things became so heated that yet another group was formed by local people, the Waterlow Park Action Group. Among other things this fiercely opposed the sale of the park's two lodges and the construction of a huge administrative information and park management centre.

By 2001 revised plans for this centre, on the site of Sir Sydney Waterlow's extensive glasshouse, won the support of the *Friends*. Pam Cooper, sometime Chairman of the Friends and then of the Action Group, is said to have achieved this result "by persuasion and negotiation rather than trading insults".

Upon the resignation of the warring factions among The Friends, the community's interest in the Park was rescued at short notice by Quentin Edwards who formed a Friends Committee. Quentin and his team then worked amicably for some three years with Camden's Head of Parks and Open Spaces on the detailed implementation of the construction project. There were intensive discussions with Camden to prepare for the Friends' future active participation in the management of the park by a successor committee under the leadership of Ceridwen Roberts.

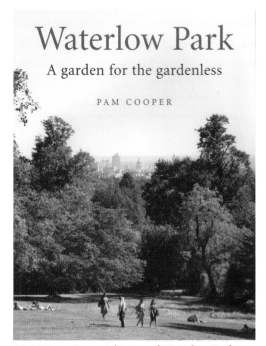

10.07 Pam Cooper's history of Waterlow Park

The Harington Scheme

Reference was made in chapter 9 to the special character of the Highgate Bowl, the area behind the High Street which for many centuries was used as grazing land for animals driven to London for slaughter in Highgate's butcheries or Smithfield Market.

A particularly appropriate use for one part of the Bowl is the Harington Scheme, a charity which provides training and education for young adults with learning difficulties and disabilities, with courses in horticulture and retail, on an attractive one-and-a half acre site in its south-eastern corner.

The idea of the Harington Scheme was first mooted by the Society's Environment Committee in 1978. There was concern that the derelict area that it now occupies, then in the ownership of the Camden and Islington Health Authority, would be sold off for development. Having an educational charity make good use of the land would help fight off development proposals and provide a real community asset.

10.09 Dame Geraldine Aves

The scheme's driving force was Dame Geraldine Aves, then aged eighty-two. Her father had worked with Charles Booth on his *Life and Labour of the People of London*. Following a degree in economics at Cambridge and a career in the Ministry of Health, in her retirement she chaired the inquiry that resulted in the Aves Report on the Volunteer Worker in the Social Services and which led to her founding the National Volunteer Centre. The obituary *Buzz* carried on her death in 1986 provides a telling example of the contribution volunteers of her calibre made to life in Highgate at this time and how interconnected was the leadership of its various voluntary organisations.

She was on the Witanhurst Working Group, the Council of the Highgate Society and its Environment Committee, and the Parochial Church Council. She was a Vice President of the Highgate Literary and Scientific Institution, Chairman and then President of the Highgate Cemetery Trust, President of the North London Hospice Group. She was the driving power behind the Harington Scheme, which she regarded as a prime example of volunteers and public authorities working together. She was its Chairman, typically insisting at her large 80th birthday party that any presents should be contributions towards the project.

She and Gwen Dains headed a steering committee of volunteers who set about obtaining a lease from the health authority, clearing the land, arranging for the supply of utilities and the construction both of a large greenhouse and the building for staff and learners which is now used by the Scheme as its main office. Tim Ronalds was appointed as site architect. Head of a successful architectural practice, this was Ronalds' first such commission, and the Scheme has remained dear to him ever since.

The trustees raised the money required to construct the new buildings and to help fund three employees, a manager, Bernard Wright, and two supervisors to oversee the training in horticulture of about fifteen learners. The aim was to combine horticultural training with work experience in the grounds of hospitals and residential homes as well as in private and commercial gardens, so improving learners' chances of finding permanent employment.

The Manpower Services Commission recognised the Harington Scheme as a training workshop and gave it financial support under its Youth Opportunities Programme. Recognising that continuing local authority support would be helpful, the name "Harington" was chosen as reflecting the interests of Haringey and of the Camden and Islington Health Authority. The Harington Scheme was registered as a company limited by guarantee and achieved charitable status on November 10th 1979. Its Memorandum and Articles of Association were registered on December 20th, 1979, its objects being:

> To relieve, rehabilitate, instruct and train in horticulture or otherwise young persons who are mentally or physically handicapped or disabled
>
> To assist in placing the beneficiaries in employment.

Many members of the Highgate Society and of the local community were actively involved. Familiar names that crop up in Harington's archives include those of Edith Morgan, Rose Mary Braithwaite, Chris Hindley, Robin Fairlie, Jenny Wright, Peter Benton, Patrick Lawlor, Norma Lacey, Mary Burns, Marcia Saunders and Nicholas Sanderson.

It was August 1980 when the first fifteen learners joined Harington. In the same year the Friends of Harington was formed, with Jenny Wright its first chairman, to organise fund-raising events and to help in other ways. Within a few years the Friends' 180 or so members were being encouraged to become actively involved in helping with teaching and travel, running a market stall outside 10A selling produce grown by the learners and trying to find permanent employment for them.

This was not always easy, so in October 1982 the trustees decided to set up the Harington Gardeners as a separate entity under the umbrella of the Scheme, offering further employment training through supported working for learners who had not found jobs at the end of their initial training. They were found paid employment as assistant gardeners, learning new skills and a work routine that would increase their chances of finding jobs when they moved on.

In 1985 Dame Geraldine Aves retired and was succeeded as the Chairman of the board of trustees by Edith Morgan, then President of the World Federation of Mental Health and a Mental Health Commissioner.

In 1985, the existence of the Harington Scheme was threatened by the decision of the Health Authority not to renew the lease but instead to apply for planning permission to develop the land. The local community swung into action: letters were written to MPs, councillors, the local and national press, charitable foundations that had been supporters and to District Health Authorities. The Scheme had established itself not only as a valuable social and educational asset, but also as a highly regarded local charity. An offer of an alternative site near the Royal Northern Hospital was firmly rejected. Eventually a new agricultural lease was negotiated for the existing site. This provided security of tenure.

With ever more learners, the Scheme added a second building designed as a temple – the classroom in the walled garden that had once belonged to the Queen Anne houses in Highgate High Street but become part of the Health Authority's estate.

It was decided that Harington Gardeners, not unlike the way the Highgate Society had, would work more efficiently with a building of its own. Edith Morgan met the then

Director of Circle 33 Housing Trust who were building sheltered housing on the far side of Cholmeley Park, and persuaded him to grant the Harington Scheme a thirty-five year lease on a left-over corner of land. So, it was the Gardeners that moved into Harington's third building that provided offices, a mess room, a changing room and stores. It was opened on July 17th 1990 by Stephen Dorrell, then a Junior Health Minister.

By 1987 the Harington Scheme had achieved national recognition. The cover of *Buzz* carried a photograph of Lord Young, Secretary of State for Employment, visiting the Scheme to mark its recognition by the Manpower Services Commission as an official Training Scheme.

In 1989 it appointed its first employment placement officer to organise work experience placements and help learners to progress into employment or, having improved their skills and self-confidence at Harington, into further education. This officer also took on the recruitment of learners, developing close links with local authorities and schools.

10.10 Lord Young visits the Harington Scheme, 1987

1993 saw a major re-building project, the Scheme's fourth and largest building which provided more indoor teaching space, social space, mess facilities and storage. This required a major fund-raising effort. The Urban Fund

awarded a grant of £100,000 and the Peabody Trust £30,000, leaving £20,000 to be raised locally. Various ingenious methods were deployed, many of which are still in use today: a supper quiz in the United Reformed Church was organised by Leila Hodge, a carol concert at St Michael's church and concerts at other venues. The Friends even raised enough money to provide a trip to the seaside for learners. Today this has developed into an inaugural residential trip to a coastal resort for new entrants.

Harington staff have always had the support of volunteers, often providing one-on-one assistance with teaching maths and English. But volunteers have also widened the Harington experience. For many years Sara Kaye organised cooking classes for learners, teaching basic cooking skills and so helping them achieve a greater level of independence. Volunteers also helped enter Harington for the Chelsea Flower Show in 2001; its courtyard garden was visited by the Queen and won a silver medal.

So far this account has made more mention of trustees than staff, but it is the staff that produce the warm, caring environment in which the learners, many with very little self-confidence having been deemed "failures" at school, can blossom and thrive. Since the millennium the Scheme has been fortunate in having Joanna Baxter as its manager. She has proved particularly expert in securing statutory funding when the criteria for support, and the funding bodies themselves, seem to change nearly every year.

One important development at this time was the introduction of retail courses. The trustees recognised that there were more "low skills" opportunities in retail than in horticulture although learners have been successfully placed in permanent jobs in the Royal Parks and at Highgate Golf Club.

Over the past six years the number and range of qualifications undertaken by learners on the training programmes has increased significantly in line with government requirements and the Scheme now offers qualifications in horticulture, retail skills, independent living skills, employability, English, mathematics and information and communications technology. Work experience and personal development play an important part in the training, particularly for those with limited academic skills. Currently an average of seventy five young people and adults benefit from the training and opportunities offered by Harington.

In the years since 2013 Harington has attracted more learners with higher support needs who are accompanied by Learning Support Assistants funded by the local authorities. This has increased income and expenditure as the staff has grown and has required an additional portacabin which it is hoped will in due course be replaced with a new permanent building.

Although its one-year rolling agricultural lease provides security of tenure, to raise large sums to finance a new build it will be necessary to be able to demonstrate to potential funders that the Scheme has security of tenure. Neither the Haringey Primary Care Trust nor its successor, the North London Primary Care Trust, felt able to negotiate on Harington's request to acquire the freehold or negotiate a longer lease.

Harington's landlord is now NHS Property Services (NHSPS) who are believed to be under a remit to realise value from non-operational land. Harington has recently persuaded them that it is not possible to introduce any residential development into the upper part of the site where the main buildings are situated without causing severe detriment to their operations; and NHSPS accept that they would never get planning permission for development on the lower part of the site, part of the protected Highgate Bowl land, where the main horticultural activities take place. In 2016 the Scheme's intention is to negotiate a longer lease with NHSPS.

Highgate Neighbourhood Forum

In 2011, the Council of the Highgate Society decided to seize the opportunity presented by the new Localism Act to establish a

10.11 Café staff with an improved menu for Archway Road

Neighbourhood Forum. It had already made a submission to the parliamentary scrutiny committee on the bill and had been successful in forcing an amendment to allow cross-Borough neighbourhood forums. Representatives of all Highgate community organisations were invited to a meeting in 10A, at which it was resolved that a Neighbourhood Forum should be formed.

Under the leadership of the Forum's first chairman, Maggy Meade-King, the organisation quickly became a separate and vibrant entity, with committee members from across the Forum's area and from a number of other local organisations, more than fifty now being affiliated to the Forum, including all the residents' associations, churches and temples, local schools and a number of action and amenity groups. All six local councillors, elected to the two Boroughs and representing three political parties were supportive from the start and the Forum was officially constituted by Camden and Haringey Councils in December 2012.

The Forum's first task was to find out what the residents and businesses of Highgate wanted for the area. An initial survey of all 8,000 households was followed by a "Placecheck" walkabout exercise and a number of "street engagement events" intended to reach members of the community who rarely join voluntary organisations or attend public meetings.

To draft the plan fifty people volunteered to form working in groups on specific topics under the leadership of Elspeth Clements. They were able to present their early ideas to community planning workshops in January 2013. This process continued under the chairmanship of Rachel Allison as the Forum worked with consultants and with officers of Camden and Haringey Councils to produce a draft Neighbourhood Plan.

10.12 Community Planning Workshop, January 2013

Early drafts were subjected to extensive consultation with the residents of Highgate, landowners, local interest groups and statutory bodies. By March 2016 the pre-submission consultation on the second draft was drawing to a close and, in the course of 2016, the aim is for the Highgate Plan to be subject to independent examination and eventually to a referendum of the electors of Highgate. If and when approved, the Highgate Neighbourhood Plan will become part of the Boroughs' statutory Local Plans.

Meanwhile, the Forum has developed an Action Plan to address wishes that have been expressed by residents during the plan preparation process but which do not fall within the remit of the plan. New groups of volunteers are working to make these a reality. The Forum is also consulting on how best to spend the proceeds of the Community Infrastructure Levy, this being a change paid by developers and which it is intended that the community should have access to. After the referendum the Forum will not disband but will continue to be engaged in these activities it has initiated and in monitoring and revising the Neighbourhood Plan through its fifteen-year life.

Conclusions

CHAPTER 11:
THE SOCIETY IN A CHANGING WORLD

Chapters 3 to 7 have provided vignettes of the people who have led the Highgate Society during its first fifty years, the social activities with which its members have entertained themselves and the campaigns that have stirred them into battle. But what do they tell us about how the Society has changed over the half century of its existence?

Is its current leadership drawn from a similar or different demographic from that of fifty years ago? Did particular activities flourish or wane in response to the enthusiasms, initiatives or retirements of individual members? Or did these ebbs and flows reflect wider political, economic and social changes? How specific to Highgate is the culture that characterises the Highgate Society? And how familiar will its way of working be to volunteers in other London "villages", or more generally to people active in different types of voluntary organisation in different parts of the country?

The demographics of leaders and members

Notwithstanding the seismic cultural changes that occurred during the 1960s, the pool from which the leadership of the Highgate Society was drawn in 1970 was not that different from the "great and the good" that led the Highgate Preservation Society[xxxi] between the 1930s and the 1950s. The owners of Athlone House, Witanhurst, Beechwood and The Elms all enrolled as members of the newly-formed Highgate Society, clearly impelled by a sense of obligation to give a little back to the community they continued to lead.

Since 1970, by contrast, an increasing number of Highgate's most sought-after homes have been acquired by a social group described by influential French economist Thomas Piketty in his *Capital in the Twenty-First Century, The*

Economics of Inequality, bankers, suppliers of top end professional services and overseas owners looking for a haven where their wealth can be held securely. Those who go to great lengths to conceal their identity and those who have no intention of making Highgate their permanent home are unlikely to provide the Society with the leadership, or even the membership, which it could once rely on from the owners of Highgate's grandest properties.

During its first decades much of the Society's leadership was been drawn from members of the professional classes who settled in Highgate after the war and more particularly those that flourished in London during the 1960's. Richard Downer, Brian Palmer, David Lowe-Watson, Brendan Nolan and Robin Fairlie made their careers in advertising and marketing. John Lacey, Tony Cox, Geoffrey Salmon, Marius Reynolds, Gordon Forbes and a high proportion of the environmental activists have been practising architects. Other members of Council have had experience in higher education, journalism, non-governmental organisations and public relations.

The decade into which the Society was born, the 1960s, is renowned for its ability to poke fun at authority and challenge tradition. *Private Eye* satirised the establishment. A person's speech, dress or musical taste no longer provide a clear guide to their social standing. That things had always been done a certain way no longer provided a justification for tradition. The vision which so enthused Ronnie Bernstein's was of particular appeal to an emerging, highly creative and questioning section of the professional and upper middle classes. Many viewed the Society as a counterweight to the socially conservative professionals and self-employed business people who until that time had dominated

Highgate society. In sociological parlance these were people whose status was bound up in their social capital (who they networked with) and their cultural capital (the knowing taste they displayed), not just their financial capital. This new spirit is captured by Peter Mostyn as follows:

Old Highgate was probably oblivious of it, but a New Age had been born with a message: Communities Matter, and there was a new swirling social current in the wake of the Lorry Route Victory. When we came home in 1965, we found that our local circle had grown ten times. 1965 brought new colours, new music and was soon to bring to Highgate a New Village. No longer just looking out of its window, Highgate took to its front gardens and the telephones if not to the streets and was about to give birth to the Highgate Society.

Though active members were drawn from a much more diverse social and cultural circle in 2016 than they were fifty years earlier, only a handful of copies of *Buzz* were dropped through the letter boxes of Highgate's few pockets of social housing. The Society's current leadership may be more conscious than their predecessors of the need to broaden the appeal of the Society. But it is not obvious how to do this.

Even in 2016 you would have difficulty inferring from the faces of those sitting on Society committees or competing against the HLSI for the *Merry Mug* that the Society draws its membership from one of the most ethnically diverse cities in the world. Notwithstanding the successes of integration over the past fifty years, members of London's different cultural groupings continue to live and spend their leisure time in neighbourhoods where they encounter people who share a common culture, however welcoming others may be.

Professionalisation

The Society of 2016 does have a sense of social responsibility. Readers of *Buzz* are regularly reminded how much more privileged Highgate is than more disadvantaged communities in Haringey and Camden, not least in having access to residents with the professional skills to protect it against inappropriate planning decisions. How important these skills are to the Society is evident from Peter Mostyn's account of his situation after his election as Vice Chairman.

There was still much to do, but we had a cabinet of all the talents; Highgate was awash with professionals of every kind.

We needed:

- a lawyer for our constitution
- an architect for our new premises
- a designer for our logo
- advertising talent for our funding appeal
- and once the appeal was over, a banker to make our money grow and not just sit in the bank

In from the start were Quentin Edwards, Geoffrey Salmon, Brian Palmer, Richard Downer, and David Whitby, all high flying, high achieving professionals. My rôle was only to convene and facilitate; theirs was to set up a Society that would last. They did. I will never forget the buzz and excitement of their talents.

Using their professional skills for the benefit of the wider community, and not just Highgate, delivers great satisfaction to many of the Society's active members. Attendees at a new members' social have always been pressed to reveal what professional skills they can offer to the Society. In 2016 skills in digital marketing, planning, law and architecture are particularly in demand.

It is impossible to over-estimate how reliant the Society is on this expertise. The mechanisms of consultation through which local authorities, government and the planning inspectorate now engage with "stakeholders" are now so complex that none but the most professionally qualified are capable of direct engagement with them. Could the Highgate Neighbourhood Plan been written were it not for one member of the Neighbourhood Forum team being a former civil servant and another a former ward councillor?

The "New Urban Colonists"

When the Society was founded in 1966 no doubt there were many old-standing Highgate residents to whom Ronnie Bernstein's vision of the community he wanted to create in Highgate – creative, energetic and gregarious, keen to debate but fast on its feet – must have seemed quite extraordinary. Over the coming twenty years Highgate was to experience an invasion by a distinct cadre of people, many of whom felt perfectly at home in such a milieu.

At this time Highgate and other London villages such as Blackheath, Dulwich and Kew were becoming the neighbourhoods of choice for professionals with a more liberal outlook. These people turned their back on many of the assumptions of previous generations, such as a signifier of success was the ownership of the modern-style home with lighter rooms, on a plot with a spacious, private garden and a garage, the sort that was found in the quieter, safer and more socially homogeneous sprawl of "suburban" London.

These newcomers were not put off as earlier generations had been by old-fashioned house designs and layouts, by the fussiness of Edwardian detail, by the modest size of gardens and lack of a garage typical of late Victorian and Edwardian streets. They were attracted by the conviviality of life in terraced streets with high residential densities, by greater proximity to shops and public spaces and easy access to the social and entertainment facilities of central London. Many of those from working class backgrounds who had benefitted from a university education found it attractive to live in a place with the sense of community in which they had grown up. Many marketers familiar with the consumer market segmentation system "Mosaic" will recognise them as examples of the Mosaic category "New Urban Colonists". These are described as living in:

areas, mostly in London, which have been gentrified since the 1960s by a new generation of young professionals quite content to trade access to the city for a higher density of population. A particular feature of these areas is the large number of well educated women, disproportionately qualified in the arts and social sciences, who tend to work in the cultural industries and caring professions. They are determined to pursue their careers and delay having children as late as possible. When children do arrive many continue to work with the assistance of nannies and au pairs or the help of expensive child care facilities.

In the early days of the Society gentrification of this sort affected much of Highgate since at that time house prices were within the reach of many young professionals, even those with children. Peter Mostyn recalls:

that everyone went to meetings as couples in the earliest days, and that it made a huge difference to the way the Society's activities flourished at its start. The average age was the late 30s, so there was an element of youthful drive. There was also a fundamental difference from today: young people could afford to live in Highgate, and because mortgages were

limited to two and a half times your income, prices were kept down.

Today the legacy of this influx is a well-educated and well-informed older cohort. By contrast most young families are now priced out of Highgate and, as a result, have been gentrifying ever less privileged neighbourhoods in London.

Mothers

As decades pass and upwardly mobile professional households have been forced to settle elsewhere in London, Highgate's population has aged. Fifty years ago, when houses prices were so much more affordable, there was less pressure on wives or female partners to contribute to household finances. Dual career partnerships were the exception rather than the rule. Young wives immersed themselves in the Society's community and entertainment programme. Having young children did not debar Nicky Gavron from setting up the Jacksons Lane Community Centre, or even entering politics, nor did having one on its way dissuade Christina Nolan from agree to taking on the role of chairman.

Perhaps it was because of the number of young mothers that much more consideration was given in the early years of the Society to children's entertainment. Mention is still made of the need to provide more for younger people, but only rarely do young mothers such as Liz Morris and Amy Brown now come up with popular ideas (p107). It is difficult to tell to what extent the decline in the Society's activities for children is the result of reduced family size, the changing demographics of its membership or a reflection of the improved provision of nursery education and children's activities at

Jacksons Lane, or of the growth of electronic games and social media.

Gender roles

In the early days, according to Peter Mostyn, while there was a strong division of labour between the sexes the female members of these couples were not shrinking violets.

People remember three "formidable women": Charlotte Salmon, Isla Merry and Barbara Edwards. Each chaired a committee, and ensured that the Society had a thriving daily life while the men did things like planning.

These women developed effective techniques for reminding men of the limits to their roles.

Geoffrey Salmon was charged with redesigning the interior of 10A; but, being a man, the women made it clear that he had no business telling women how to design a kitchen. They were adamant that there had to be the best possible kitchen, and dragged him to the West End to look at kitchen shops, though there was no money to pay for it.

However during the fifty years of the Society the role of this group of forceful and educated women changed dramatically and Michael Hammerson explains that in due course it was not only men "who did the planning".

Susan Cox and Joan Neale, who worked indefatigably to secure good planning, particularly in the pre-digital age, when Joan and Susan would go off every week to Camden and Haringey Town Halls, armed with sheaves of tracing paper, and bring back tracings of all the documents accompanying every planning application affecting Highgate. They were a formidable pair, who managed to convey the outward appearance of harmless middle-class ladies, but who could run rings round the greatest planning brains in the land.

Once it would have been considered natural that a woman such as Nicky Gavron would lead the campaign for children's play groups, that Marion Uglow should coordinate services for the elderly and that women should organise the Watercolour group and Music in Highgate Homes. However from 2000 Catherine Budgett-Meakin, Kirsten de Keyser and Jan Morgan have each been elected to the position of chairman. Elspeth Clements was invited to lead the Planning Group and Gail Waldman to be one of the expert witnesses at the Athlone House appeal.

However pervasive the change in attitudes, changes in behaviour can sometimes lag behind. Most male members of the Society would concede that it is women members who tend to take the leading role in the catering for social events and who then restore order to the 10A kitchen once they are over. Is it because few volunteer or because they are seldom asked that so few men pass round plates of canapes during new members' parties? But as female sociologists lament most men do not do their share at home either.

Pensioners

Improved health in later years may be one of the factors responsible for the greater involvement of the recently retired. The success of the Society's environmental campaigns recorded in chapter 9 would not have been possible without the professional expertise of its older members, as indeed is the case with the editorship and distribution of *Buzz*. The older profile of the Society also accounts for the popularity of particular activities such as Music in Highgate Homes, house walks when they were organised and Saturday morning coffee at 10A. Unfortunately there is a risk of marginalisation of those older members who do not access e.mail.

The professionalisation of leisure

It could be argued that the running of the society has been as much affected by the professionalisation of leisure as by the professionalisation of work. There can be few young or middle aged readers, especially those with children, who will not have marvelled at the energy with which their counterparts described in chapters 3 and 4 threw themselves into the myriad social and creative activities of the Society's earlier decades. Was professional work as demanding then, were hours less long? Has the advent of the smart-phone constrained leisure time? Were parents then as pre-occupied as they are now in monitoring how well their children are doing at school or ferrying them so constantly between after school activities?

Reading the accounts of the creative activities of the Society's early years, at a time when television was still a novelty and social media beyond imagination, one is struck by how willing Highgate residents were to have a shot at exploring something new, trying new recipes, acting in plays, making new clothes. In common with members of other voluntary organisations, members of the Society can become anxious about the burdens imposed on them by health and safety regulations and by fears over children's safety.

As the pursuit of leisure has involved greater commitment to training and investment in specialised clothing and equipment, have we become more reluctant to publicly expose ourselves in activities in which we are not already expert? Do we then leave the leisure activities

that the Society used to organise for its members to celebrity specialists, to professionals or only very serious enthusiasts? In its early years the Society's members seemed far more confident throwing themselves into new challenges than their counterparts do today.

Traffic, parking and the travails of the High Street

During the period when the Society was founded, conventional wisdom predicted that levels of car usage would necessarily grow in parallel with rising incomes. The volume of freight carried by road would increase in line with consumption. Investment in new road infrastructure, such as London's proposed motorway box, was essential to avoid unacceptable levels of congestion and eventual gridlock. The founders of the Society were part of a group, tiny and contrarian in their time, who challenged these assumptions – that unrestricted car use was sustainable in a city the size of London.

The Society's founders would be gratified to find that today their arguments constitute the new orthodoxy and that worrying reports of damaging new road schemes have almost disappeared from the pages of *Buzz*. Highly relevant to this change is not just containerisation, the consequent relocation of freight handling from the London docks to Tilbury and Felixstowe and the construction of the M25 and new A14, but also the introduction of the Controlled Parking Zones to much of inner London from 2002, the introduction of the Congestion Charge in 2003 and major improvements in the comfort and reliability of London's buses.

Credit is due to TfL and its predecessor London Transport for more comfortable buses and the adoption of satellite technology for improving reliability. In the 1960s few of the more wealthy car-owning families of Highgate would be regular users of a mode of transport associated with lower income groups. By 2016 most active members of the Society, though they still have access to a car, are likely to be regular users of buses and tubes, perhaps because so many of them benefit from Freedom Passes. Greater awareness of the risks entailed by climate change have also had an impact. As a result there is now near universal support in the Society for moves to give public transport priority over the car.

These factors have all contributed to a change in Londoners' cultural attitudes. The spiralling cost of insurance, the difficulty in finding a parking space, car clubs and the ability the internet offers to find the nearest available taxi have all contributed to the number of young adults who no longer want to own a car even if they could afford one. Peak private car ownership may have already passed, notwithstanding London's population growth.

By 2016 transport planners were beginning to question whether this decline in private car ownership will necessarily result in lower traffic volumes. This is perhaps because of the number of vans required to cater for internet shopping and of Uber offering an easy, inexpensive and rapid alternative to public transport.

On the other hand, parking is supplanting congestion as a topic of debate on transport policy. Whereas CPZs were introduced to make it easier for residents to park close to their front doors, by 2016 an equally pressing issue is the difficulty shoppers face when visiting the High Street. The absence of visitor parking must have a major impact on the competitiveness of Highgate as a shopping destination and contributes to the High Street losing out to purpose-built shopping centres and supermarkets where greenfield sites provide sufficient space for free parking.

Spiralling shop rents also threaten the viability of independent traders and the attractiveness of the High Street as a whole. The Society has made some efforts to persuade landlords to curb rent increases, though in the case of Raj, who ran the corner shop, ultimately with little success. It has added its voice to the campaign for the reform of business rates implemented in the 2016 budget. The Society has also made efforts to establish a business circle (p81) believing that the absence of a management plan for the High Street requires a higher level of co-operation between retailers. Many members refuse on principle to buy goods from the local branch of a national supermarket chain, preferring instead to patronise independent traders.

Globalisation

Visitors to Highgate High Street cannot but be struck by the number of estate agents that the Village seems able to support. Their ubiquity is the direct result of the prolonged increases in house prices in London's prestige neighbourhoods which result from London's position as the world's leading business and financial centre. The period since 1980 has also been marked by a seemingly exponential increase in the number of the world's footloose rich for whom Highgate and Hampstead are preferred locations to buy a property for their own use, as an investment or, as many people suspect, to avoid paying taxes.

So exacting are these newcomers' requirements that major modifications often cost more than tearing down an existing property and re-building from scratch, providing the necessary permissions can be granted. Early chapters of this book reveal that this did not used to be a common practice and certainly less of a concern than traffic. This trend has built up inexorably since the 1960s until it now forms the largest single element in the workload of the Environment Group.

The use of formal measurement criteria to assess performance or value is an increasingly common feature of contemporary life and the valuation of houses is no exception. In a culture where there is no common criterion of beauty, a house's valuation is increasingly based on square footage, the maximisation of which becomes more important than the frequency with which particular, seemingly mandatory facilities are used. Unable to rebuild upwards, and with limited scope for sideways extension, basements become an easier means of adding to a property's square footage and justifying a higher valuation, notwithstanding the disruption they cause to neighbours.

Often enlargement can be achieved only by excessive extension to a house's footprint or by cutting down mature trees to enable significant building over or under back gardens. The prize at stake justifies the employment of large teams of specialists to argue on the behalf of owners whose pockets are deep enough to support the cost. Mounting effective counter arguments imposes a growing professional and financial challenge to the Society.

Heritage

Changes to planning legislation during the period 2015/6 can easily lead to the assumption that the threat to heritage assets has never been more serious. Chapter 2 challenges that assumption. Its shows how the need for opposition to the destruction of heritage buildings was far greater in the years before the formation of the HPS and the Highgate Society than it is today and how novel this opposition

was. This is notwithstanding the 800 who attended the public meeting organised by the Save Highgate Committee at Highgate School in 1962.

To a degree, improvements in the legislation surrounding environmental protection reflect very welcome changes in public attitudes towards the conservation of both the physical and natural environment. Styles of architecture which were considered "old-fashioned" during the 1960s have subsequently been rediscovered by "New Urban Colonists" and a new respect is given to the aesthetic value of late Victorian and Edwardian terraced housing. In the highest political circles however a contrary opinion is being expressed, that the conservation of Britain's heritage is acting as an unacceptable brake on the country's economic growth.

As is evident from the planning disputes over Witanhurst, Athlone House and the Highgate Bowl, the relationship between the community and wealthy international would-be newcomers is more strained that it was when the former owners of Athlone House, Witanhurst, Beechwood and The Elms were members of the Highgate Society in its early years. The new global rich who buy homes in Highgate are more likely to do so only because of the houses that are available and proximity to Highgate and Channing schools.

Their reason for choosing to live in Highgate is not necessarily because they wish to become part of the Highgate community, though some of course do. Many think of themselves as living in London: Highgate is just the location where they have succeeded in finding a home that meets their specialised needs, often the protection that comes from living behind railings and electronic gates and from state-of-the-art security systems. Interestingly, the increasingly number of celebrities that have chosen to live in Highgate tend to select prestigious period properties close to the Village often think differently, being more willing to lend their name to community campaigns.

Whereas the early years of the Society were characterised by a common set of values, and the broader interests of the community commanded near universal respect, representatives of the community now find themselves increasingly in conflict with those newcomers on grounds of taste as well as ethics. Objecting to a new development the Society finds itself in opposition to teams of barristers and so-called expert witnesses who appear to be seeking to justify the seemingly unjustifiable on behalf of clients for whom financial gain has become far more important than the respect of the local community.

An increasingly cosmopolitan world, one might suppose, necessarily results in an increasingly varied set of views as to what constitutes good taste and acceptable styles of development. A proposed development may be criticised by many as inappropriately ostentatious. Yet to the owner, developer or client the fact that a house so visibly displays the material success of its owner may be one of its strongest attractions.

What to the Society and the planners may be criticised as vulgar on account of its lack of restraint may itself incorporate some of the values which, in their time, characterised more than one or two of the heritage buildings which the community prizes today. Such clashes in taste are inevitable when homes are being designed for people originating from parts of the world with radically different aesthetic and moral values, political conditions and climates.

Nevertheless their great wealth, the growing trend for property to be viewed as an element in an investment portfolio rather than as space for living, and the size of the financial

rewards that follow a successful planning application can reward developers and owners for "playing" the planning appeal system. The refusal to accept the rejection of a planning application by a system which was designed as a means of securing justice all too often engenders the attitude of a "second or even third throw of the dice" in a manner which would have been considered ethically unacceptable in earlier days. A decline in ethical standards is also given as the reason for the lack of transparency regarding the identity of the beneficial owner of companies applying for or appealing against planning decisions, as for example in the case of previous owners of Athlone House.

Changes in the public policy

Although changes in the objects and practices of environmental campaigns have received much coverage in this book, the accounts of the formation and subsequent development of voluntary organisations such as the Harington Scheme, Highgate Cemetery and Jacksons Lane Community Centre provide some of the clearest illustrations of the changes during the past fifty years in the role of the voluntary sector.

Though these ventures could not have been formed and would not have flourished without the dedication and skills of local volunteers, their success is witness to the evolution of a new political consensus - that many "caring" services are delivered more effectively by not-for-profit organisations, funded from the public purse, than they are by local councils. Whilst some of these entities, such as the Friends of Waterlow Park and the Hampstead Heath Consultative Committee, have a purely advisory role, others have grown only as a result of their ability to secure public funding for the provision of specific services.

The trusteeship of these organisation involves a very high level of professional expertise in budgeting, procurement and building management as well as general management abilities, a rather different set of skills than those needed to get the organisations off the ground and those needed to run the Highgate Society. This is one reason why it has never been thought appropriate that these activities should be undertaken from within the Society, not least because the Society has no tradition of hiring or managing paid staff.

During the fifty years since the formation of the Society changes in the way in which the planning system is administered have had a significant impact on the skills needed to engage with it. Early issues of *Buzz* focused on the representations made by the Society's planning group to Haringey and Camden's planning departments. These were relatively easy to write because of the simpler and more transparent nature of the system. Today, when the discretion of local authority planning departments is so restricted by the dictates of central government, Michael Hammerson, the author of *Buzz's* environment report, argues that the successful protection of Highgate's heritage depends as much on campaigns to amend national planning legislation as on the representations that the Society continues to make to local planners.

If communities lose the rights they won in the 1930s to determine how their areas are developed there will be more opposition to development from communities who feel themselves to be disenfranchised. This opposition will be compounded by the current expansion of permitted development.

Governments, Michael Hammerson argues, should realise that if communities are given a real voice in how their areas are developed - and experience is already showing that the much-

vaunted Localism agenda is failing to achieve this - there will not only be more development, but better development.

Among members of the Society's Planning Group there continues to be a belief that every member of the Highgate community – or indeed every other community, whether or not benefiting from legal protection for its environment – should join their local amenity group. Fighting for one's heritage and one's living and working environment should not be the privilege of the better-off but both a duty and a right which applies to all. It can too easily be assumed that the designation of Conservation Areas status implies that a neighbourhood is worthy of protection, an entitlement denied to non-designated areas, in which case communities without such protection are fair game for any form of development. Every community should be entitled to bring the standard of planning in its area up to the status of a Conservation Area: in other words that Conservation Area protections should apply to all.

Effective response to applications for development and to threats to local heritage can no longer be effectively undertaken by well-meaning and well-connected leaders of the community, meeting together on ad hoc and occasional basis. Such is the complexity of the design process, of measurement and modelling, of technical reports, planning legislation and the appeal system, that what should properly be voluntary activity is now in danger of requiring an almost full time sense of vocation.

The sacrifice of personal life involved in work of this sort may be difficult to sustain amid the pressures of modern-day life. Yet the power of social media and the receptivity of the local community means that it is easier than it ever was to mobilise mass opinion in support of a particular campaign. This has been evident over the campaign to save Athlone House and to contest the proposed changes to the Archway gyratory. These tools also re-shape the manner in which the Society and other voluntary organisations operate.

In an era when the National Trust's membership exceeds three million, there is no doubt that there is widespread public support for the objectives of local amenity societies. This should give encouragement to the "old guard" of campaigners. Will the committee-based structures on which organisation such as the Highgate Society have relied for fifty years continue to deliver success? Or will it need to adapt to a different participatory style, more common in contemporary politics, where supporters are drawn in to single-issue campaigns with very specific, often short term objectives, informally organised and much more reliant on social media? Maybe the baton will be taken over by subsequent generations but operating in a different formation.

Helen Wills playing at Witanhurst during the 1930s

INDEX

Figures in bold denote illustrations – see pp166-167 for further details

50/50 Club 88

A

Abse, Danny 57
Adam, Robert 15, 129
Adeney, Martin 2
Ades, Tim 34, 52
Advertising in Buzz 51
Alexandra Palace 48, 70, 109
Alice, Princess, Duchess of Argyll 86
All Saints Church 50
Allen, Sheila 139
Altaras, David 133
Amenity and Planning Committee 32, 34
Angel Yard 56
Archway 22, 139
Archway Bridge 29, 86, 120
Archway gyratory 84, 117, 120, 157
Archway Road
23-26, 29, 43, 54, 73-4, 81, 86, 92, 93, 98-9,
113-5, 119, 120, 121, 123, 139, 145
Archway Road Association 24, 26-27
Archway Road Community Directory 98
Archway Road Residents and Business Association
.... 73, 92
Arts and Crafts 36, 57, 61
Arts Lending Library 41, 57
Arundel House 55
Arup, Ove 22
Aspects of Highgate 93
Athlone House
.... 15, 21-22, 129, 130, 131, 132-3, 147, 154-7
Athlone House Working Group 21, 130-3
Atkinson, Harley 79
Automobile Association 25
Avent, Jon 133
Aves, Dame Geraldine 80, 126, 136, 142

B

Bacon, Francis 55
Baker, Tony 2
Baker's Lane 27, 29
Ball, Colin 131

Barbershop Quartet 51
Barnet, London Borough of 94
Barnett, Henrietta 14
Barron, Donald 64
Basements 10, 20, 74, 92, 114-116, 129, 154
Basevi, George 15
Basevi, Nathaniel 15
Bates' Nursery Land 125
Beechwood 15, 147, 154
Benham & Reeves 98
Benton, Peter 143
Bernstein, Ronnie
22, 24-5, 30-34, 35, 36-9, 48-9, 52, 59, 65-6, 78, 98,
148-9
Betham, Adrian 89
Betjeman, John 87, 137
Better Archway Forum 121
Bishop of London 17
Bishopswood Road 98
Blackheath Society 109
Blackshaw, Tye 2
Blood Transfusion Service 43, 49, 66, 78
Bor, Walter 77, 80
Boswell, John 133
Bowers, Fleur 34, 61
Brains Trust 42
Braithwaite, Rose Mary 143
Brent Cross 81
Breughel, Pieter 78
Bridge Club 36, 41, 48-9, 57, 99
British Broadcasting Corporation 26, 90
Broadlands Road 53, 78, 95, **116**
Brooke, Roger 15, 129
Brown, Amy 107, 150
Brown, Sir James 23, 33, 38, 47, 49
Buckingham Palace 15
Budgett-Meakin, Catherine .. 2, 45, 93, 105-6, 151
Budgett-Meakin, Denzil **11**, 23, 33, **45**
Builder Center 99
Bull, The 93, 110
Burgh House 63
Burns Night 41, 47, 53, 57, 107
Burns, Mary 143
Burt, Ivor 78, 86, **87**
Bus route 214 .... **16**, 122-3

Bus route 271 .... 88, **97**, 117, **122**

Bus route 603 122

Bus route C2 123

Buss, Lillian 47, **56**, 57

Butterfield, Michael 29

C

Caddy, Elizabeth **62**, 77

Caesar, Ed 129

Café Rouge 64, 107

Caird, John 108

Camden & Islington Health Authority
.... 126, 129, 141-3

Camden Town 23, 109

Camden, London Borough of
44, 53-56, 62, 66-8, 70-6, 86-9, 91, 97-99, 104-5, 111-6, 122-4, 126, 129-33, 136-8, 141-3, 146, 149, 151, 156

Camden, Mayor of **47**

Capital Gardens 127

Carols in Pond Square
.... 18, 36, 53, 80, 87, **88**, 102, 107-8, 144

Castle Yard 22, 27, 28, 122

Centaur Gallery 48, 57

Channing School 21, 23, 65, 154

Channon, Paul 72

Charitable status 95-6, 102-4

Children's activities
...... 35, 41-44, 48-9, 57, 60, 107, 139, 140, 150-2

Chipperfield, David 130

Cholmeley Park 24, 91, 114, 126, 144

Cholmeley, Roger 14

Church Road **26**, 27, **124**

City of London
... 16, 55, 68-70, 93, 110-112, 115, 121, 123, 131

Clark, Marguerite 80, 90, 94

Clements, Elspeth 104, 146, 151

Cohen Family **43**

Cohen's Field 22, 129

Coleridge, Samuel Taylor **14**

Community Services
.... 34, 36-7, 40, 43, 48, 56, 66, 78

Conservation Area
.... 44, 54, 74, 89-90, 99, 104, 113-4, 156

Conservation Area Advisory Council
.... 104, 127, 130

Constable, John 14

Controlled Parking Zones 117, **124**, 153

Cooper, Pam **141**

Corbyn, Jeremy 139

Cory-Wright, Arthur 15

Country Life 128

Courtenay Avenue **116**

Cox, Jenny 137

Cox, Lady Susan 22, 45, 78, 151

Cox, Tony 148

Crafts 36, 41, 48, 57, 79

Cromwell Avenue 55

Cromwell House 14, 56, **67**, 68

Crosfield, Lady Domini 22

Crosfield, Sir Arthur 15, 21-2, 127-8

Crouch End All Stars 51

D

Dains, Gwen 142

Daniels, Leon 122

Dartmouth Park Hill 24, 55

Day Morris 98

de Joia, Bobby 69

de Keyser, Kirsten 151

Debating **42**, 65

Deeble-Rogers, Hilary 138

Denewood Road **71**, 116

Dodd, Jeanne 79

Doggart, John 106

Dorrell, Stephen 144

Doulton, Alfred 24-27, 33

Downer, Richard 34, 38-41, 98, 148-9

Doyle, Gavin 62, 88, 107

Dungavell, Ian 2, 139

Dwyer Ltd 130

E

East London Assessment Study 72

Easter Egg Hunt 107

Eccesiastical Commissioners 15

Eccles, David MP 25
Edwards, Barbara 37, 40, 48, 151
Edwards, Quentin 23, 31, 33, 37, 98, 141, 149
Elections to Council 32, 50
Elms, The 73, 147, 154
English Heritage
15, 69-70, 74, 76, 88-9, 91, 94, 111, 113-4, 131, 138
Environment Committee 11, 44-5, 52-4, 66-7, 71,
75, 77-8, 88-90, 104, 116-7, 120, 132, 136-7, 142
Evans, Harold 34
Evening Standard 90

F

Fair in the Square 36, 47, 60, 81, 87-8
Fairlie, Robin . 2, 81, 90, 95, 102-3, 121, 143, 148
Falloden Way 24, 27
Fame Academy 90
Featherstone, Lynne MP and Baroness 98
Fielding, Rev John 138
Finchley Road 24, 26
Fitzroy Park 15, 22, 91
Flask, The **17, 60**, 61, 76, 93
Fletcher, Eric MP 25
Forbes, Gordon 103, 148
Fowler, Edward 33
French Circle 64, **108**
Friends of the Earth 70
Furnival House 91, 126

G

Gammans, Lady 25
Gardiner, Stephen 74
Gatehouse, The 28, 51, 57, 75-6, 80, 93
Gavron, Nicky 2, 43, 104, 136, 139, 150-1
Gay, John **42**, 48, 52, 77, 128, 138
Gay, Marie 42, 52, 61
Gestetner, Sigmund 20, 22
Ghanaian Embassy 68
Goldsmith, Zac MP 114
Good Neighbour Scheme 37, 42, 66
Gordon, Ed 79
Gospel Oak 112
Gould, Stephen 90
Graffiti 94, **95**, 97

Graham, Sandy 56, 66
Grange Road 116
Great Ormond Street Hospital 107
Greater London Authority 105, 122
Greater London Council 36, 45, 52, 66, 68, 91,
137, 140
Grove, The 14, 22, 32, 124
Guardian, The 113
Guryev, Andrey 129

H

Hall, Derek 88, 95, 107, 121
Halloween 57, **107**
Ham and High, The 20, 27, 41, 48, 138
Hammerson, Michael
.......2, 51, **53**, 67, 76, 89, 104, 109, 132, 151, 156
Hampstead Garden Opera 111
Hampstead Garden Suburb 14, 21
Hampstead Garden Suburb Residents Association .. 23
Hampstead Garden Suburb Trust 109
Hampstead Heath
10, 14-5, **17**, 20, 22-3, 25-6, 29, 45, 68-9, 109,
112, 128-31, 133, 155
Hampstead Heath and Old Hampstead Protection
Society: see Heath & Hampstead Society
Hampstead Heath Consultative Committee
.... 69, 93, 155
Hampstead Lane **17**, 22, 29, 88, 129
Hampstead Lane, No 5 89
Haringey, London Borough of
11, 43-4, 53-6, 62, 66-8, 70-2, 74, 86, 90-1, 94,
98-9, 104-5, 109-110, 114-5, 122-6, 136, 139-40,
143, 145-7
Haringey, Mayor of 81, 86
Harington Gardeners 99, 143
Harington Scheme
.... 50, 52, 61, 78, 106, 126-7, 136, 142-4, 155
Harington, Friends of 143
Harris, Vincent 91
Harrison, Gary 130
Hazeldine, Ruth 79, **108**
Heath & Hampstead Society / HOHPS
20, 23, 25, 29, 45, 68-9, 73-4, 90, 102, 109, 112,
128, 130
Heath Hands **69**

Henghes, Ian 116

Herbert, John 41

HiCAN 105

Highgate Avenue 94, 139

Highgate Bowl

.... 29, 44, 53, 125, 126-7, 142-145, 154

Highgate Bowl, Friends of **126, 127**

Highgate Business Circle 81

Highgate Calendar **57**, 58, 95

Highgate Cemetery

38, 42, 52, 54, 77-8, 108, 125-6, **135**, 136-139, 142, 155

Highgate Cemetery, Friends of ... 50, 96, 98, 137-8

Highgate Chamber Music Society 101

Highgate Choral Society 117

Highgate Council of Churches 50

Highgate Decorative and Fine Arts Society 51

Highgate Fine Art 98

Highgate Golf Club 144

Highgate Group Practice 123

Highgate High Street

10, 13, 14, 21-22, 24, 27, 36, 44, 46, 51, 57, 61, 64, 72, 76, 88, 107, 113, 117, 125, 142-3, 152-3

Highgate Hill 21, 24, 26, 29, 53, 55, 86, 121

Highgate Horticultural Society 50, 91

Highgate Literary and Scientific Institution

18, 21, **37**, 38, 40-1, 43, 45-6, 49, 50, 61-2, 64, 78, 97, 110, 137, 148

Highgate Neighbourhood Forum

.... 89, 105, 122, 127, 135, **145-6**, 149

Highgate Neighbourhood Plan

.... 105-6, 144, **146**, 149

Highgate New Town 49

Highgate Picture Lending Exhibition 41

Highgate Preservation Society

.... 20, **21**, 22-24, 26, 29-30, 33-4, 147, 154

Highgate Primary School 26, 138

Highgate School

14, 22, 24, 27, 30, 33, 42, 61-2, 64, 88, 98, 107, 122, 126, 154

Highgate Society Chamber Orchestra 43

Highgate Travel 98

Highgate Underground Station . 92, 110, 114, 121

Highgate Village Millennium Party 86

Highgate Wood .. 55, 69-70, 74, 93, **94**, 110, 115

Highgate-on-Sea **106**

Highpoint **19, 20**, 21-22, 109

Hill Homes 50, 78, 79

Hill, Margaret 50, 78

Hillcrest 49

Hillside 55

Hillside Gardens 27, 94

Hindley, Christopher 142

Historic England 111

Hodge, Leila 65, 77, 144

Hodge, Margaret MP and Dame 65

Holly Court School 74

Holly Village 53

Hornsey Borough Council 22, 26-29

Hornsey Historical Society 50, 109

Hornsey Journal 24-28, **35**

Hornsey Lane **17**, 55, 86

House of Lords Select Committee 67

Hurd, Percy 20

I

IMG 111

Inner London Education Authority 45

Ireton House 55

Ireton, William 55

Isaaman, Gerald 42, 48

Isaksson, Anne 107

Islington 25, 29, 113, 121

Islington, London Borough of

.... 44, 65, 104, 117, 121

Islington, Mayor of 86

Iveagh, Lord 15, 91, 111

J

Jackson, Glenda MP **65**

Jacksons Lane 43, 51, 55, 94

Jacksons Lane Community Centre

50, 76, 81, 86, 88, 114, 136, 138-9, **140**, 151, 155

Jardine, Isabel 57

Jay, Peggy **49**

Jazz Ball **51**, 56

Jazz Band 59, 86

Jones, Jackie 106

Judd, Marion 53

K

Kara-Rajani, Raj 46, 86, **92**, 153
Karet, Tamar 117
Kaye, Sara **51**, 110
Keats, John 14
Keep Highgate Tidy 41, 69, 71, 89, 93, 94, **95**
Kensington Society 23
Kenwood House and Estate 14, 15, **16**, 68-70, 73-4, 78, 91, 111
Kenwood Lakeside Concerts 41, 111
Kenwood Landscape Forum 70, 91

L

Lacey, John **30**, 32-3, 39, 51, 66, 69, 78, 148
Lacey, Norma 143
Landmark Trust 72
Lauderdale House 50, 53, 57, 62, 64, 136, 141
Laurie, Hilary 2
Lawlor, Patrick 143
Lebanon, Circle of 138
Letwin, Oliver MP 57, 65
Lewis, Oswald MP 65
Life Drawing Group 6, 42, **79**, 80, 99
Little, Margaret 130
Livingstone, Ken MP 122
Localism Act 75, 105, 114, 145, 156
London County Council 19-21, 24-5, 29, 53, 90
London Evening News 25
London Forum 68, 77, 102, 110
London Residuary Body 68
London Underground 70
Lowe-Watson, David 23, 34, 148
Lubetkin and Tecton 20
Luncheon Club 36
Lyttelton Road 24, 27

M

Mackintosh, Andrew 30
Mansfield, Melian 140
Marcus, Helen 68
Marples, Ernest MP 23, 25-6, 28, 65
Marriott, June 138
Marsh, John 107
Marvell, Andrew 57

Marx, Karl 44, 136
Mary Feilding Guild 66
Mason, Towyn 86
Mayer, Adrian 98
Mayer, Kaia 57
McCartney, Jenny 116
McKellen, Ian 139
Mead, Ulla 79
Meade, John 105
Meade-King, Maggy 146
Meck, Madame 41
Membership Committee 45
Menuhin, Yehudi
.... 32, **34**, **38**, 45, 47, **50**, 51, **52**, 53, **59**, 61
Merry Mug **46**, 50, 110, 148
Merry, Isla 40, 46, 81, 151
Merton Lane 74
Miles, Bernard **52**
Ministry of Health 21, 142
Ministry of Transport
.... 23, 26, 28-9, 36, 73, 98, 120
Mitchell, Andrew 66
Monday Club 35, 41, 62, 78, 99
Moorgate 122
Morgan, Edith 143
Morgan, Jan 86, 90, 151
Morland, George 14
Morris, Bryan 137
Morris, Liz 107
Morris, Rosemary 47
Morris, Simon 86
Mostyn, Peter 33, 98, 149-151
Mother and Baby Class 35, 43, 48, 62
Motorways 10, 23, 29, 35, 49, 92, 109, 120, 152
Murray, William, 1st Earl of Mansfield 15
Murugan Temple **109**
Music in Highgate Homes
.... 36, 51, 79, 108, 117, 151
Muswell Hill Road 111, 123

N

Neale, Lady Joan **45**, **67**, 77, 151
Nevinson, Nancy 41
New Hampstead Society 26
New Members Party 80, 107, 149

New Yorker 129
Nolan, Brendan 34, 47, 77, **81**, 117, 148
Nolan, Christina ..**47**, 48, 71, 81, 88, 94, 108, 150
North Hill
.... 20-22, 24, 28, 70, 74, 78, 110, 120, 123-4
North London Hospice 50, 53, 142
North Norfolk District Council 114
North Road ... **13**, 22, 24, 27, **28**, 76, 117, 122, 124
Northern Heights Publications **109**

O

Oakes, John 59, 121
Old Hall 55
Olympicnics **52**

P

Paddington 122
Pain Quotidien, Le 93
Palmer, Brian 38, 148-9
Panke, Stephen 61, 65
Parkfield 15, 127
Parking 76, 88, 97-8, 123, 129, 153
Parkland Walk 45, 53, **54**, 72
Pateman, Jean 98, 136, **137**, 138
Patton, Freda 98
Pauncefort Almshouses 27
Pearl Garages 29
Pedestrian Crossings 10, **36**, 78, 124
People on the Hill 47, 117
Pepler, George 21
Phillimore, Terry 113
Phillips, Ruth 34, 51, 59
Piketty, Thomas 147
Planning Surgery 9, **89**
Playgroups 35, 43, 48, 56, 62, 139, 151
Plews, Katie 76, 87
Poets 14, 42, 44, 50, 57, 61, 80
Pond Square
22, 30, 36-7, **54**, 55, 76, 86, **87**, 88, 107, 113,
122, **123**
Pond Square Residents Association 88-9
Pond Square Working Group 76, 88
Poole, Ray 94
Price, Rex 88

Prickett & Ellis, Underhill **14**, 98
Private Eye 133, 148
Public toilets 97, **99**, 116, **117**
Purey-Cust, Admiral Sir Herbert 21

Q

Queens Wood 68, 71, 74, 94

R

Read, Mike 79
Reckitt, Francis 15
Recreational Charities Act 103
Red Hedgehog, The **114**
Reid, Joanna 127
Repton, Humphry 15
Reservoirs Act 1975 112
Reynolds, Marius 111, 148
Roberts, Ceridwen 141
Roche, Barbara MP 74, 81
Ronalds, Tim 142
Rose & Crown, The 93
Rose, Susan 132
Rossi, Hugh MP 28
Royal Automobile Club 25
Royal Mail Sorting Office 74
Russian Trade Delegation 29, 41
Rykwert, Professor Joseph 133

S

Safer Neighbourhoods 98
Sainsbury, John 15
Saint Anne's Church 50
Saint Augustine's Church 50, 114
Saint Columba's 73
Saint Joseph's Church 51
Saint Michael's Church
.... 50, 55, 86-8, 96, 117, 138, 144
Saint Michael's School 26, 56, 86
Salmon, Geoffrey 38, 110, 148-9, 151
Salomons, Edward 15
Samuel, John 50, 77-8
Samuels, Alex 26
San Carlo 98

Sanderson, Nicholas 143

Saunders, Marcia 143

Save Britain's Heritage 131

Save Highgate Committee

.... 24-26, 28, 30, 34, 119, 154

Schwitzer, Joan 50

Schwitzer, Mat 50, 64, **77**, 79, 108

Scottish Dancing 57, 107

Second Nature 98

Sells, Peronet 15

Seow, Yitkin 47

Shelbourn, David 90

Sheldon Avenue 28, 115

Shelton, Shirley 113

Shepherds Hill 23, 111

Skippon, Leslie 38

Slater, Margot 77

Social and Entertainment Group 36, 47, 57, 65

Social Services Committee 10

South End Green 112

South Grove

.... 37, 39, 43, 55, 61, 64, 76, 86, 107, 122, 124

Southwood Avenue 94

Southwood Lane

17, **18**, 22, 27-8, 36, 75, 90, 92, 94, 109, 114, 124

Southwood Lawn Road 94

Southwood, Chris 126

Spaniards Inn 14

Spaniards Road 26, 73, 88

Spectator, The 116

Stagg, Sandra 88

Statistical Surveys **73**, 105, 120, 122, 136, 146

Stern, George 120

Stevenson, Juliet 93

Stormont Road 116

Sulston, Andrew 116

Summerskill, Baroness 36

Sustainable Homes **106**

Swain's Lane **17**, 72, 124, 136

Swearing on the Horns 59-61

Swiss Cottage 23, 73, 122

T

Tavener sweets 15

Tesco Express 92

Thatcher, Margaret MP and Baroness 10

Theatre 36, 41, 50, 80, 108, 110, 140

Thomas, Margaret 38

Times, The 25

Tindall, Gillian 42

Tiomkin, Dmitri 41, 43

Toeman, Diana 45

Tottenham 90

Transition Highgate 106

Transport for London 84, 114, 117, 123-4, 152

Tree Preservation Orders 44, 70

Trewin, Ion 34, 45, 48

Trewin, Sue 49

Trick or Treat 107

U

Uglow, Marion **78**

Unger, Hans 111

United Cemeteries 136, 137

United Reformed Church

.... 43, 50, 53, 56, 62, 66, 86, 96, 139, 144

Unwin, Sir Raymond 14, 21

Upcott, Sir Gilbert 21, 26

Upper Holloway 25, 27

Upstairs at the Gatehouse . **75**, 76, 86-7, 110, 117

Usborne, Ann 34, 52, 58

Usborne, Peter 48

V

van Vessem, Cornelis 80, 107

Victoria, The 93

View Road 33, 36, **115**, 116, 124, 137

Village Flower Stall 76, **113**

W

Waldman, Gail 132, 151

Waley-Cohen, Edward 129

Waley-Cohen, Robert 15, 21-2

Walks and Talks 61, 91, 109

Walter Castellazzo Designs 98

Watercolour Group 53, **63**, 99, 117, 151

Waterhouse Family, The 59

Waterlow Park
.... 38, 53, 55, 71, 75, 86, 136, **141**, 155
Waterlow Park Action Group 141
Waterlow Park, Friends of
.... 52, 73, 75, 136, 141, 155
Waterlow, Sydney 53, 141
Wearden, Clifford 71
Webber, Richard 108, 124
Wedding Day Whoopee 52
Weight, David 64
Wellington, The 22, 28, **74**, 76, 120
Wesker, Arnold 139
West Hill
21, 29, 41, 54, 70, 74, 76, 112, 122, 124, 127,
129, 137
West Hill, 78-79 .... 70, 72, 74
Wetherspoons 75
Whinney, Vanessa 34, 51, 77, 98, 105
Whitby, David 39, 149
Whitby, Sally 139
Whitestone Pond 26, 73
Whittington Hospital 53, 117

Whittington Hospital, Friends of 50
Williams, Sir Robin 99
Wilson, Marjorie 47
Wine Committee **48**, 57, 64, 80, 107
Winter, John 137
Witanhurst
15, 21-22, 49, 53, 90, 115, 124, 127, **128**, 129,
142, 147, 154
Wolff, Simon 73
Wolton, Deborah 132
Wood Green 90, 122
Woodman, Elizabeth 64, 108
Woodside Avenue 26
Wrestlers, The 76, 93
Wright, Bernard 142
Wright, Jenny 87, 142
Wright, Michael 53, 137

Z

Young, Lord **144**
Yuille, Judith 137, **138**

LIST OF ILLUSTRATIONS

PAGE REF.   ILLUSTRATION

11 0.01 *Letter from Borough Planning Officer to newly elected Chairman of the Environment Committee*

13 1.01 *Canopy, legacy of butcher's shop, Highgate High Street*

14 1.02 *Prickett & Ellis, Underhill*

14 1.03 *Chapel, Highgate School, 1867*

14 1.04 *Commemoration of Samuel Taylor Coleridge, 3 The Grove*

15 1.05 *Athlone House, Hampstead Lane, c 1880*

16 1.06 *Kenwood House*

16 1.07 *Route 214 bus at Liverpool Street*

17 1.08 *Original road sign outside The Flask pub*

17 1.09 *Rus in urbe, Hampstead Heath*

17 1.10 *Signifiers of Highgate's rural origins*

18 1.11 *Southwood Lane, Highgate Village*

19 2.01 *Highpoint I, when newly built, c 1935*

20 2.02 *Highpoint I*

21 2.03 *Membership application form, Highgate Preservation Society*

26 2.04 *Church Road*

27 2.05 *Press cutting: Highgate one-way system*

28 2.06 *Opposition to one-way system*

28 2.07 *The Highgate one-way system*

28 2.08 *Accident, North Road*

29 2.09 *The section of Archway Road that was upgraded*

30 2.10 *John Lacey, President, Highgate Preservation Society*

31 3.01 *Declaration by early members of the Society*

32 3.02 *Inaugural public meeting of the Highgate Society*

34 3.03 *The Society's first president, Yehudi Menuhin*

35 3.04 *Ronnie Bernstein, QC, the Society's founder and first chairman*

35 3.05 *Hornsey Journal, 6th May 1966*

35 3.06 *Poster protesting at the plans to build a "motorway" through Highgate Village*

36 3.07 *Pedestrian crossing installed in 1966 at junction of Southwood Lane and High Street, 2016*

37 3.08 *Highgate Literary and Scientific Institution*

38 3.09 *Fundraising letter from Yehudi Menuhin*

39 3.10 *10A South Grove*

40 3.11 *10A prior to refurbishment*

40 3.12 *Appeal for refurbishment of 10A*

42 3.13 *Debating the Common Market, 1971*

42 3.14 *John Gay, photographer*

42 3.15 *Invitation to meet the Cohen family, 1972*

45 3.16 *Susan Cox and Joan Neale*

45 3.17 *Denzil Budgett-Meakin, with wife Kathleen and daughter Catherine*

46 3.18 *Contest for Merry Mug*

47 4.01 *Christina Nolan with Mayor and Lady Mayor of Camden, Burns Night, 1976*

48 4.02 *Wine tasting pre-decimalisation*

49 4.03 *Peggy Jay chairing the Witanhurst committee*

50 4.04 *Yehudi Menuhin opening the Highgate Art Fair*

51 4.05 *Sara Kaye*

51 4.06 *The first advertisement in Buzz*

52 4.07 *Yehudi Menuhin marks 20th anniversary of the Highgate Society, 1986*

52 4.08 *Poster promoting the Olympicnics, 1980*

52 4.09 *Bernard Miles at Wedding Day Whoopee, 1981*

53 4.10 *Michael Hammerson*

54 4.11 *Parkland Walk*

54 4.12 *York stone paving, Pond Square*

56 4.13 *Lillian Buss*

57 4.14 *Calendar page drawn by Caitlin Egen, then aged 10, Hillway N6*

59 5.01 *Yehudi Menuhin and quartet, 1986*

60 5.02 *The Flask public house*

62 5.03 *Elizabeth Caddy*

63 5.04 *The Watercolour Group at work*

65 5.05 *Glenda Jackson and Oliver Letwin debating under the chairmanship of Ronald Bernstein*

67 5.06 *Joan, Lady Neale*

67 5.07 *Cromwell House, 2014*

69 5.08 *Heath Hands at work, 2016*

71 5.09 *Veteran oak in Denewood Road, relic of old hedgerow*

73 5.10 *Surveying lorries in the High Street*

74 5.11 *Demolition of the Wellington Inn*

75 5.12 *The Gatehouse, 2012*

75 5.13 *Upstairs at the Gatehouse: "Singing in the Rain", 2014*

77 6.01 *Mat Schwitzer giving lecture at 10A*

78 6.02 *Marion Uglow*

79 6.03 *Harley Atkinson with the Albany Piano Trio, Music in Highgate Homes, October 2015*

79 6.04 *Life Drawing Group at work*

81 6.05 *Brendan Nolan, Editor, Buzz, 1997 - 2009*

86 6.06 *Centenary celebrations, Archway Bridge*

87 6.07 *Ivor Burt, President 2001 - 2010*

87 6.08 *Rock House, Pond Square in spring*

88 6.09 *Carols in Pond Square, 2015*

89 6.10 *Saturday planning surgery, 10A*

92 6.11 *Raj Kara-Rajani*

93 6.12 *Archway Road shops and bridge*

94 6.13 *Highgate Wood Heritage Day*

95 6.14 *Litter pickers*

95 6.15 *Graffiti, Broadlands Road*

97 7.01 *Buses struggling to find a berth in Pond Square*

98 7.02 *Organising group for the fortieth anniversary ball*

99 7.03 *Campaigning to keep the toilets open, 2005*

106 7.04 *Highgate-on-Sea*

106 7.05 *Sustainable Homes event, 10A*

107 7.06 *Halloween, 2009*

108 7.07 *Ruth Hazeldine and Elizabeth Woodman baking for the French Circle*

109 7.08 *House visit to the Murugan Temple, Archway Road*

109 7.09 *Section two of the Circular Walk*

110 7.10 *Scoring at the HLSI / Highgate Society Quiz, 2004*

113 7.11 *The flower stall, 2015*

114 7.12 *The Red Hedgehog, Archway Road, 2016*

115 7.13 *Gilded spikes, View Road*

116 7.14 *21 Broadlands Road*

117 7.15 *Neo-classical pastiche, Courtenay Avenue, 2012*

116 7.16 *Sky News covers opposition to toilet closure*

120 8.01 *Draft proposals for a dual carriageway, Archway Road, 1962*

120 8.02 *Anger felt along the Archway Road*

122 8.03 *Campaign to relocate 271 bus turnaround*

123 8.04 *Parking in Pond Square*

124 8.05 *Controlled Parking Zone, Church Road*

126 9.01 *The Highgate Bowl*

127 9.02 *Celebrating the inspector's judgment on the Bowl case, November 2014*

128 9.03 *Witanhurst, seen from Hampstead Heath, c 1980*

128 9.04 *Service quarters of the new Witanhurst*

129 9.05 *Athlone House from Hampstead Heath*

131 9.06 *Athlone House during the 2000s*

131 9.07 *Saving Athlone House campaign*

131 9.08 *The campaign to save Athlone House, the Society's first to use social media*

135 10.01 *Highgate Cemetery*

137 10.02 *Jean Pateman*

138 10.03 *"Mums Army Fights Back"*

139 10.04 *Nicky Gavron*

140 10.05 *Jacksons Lane Community Centre*

140 10.06 *Society members after class at Jacksons Lane*

141 10.07 *Pam Cooper's history of Waterlow Park*

141 10.08 *Statue of Sir Sydney Waterlow, Waterlow Park*

142 10.09 *Geraldine Aves*

144 10.10 *Lord Young visits the Harington Scheme*

145 10.11 *Café staff with an improved menu for Archway Road*

146 10.12 *Community Planning Workshop, January 2013*

ILLUSTRATION CREDITS

Ed Gordon
6.03, 6.04

Evening Standard
9.04

Ham and High
2.08, 6.09, 7.06, 11.03

Harington Scheme
10.09

Highgate Cemetery
10.02

Highgate Society
0.01, 2.10, 3.01 - 3.04, 3.09, 3.11 - 3.13, 3.15,
3.17, 3.18, 4.01 - 4.10, 4.13, 4.14, 5.01, 5.03,
5.05, 5.06, 5.10, 5.11, 6.02, 6.05 - 6.07, 6.14,
6.15, 7.02, 7.03, 7.07, 7.10, 8.01, 8.02, 8.04,
9.02, 9.03

Hornsey Journal
3.05

Ian Henghes
7.05, 10.12

John Gay
9.01

Maggy Meade King
15.11

Michael Hammerson
1.01, 5.09, 6.08, 6.13

Nicky Gavron
10.03

Rebecca Bramwell
4.11

Richard Webber
1.02 – 1.12, 2.02, 2.04, 2.09, 3.07, 3.08, 3.10,
4.12, 5.02, 5.07 - 5.09, 5.12, 6.10 – 6.12, 7.01,
7.08, 7.09, 7.11 – 7.15, 8.05. 9.05 – 9.07, 10.01

Shiv Sharma
10.07

Susan Cox
5.04

Terry Gilliam
9.08

Tony Gay, The Journal
10.10

Unknown
2.01, 2.03, 2.05 – 2.07, 3.05, 3.06, 3.14, 5.02,
4.11, 6.01, 8.03

Upstairs at the Gatehouse
5.13

Vanessa Whinney
5.04, 7.04

18th century houses in North Road

OFFICERS OF THE HIGHGATE SOCIETY

The following lists have been created from the pages of back issues of *Buzz*. Some will be simplified as the committee structure was more complex than can be presented here. In addition to chairs each of these committees and groups had many committee members over the decades, some of them extremely active, but because they chaired no groups, their names do not appear; outstanding examples are Susan Cox and Joan Neale, who were the backbone of the Environment Committee, and the reasons for so many of its successes, over four decades.

Other, shorter-lived or ad hoc committees have also played an often vital role in the life of the Society – for example: Walks and Talks, Social and Entertainment, Traffic and Transport (as a subgroup of the Environment Committee), Highgate Business Liaison, Carols in Pond Square.

Space does not allow the publication of the names of everyone who has served the Society to a significant degree to be published here. Complete lists of the composition of committees can be found in the issues of *Buzz*, a complete set of which is stored at 10A South Grove.

PRESIDENTS

1	Yehudi Menuhin	*1970-1982*	4	Ivor Burt	*2001-2010*
2	Ronald Bernstein	*1983-1993*	5	Stephen Panke	*2010-*
3	John Samuel	*1993-2001*			

CHAIRMEN

2	Ronald Bernstein	*1967-1968*	15	Gavin Doyle	*1991-1994*
6	David Lowe-Watson	*1968-1970*	5	Stephen Panke	*1994-1996*
7	Isla Merry	*1970-1973*	16	Janice Morgan	*1997-2000*
8	Marius Reynolds	*1973-1975*	17	Derek Hall	*2000-2003*
9	Christina Nolan	*1975-1976*	18	Robin Fairlie	*2003-2006*
10	Michael Hughes	*1976-1979*	19	Gordon Forbes	*2006-2009*
11	John Oakes	*1979-1982*	20	Catherine Budgett-Meakin	*2009-2012*
12	Matej Schwitzer	*1982-1985*	21	Kirsten de Keyser	*2012-2014*
13	Michael Wright	*1985-1986*	5	Stephen Panke	*2014-2015*
14	Christopher Ryder	*1987-1991*	16	Janice Morgan	*2015-*

VICE PRESIDENTS

Alfred Doulton	1970-1978
Sir James Brown	1970-1979
Ronald Bernstein	1970-1982
John Lacey	1970-2005
David Lowe-Watson	1970-2006
John Samuel	1975-1993
Edward Fowler	1979-1994
Michael Hughes	1980
Lillian Buss	1983-1996
Susan Cox	1983-2003
Joan Neale	2000-2002
Stephen Panke	2003-2010
Gavin Doyle	2003-2014
Michael Hammerson	2003-
Marius Reynolds	2007-
Christina Nolan	2008-

VICE-CHAIRMEN

Peter Mostyn	1967-1968
Edward Fowler	1967-1969
Michael Hughes	1968-1970
John Samuel	1969-1975
Marius Reynolds	1970-1971
John Southwell	1970-1971
Edward Fowler	1971-1973
Ian Davis	1972-1973
Isla Merry	1973-1975
Barbara Edwards	1975-1976
Colin Dollimore	1975-1978
Quentin Edwards	1976-1979
Tim Ades	1978
Robert Adams	1979-1980
Tim Ades	1979-1980
Tony Baker	1981-1982
John Olphert	1981-1983
John Oakes	1983
Derek Merton	1983-1985
Marius Reynolds	1983-1986
Millicent Ballantyne	1985-1986
Jan Burt	1987-1988
Sue Vinson	1987-1990
David Weight	1988-1991
Millicent Ballantyne	1990-1991

Ann Riddell	1991-1993
Jenny Wright	1991-1994
Donald Barron	1993-1996
Marguerite Clark	1994-1997
Ivor Burt	1997-2001
Elizabeth Millar	1997-2006
Liz Morris	2006-2010
(Vacant)	2011-2013
Pippa Rothenberg	2014-

TREASURERS

Harley Atkinson	2000-2004
Alan Taylor	2004-2005
Paul Dowsey	2005-2007
Michael Read	2008-2010
Amy Brown	2010
Michael Read	2010-2013
Kabir Ali	2013-2014
William Britain	2014-

SECRETARIES

Barbara Edwards	1967-1968
Doreen Mostyn	1968-1970
Freda Patton	1971-1972
Jeanne Thain	1972-1973
Shirley Forsling	1974-1975
Douglas Fairhead	1975
Tim Ades	1976-1978
Barbara Fletcher	1978-1979
Matej Schwitzer	1979-1982
Brian Holland	1982
Denise Ward	1982-1984
Carol Wilson	1984
John Olphert	1984-1985
Shirley Hinton	1985-1987
Marguerite Clark	1987-1990
Catherine McLay	1991-1994
Vanessa Whinney	1994-1996
Sarah Miller / McLachlan	1997-2000
Avril Castellazzo	2001-2003
Michael Read	2004-2007
Vanessa Whinney	2007-2010
Pippa Rothenberg	2010-2013
Dominic James-Moore	2013
Capri MacDuffie	2013-2014
Harley Atkinson	2014-

CHAIRMEN OF COMMITTEES

ARTS

Charley Salmon	1966-1968
Judy Hildebrand	1968-1970
Richard Toeman	1970-1972
Mrs E Meetham	1972
Brian Palmer	1972
Jan Burt	1973-1975
Robert Adams	1975-1979
Judith Steiner	1980-1985
Elizabeth Kay	1985-1987
Daphne Russell	1987-1990
Donald Barron	1990-1995
Katie Plews	1996-2005

COMMUNITY SERVICES

Mary Hucks	1967-1970
Jill Lock	1970-1973
Jenny Wright	1973-1976
Lucy Haynes	1976-1979
Angela Hughes	1979-1982
Diana Sharp	1983-1985
Elizabeth Fletcher	1985-1986
Marion Uglow	1986-1990
Anita Morgan	1991-1994
Sandy Graham	1994-1996
Marion Uglow	1997-

ENVIRONMENT COMMITTEE /PLANNING GROUP

John Lacey	1966-1967
David and Dawn Lowe-Watson (Traffic, 1966-1967)	
Michael Hughes (Traffic, 1967)	
(Traffic & Transport merged with Planning Group 1977 to form Environment Committee)	
Michael Hughes	1968
Marius Reynolds	1968-1970
Colin Dollimore	1970-1971
Michael Hughes	1971-1973
Denzil Budgett-Meakin	1973-1974
Susan Cox	1975
Michael Wright	1975-1977
Patrick Lawlor	1977-1979

Ian Davis	1979-1980
Quentin Edwards	1981-1982
John Lacey	1983-1986
Michael Hammerson	1986-2003
Gordon Forbes	2003-2006
Michael Hammerson	2006-2010
Elspeth Clements	2011-

FRENCH CIRCLE

David Weight	1990-1996
Matej Schwitzer	1996-1998
Elizabeth Woodman	1998-2010
Ruth Hazeldine	2010-2011
Elizabeth Woodman	2012-2014
Ruth Hazeldine	2014-

KEEP HIGHGATE TIDY

Ruth Phillips	1993-1994
Freda Patton	1995
Christina Nolan	1996-1998
Sue Hall	2000-2003
Marguerite Clark	2007-2010

MEMBERSHIP

Peter Hildebrand	1967-1969
Richard Toeman	1969-1970
Mark Myers	1971-1973
Diana Toeman	1973
Robert Adams	1973-1974
Diana Toeman	1975-1977
Barbara Edwards	1977-1979
Gladys Anderson	1979-1984
Lucy Haynes	1985-1990
Jenny Wright	1990-1994
Richard Waddington	1994-1997
Janice Morgan	1997-1998
Freda Patton	1998-2008
Janice Morgan	2008-

MONDAY CLUB

Elizabeth Caddy	1967-2002
Robert Last	2002-2004
Sue Weisberg	2004-

MUSIC IN HIGHGATE HOMES

Sara Kaye   1985-

NORTHERN HEIGHTS PUBLICATIONS

Richard Webber   2012-

WATERCOLOUR GROUP

Margaret Cornelius	1988-1994
Doreen Wainwright	1994-2000
Vanessa Whinney	2001-2004
Roger Scopes	2005
Jill Wilkinson	2005-

WINE COMMITTEE

Alastair McGeorge	1971-1972
(1972-1979 not recorded)	
Lillian Buss	1979-1986
Rosemary Davis	1986
Millicent Ballantyne	1987
Jan Burt	1987-1988
Matej Schwitzer	1988-1990
Marguerite Clark	1991-1993
Lucy Haynes	1993-1996
Camille Gibson	1996-1998
Marguerite Clark	1999-2012
Sue Hall	2012-

10A SOUTH GROVE: HOUSE MANAGERS

Anthony Mulgan	1968-1969
Jan Burt	1969-1972
Sylvia Howe	1972-1975
Shirley Forsling	1975-1978
Michael Hughes	1978
Primrose Orgel	1978-1979
John Olphert	1979-1980
Jasper Fuller	1981-1894
Sandy Graham	1985-1987
Pauline Acheson	1987
Ann Riddell	1988-1991
Judy Doyle	1991-1994
Catherine McLay	1994-2006
Dan Hirsch	2007-2012
Richard Spencer-Smith	2012
Gail Waldman	2013
Catherine Budgett-Meakin	2013-2014
Pippa Rothenberg	2014-

10A SOUTH GROVE: BOOKINGS MANAGERS

Diana Toeman	1975
Jeanne Thain	1975-1978
Marjorie Fuller	1978-1985
Marion Uglow	1985-1986
Lois Godfrey	1986-1987
Sylvia Read	1987-1991
Catherine McLay	1991-2011
(since 2011, merged with House Management)	

END NOTES

i   Records exist for forty different inns and taverns of which over fifteen have survived until 2016. These taverns attract clientele from across a wide area of North London.

ii   "Highgate School – A History", Thomas Hinde, James and James, 1993

iii   These comments were made during one of a number of discussion groups held by the Economic and Social Research Council's "Alpha Territory" project.

iv   "Highgate – Its History since the Fifteenth Century", John Richardson, Historical Publications, 1983

v   The difficulties of establishing the identity of the beneficial owner of Witanhurst were described by Ed Caesar in the June 2015 edition of "The New Yorker". His name is Andrey Guryev.

vi   John Sainsbury lived in Bishopsfield in Broadlands Road, the site now occupied by Apollo House.

vii   The current sign was restored by Camden Council during the 1990s.

viii   It might well be argued that due to the number of years many of its residents have lived in the village and its dense network of community organisations, Highgate shares another feature, more pronounced in village communities, a back story of historic alliances and disputes between its various community organisations which is largely hidden from younger, more recently arrived residents.

ix   This concept is associated with the work of the urbanist Jane Jacobs in the 1970s and that of sociologist Pierre Bourdieu in the 1980s.

x   That the responsibility for planning should lie with the Ministry of Health was a legacy of the time when improved housing conditions were perceived as critical means of improving sanitation and hence public health.

xi   The same opportunities for rerouting the 271 bus route were still being discussed in a consultative meeting with TfL as late as March 2016.

xii   The Borough of Hornsey formed part of what in 1968 became the London Borough of Haringey. In addition to the Haringey part of Highgate, the Borough included Muswell Hill and Crouch End, where its administrative offices were situated on the Broadway.

xiii   Criticism of Marples also focused on his conflict of interest. Before becoming a minister he had been Managing Director of the construction company Marples Ridgway. Though Marples agreed to sell his shareholding after been appointed Minister of Transport it was reported after Marples Ridgway had won the tender to build the Hammersmith Flyover that the Ministry of Transport's engineers had endorsed the London County Council's rejection of a lower tender.

xiv   The elevated Westway is a legacy of the motorway box concept.

xv   The County of Middlesex covered much of North West London, including the borough of Hornsey, prior to local government reorganisation in 1968.

xvi   Written for a Bernstein family booklet produced for Ronnie's eightieth birthday in 1998.

xvii   According to Peter Mostyn in "1966 and All That"

xviii   Published in *Buzz*, summer 2006

xix   Competitors seated from left are for Highgate Society Michael Wright, unknown, Stephen Benson and unknown. Adrian Mayer is the chair. For the HLSI are Edward Fowler, Gwynydd Gosling, Ian Roy and Jenny Johnson.

xx   This was repeated in the Gatehouse in February 2016 as part of the fiftieth anniversary celebrations.

xxi   From left are seated Kit Ikin, Peggy Jay, Michael Powers and Sir Anthony Cox. The event took place at the HLSI.

xxii   In the days before "right to buy" legislation the population of these estates was less middle class than they became in later years.

xxiii   The lady standing immediately behind Yehudi Menuhin is Jenny Wright, founder of Jacksons Lane Community Centre.

xxiv   Better known to many as Ruth Hazeldine

xxv   Kari Hegarty and Susan Maxwell

xxvi   The musicians are Pippa Harrison (piano), Gemma Sharples (Violin) and Verity Evanson (Cello).

xxvii   John H. Lloyd's "History, Topography and Antiquities of Highgate" (1888, page five) cites a public notice promoting a fair on Pond Square in July 1744.

xxviii   From left Janet Munro-Nelson, Katie Plews, Betty Pires, Christina Nolan

xxix   A Section 106 agreement enables a local planning authority to make the granting of its permission to a developer in respect of a particular application to be conditional on the developer agreeing to provide some public benefit. This may not necessarily be directly related to the planning application itself but land nearby.

xxx   Friends of Highgate Cemetery Trust newsletter, December 2015, author Malcolm Holmes

xxxi   Though not perhaps from its Committee of 1936 which included a lord, a lady, three knights and two sitting or former MPs and when the President was also an MP and the Chairman a knight.